Big-City Politics, Governance, and Fiscal Constraints

GEORGE E. PETERSON
Editor

Big-City Politics, Governance, and Fiscal Constraints

THE URBAN INSTITUTE PRESS
Washington, D.C.

Library of Congress Cataloging in Publication Data

Big-City Politics, Governance, and Fiscal Constraints/George E. Peterson, editor.

1. Municipal government—United States. 2. Voting—United States.
3. Minorities—United States—Political activity. Political participation—United States. I. Peterson, George E.

JS323.B54   1994   94-3711
320.8'5'0973—dc20   CIP
DNLM/DLC

ISBN 0-87766-573-7 (paper, alk. paper)
ISBN 0-87766-572-9 (cloth, alk. paper)

Printed in the United States of America.

THE URBAN INSTITUTE is a nonprofit policy research and educational organization established in Washington, D.C., in 1968. Its staff investigates the social and economic problems confronting the nation and public and private means to alleviate them. The Institute disseminates significant findings of its research through the publications program of its Press. The goals of the Institute are to sharpen thinking about societal problems and efforts to solve them, improve government decisions and performance, and increase citizen awareness of important policy choices.

Through work that ranges from broad conceptual studies to administrative and technical assistance, Institute researchers contribute to the stock of knowledge available to guide decision making in the public interest.

Conclusions or opinions expressed in Institute publications are those of the authors and do not necessarily reflect the views of staff members, officers or trustees of the Institute, advisory groups, or any organizations that provide financial support to the Institute.

URBAN OPPORTUNITY SERIES TITLES

ACKNOWLEDGMENTS

Preliminary versions of all but two of these chapters were originally presented at an Urban Institute conference. We thank the Ford Foundation for its financial support of that conference and of the wider Urban Opportunity Program of which the conference was a part. We also thank the distinguished Advisory Committee that helped guide the work of the Program. The Committee chair was Neil Goldschmidt. Committee membership included Elijah Anderson, Henry G. Cisneros, Mathea Falco, Nathan Glazer, Elliott S. Hall, Katharine C. Lyall, Richard P. Nathan, Alan L. Otten, Franklin Raines, Isabel V. Sawhill, and John C. Weicher. In addition we thank the John F. Kennedy School of Government, Harvard University for commissioning the work that appears here as chapters 8 and 9, and for allowing us to include these chapters in the volume. Finally, we thank Carlotta Molitor for conference planning and logistics and Susanne White for helping with manuscript preparation.

CONTENTS

Tables

Figures

FOREWORD

Opportunity is a distinctively American value. Immigrants of all eras who have chosen to come to this country have been drawn to a place where those willing to work can find economic advancement and where groups of all kinds have the right of access to the institutions that support social mobility. For most of U.S. history, the laws defining equal opportunity have become increasingly inclusive and its practice in crucial aspects of life (housing, employment, education) more common.

The city occupies a central role in this conception. It has been in U.S. cities that opportunities have accelerated and barriers to social and economic mobility most effectively breached. Two trends now threaten the ideal of opportunity.

First, opportunities for advancement in our cities have narrowed, especially for those at the low end of the socio-economic ladder. This is largely a result of the slowdown in aggregate economic growth, international economic forces, and the weakening of institutions— particularly the urban institutions that historically have furthered economic and social opportunity.

Second, the consensus surrounding equal opportunity has weakened. The term itself has become closely identified with a particular strategy of remedial action. As a result, the political debate over how, and to what extent, society should compensate for past unequal opportunity has tended to undermine agreement about the importance of an equal opportunity structure. The alternative to this structure might be labeled a competitive opportunity system, in which groups or individuals compete for access to the fewer opportunity routes now open, based on their own inherited endowments.

The Urban Opportunity Program, supported by The Ford Foundation, was charged with reconsidering the last quarter century of changes in urban markets and institutions, from the perspective of the opportunity structure. Toward this goal, The Urban Institute sponsored a series of conferences on different aspects of urban opportunity. Four broad subjects were covered: drugs, crime, and social isolation; urban labor markets and barriers to job mobility; housing markets and residential mobility; and big-city politics and fiscal choices. Most chapters in this volume grew out of or were inspired by one or more of these conferences.

The contributing authors examine the politics, governance, and fiscal constraints faced by big cities over the past quarter century and the political transition now going on in many of them. Big-city mayors and other political leaders face the triple challenge of assembling a winning coalition; translating this into an effective governing coalition; and coping with a tightening local budget constraint. The challenge is still greater when elections have produced a change in ethnic control of local government, bringing into power new groups that want to use government spending to meet their constituents' demands but are resisted by those controlling the economic resources.

The story told here is not encouraging. Minority representation increased during the 1980s but did not bring with it the substantial improvement in the lives of poor and minority residents that had been widely assumed would follow. In addition, ethnic and political fragmentation over at least the past decade has made it increasingly difficult to form a stable winning or governing coalition. And all this has taken place against a backdrop of fiscal austerity. According to the evidence presented here, demographic and economic change has led to worsening of the typical big city's underlying health since the late 1970s, a trend that has been exacerbated by reduced federal funding for urban areas.

There are no easy solutions to the real world problems addressed here. However, these national experts provide a diagnosis of today's problems in big-city politics, governance, and finances, and lay out the framework within which policy solutions will have to be sought.

William Gorham
President

Chapter One

INTRODUCTION

George E. Peterson

Over the past quarter century, demographic and economic changes have challenged big cities' capacity for governance. Observers have alternated in their predictions as to how the politics of the new urban conditions would be resolved. Writers analyzing the political and fiscal position of cities in the mid-1980s sounded almost optimistic about the capacity of the typical big city to adapt to an environment that many had predicted would lead to crisis. City electorates were increasingly successful in electing minority mayors, and minority representation in the institutions of city government generally was increasing. Both trends were assumed to portend greater responsiveness to and success in dealing with the needs of poor and minority residents. In addition, some observers noted the unexpected fiscal resilience of cities in the face of the federal aid cutbacks of the Reagan era, implying that budgetary stability might give the cities room for political accommodation in meeting the demands of new voters.

Political events did not unfold as predicted, however, or as the demographic facts might seem to dictate. The agendas of the coalitions originally responsible for increasing the representation of minorities in city hall are far from being realized, and, in most cases, the coalitions themselves vanished. Despite substantially increasing black populations in most central cities, African-American mayors have been replaced by white mayors in four of the nation's five largest cities. This book looks in particular at the politics and governance of five cities originally chosen for study because of their ethnic diversity: Chicago, Los Angeles, Miami, Philadelphia, and San Antonio. All five cities now have mayors who are white non-Hispanic males who succeeded minority incumbents.

The meaning of these changes is open to interpretation. One line of argument places emphasis on the economic and fiscal constraints of central cities, and the inevitable disappointment of minority voters when they discovered how severely the constraints limited minority

mayors' freedom of action. Compared to other periods of ethnic succession in big-city politics, there were fewer spoils available for redistribution and great sensitivity to the demands of business and
middle-class taxpayers who had the realistic option of moving out
of the city. Minority turnout typically declined sharply after the
initial successful campaigns of a minority mayor, suggesting that the
reality of governance generated less enthusiasm than its prospect. An
alternative interpretation of recent mayoral elections assigns greater
weight to the inherent fragility of the first-generation minority coalitions. Initial ethnic-group solidarity masked important differences
within minority groups by economic class, generation, and political
style. As these were revealed, it became increasingly difficult to
mobilize minority support for a single figure. The fusion of different
minority groups—African-American, Hispanic, and Asian—into an
effective political coalition of color has rarely been achieved, even
for one generation.

Yet a third interpretation sees in the outcome of recent mayoral
elections a political pragmatism that stretches beyond race. Many of
the new mayors ran on less confrontational platforms, relied less on
symbolic representation of ethnic groups, tried to convey a can-do
attitude toward city management and city problems, and openly
sought the cooperation of business as an implementation partner.
This is as true of cities with newly elected black mayors, such as
Dennis Archer in Detroit, Norman Rice in Seattle, Wellington Webb
in Denver, or Sharon Sayles-Belton in Minneapolis (the last three
mayors of cities with modest black populations) as it is of cities
where minority mayors have been displaced. The political reality of
the 1990s may reward the plausible promise of concrete achieve-
ments.

This book seeks to understand the forces behind the turning point
in big-city mayoral elections that occurred at the beginning of the
1990s. It does so by closely examining the processes that led to
political change in five cities, and considering from a national perspective some of the key issues that local political contests reflected.

THE MAJOR MESSAGES

Four major messages stand out among the detailed analyses that
follow. The first is that the increased minority representation which
undoubtedly took place in the 1980s did not bring with it substantial

improvements in the lot of poor and minority city residents taken as a whole. The second is that the story of urban politics in the 1980s was one of increasing fragmentation, so that in many cities by the end of the decade there seemed to be no natural majority to facilitate effective governance. The third is that, although the fiscal health of big cities generally did not deteriorate over most of the 1980s, it never regained the level obtaining in the late 1970s and almost certainly deteriorated at the beginning of the 1990s. Most cities may have avoided budgeting crises, but they had less and less room for funding policy changes. The final message is that, although minority representation did increase over the 1970s and 1980s, the new politics of class and income progressively leaves out the more disadvantaged groups and further reduces the likelihood of new coalitions developing that give true priority to the needs of the disadvantaged.

FAILURE OF INCREASED MINORITY REPRESENTATION TO BRING COMMENSURATE IMPROVEMENT FOR MINORITY RESIDENTS

That minority representation increased throughout the 1970s and well into the 1980s is documented throughout the book. There was a dramatic rise in minority voter participation and in the number of cities with minority mayors over the 1980s. The minority mayors were originally elected primarily on liberal platforms, with very strong minority support combined with liberal white support. In Philadelphia (chapter 2 by Carolyn Adams) the first black mayor was elected in 1983, when 98% of the city's eligible blacks were registered, constituting almost 44% of all Democratic party registrations. In Chicago (chapter 3 by Dianne Pinderhughes) the first black mayor was also elected in 1983, predominantly with black support. In Los Angeles (chapter 5 by Byran Jackson and Michael Preston) the first black mayor was elected much earlier, in 1973, with a winning coalition of blacks, Jews, and liberal whites and Hispanics.

In cities with large Spanish-speaking populations the story is similar. In San Antonio (chapter 6 by Carlos Muñoz) Henry Cisneros became the first Mexican-American mayor of San Antonio for 140 years, drawing almost 100 percent of the Mexican-American vote and 45 percent of the white vote. Miami (chapter 4 by Genie Stowers and Ronald Vogel) elected its first Cuban-American mayor in 1985, a year in which 38 percent of the registered voters were Hispanic, 30 percent non-Hispanic white, and 18 percent African-American.

This electoral power was rewarded with political participation, including representation on citizen commissions and other institutions created to oversee or manage a vast range of city functions. But that participation did not reap the social and economic rewards for minority residents and communities that many expected from it. Absolute gains were made. But racial minorities and the poor gained considerably less than they anticipated and less than other ethnic groups have won in the past by taking control of local political machinery.

In Philadelphia, for example, blacks became much more heavily represented in cabinet and high administrative government positions under the first black mayor, W. Wilson Goode. Contracts to minority business increased. But community services in the poorer areas were cut, the black community's highest priority of improved housing received scant attention, and the building of neighborhood facilities was subordinated to downtown development.

In Los Angeles, blacks were overrepresented in the municipal workforce in 1973, and by about the same proportion in 1990, but they were still significantly underrepresented in 1990 in the top three levels of the bureaucracy. Black neighborhoods benefited least from the mayor's efforts to encourage economic development.

In San Antonio, after having had a Mexican-American as mayor for six years, only 4 percent of Mexican-American residents had incomes over $35,000 a year. In Miami, Cuban-Americans constitute the most powerful minority on the local political scene. They have clearly benefited from their increasing political power. But they are different from minority groups in most U.S. big cities, because they are fundamentally middle class in incomes and in values. Cuban political power has preempted the African-American community from sharing political power and made far less likely policies focused on the lives and neighborhoods of poorer residents of the city, whatever their ethnic group.

Milwaukee (chapter 7 by Peter Eisinger) provides something of a contrast. One of the most segregated and racially divided cities in the country, it went from the long-time tenure of Mayor Henry Maier ("no friend to blacks") to the election of John Norquist in 1988, a liberal Democrat advocating and working to promote minority economic development. According to author Peter Eisinger the political climate in Milwaukee is currently favorable to such an agenda. Eisinger finds that minority programs, including affirmative action initiatives in public employment and several targeted economic development programs, in fact led to substantial increases in the employment of minorities relative to whites in the city and county of Milwaukee in the late 1980s.

He does not find the prospects for the future particularly encouraging, however, for two reasons. First, the private sector is perforce the major influence on the employment picture. Jobs are not growing nearly as fast as the minority population, and the private sector is still rife with discriminatory employment and financing practices. Second, many of the initiatives that underwrote significant minority employment in both public and private sectors were funded by programs that no longer exist. "The loss of intergovernmental revenues makes an expanding—and even continuing—commitment to minorities and neighborhoods a potentially fragile proposition." This analysis suggests that the economic constraints on big-city mayors are such that they can have only modest to moderate impact on the issues that matter most to minority residents, like jobs, regardless of their political priorities.

INCREASING POLITICAL FRAGMENTATION

The electoral histories of the past 20 to 30 years traced in this book, with changing racial and ethnic representations in the voting and nonvoting populations show that the interactions between shifting racial/ethnic and class politics rendered the coalitions necessary to win political office ill-suited to the task of governing, leading to a continuing search on the part of the elected leaders for an effective governing coalition. None of the chapters carries much hope that the 1990s will see stable governing coalitions that also give priority to the needs of poorer, more disadvantaged residents and neighborhoods.

A look at how the winning coalitions in local elections in big cities changed over the 1980s highlights the increasingly disparate forces needed to achieve victory at the polls and the change from explicitly race-based politics to a politics governed by income and class divisions. An important part of this evolution in many cities is the split within the black community resulting from the emergence of a black middle class interested in economic advancement rather than racial solidarity. Three of the cities profiled in this book are discussed briefly below to illustrate the point.

PHILADELPHIA

Until the mid-1970s, black political participation was channeled through the Democratic party, with blacks voting for Democratic candidates irrespective of race. This changed during the late 1970s, as the black representation in Philadelphia increased, helped by the confrontational stand taken by then-mayor Frank Rizzo in supporting white working class areas in their fight against accepting subsidized housing in their neighborhoods. In the 1979 election a group of black ward leaders endorsed their own independent slate of candidates. A white man won the election for mayor, but recognizing the new political muscle of the black community, he appointed a black man, W. Wilson Goode, as managing director of the city. The black community responded by rapidly increasing voter registration and turnout rates. Goode—who had earned a solid reputation for honesty and efficiency—was elected on a classic reform platform by a coalition of blacks, neighborhood groups, Democratic regulars in white working-class wards, and downtown business. The black community was more financially involved in Democratic politics than ever before, and 98 percent of the eligible black voters were registered to vote.

Adams, in chapter 2, sees a single event in 1985—Goode's decision to bomb a small extremist commune known as "MOVE," killing all 11 people inside the commune and destroying two city blocks of a largely black neighborhood—as a major turning point in Goode's political fortunes. "No longer did Goode enjoy the unqualified support of black Democrats, some of whom saw [the decision] as a racist act. . . . Business leaders were appalled at the lapse in managerial control. . . . And many white liberals were shocked at the use of such brutal force to quell a neighborhood disturbance."

But in light of national trends one has to wonder whether Goode's traditional constituency would have broken down anyway. The later years of his mayoralty were marked by a political standoff between the mayor, pushing for economic development and budgeting austerity, and the city council, dominated by populist politicians. In 1987 Goode retained the mayor's office, but only barely. He drew 97 percent of the black vote, but black voter registration had declined substantially.

Even that electoral base could not hold. As Adams herself points out, the widening disparity across the nation in household incomes began to affect local politics, and "no mayor, regardless of race, could satisfy both blacks in business and the professions and the disadvantaged." In 1991, a white candidate, Edward Rendell, won the Democratic party nomination and the election. There were two black and two white candidates for mayor, and the black vote split four ways. Adams traces the declining trend in black political cohesion through voting patterns in the city's most heavily black wards. The percentage of registered Democrats voting for black candidates in these wards reached a high of 62 percent in 1983 and had dropped to 33 percent in 1991.

The "alarming reality," according to Adams, "is that there is no longer any dominant coalition." Rendell, running on a platform of hard-headed fiscal management, convinced the electorate that he was the person to bring Philadelphia back from the financial crisis that had overtaken the city as Goode neared the end of his last term. His administration so far enjoys widespread voter support. But Adams fears this may be a "temporary truce" imposed by the fiscal crisis unless "political leaders use the respite to build new coalitions that self-consciously cross classes, racial lines, and neighborhoods."

CHICAGO

The period between 1975, when Richard J. Daley was elected mayor for the last time, and 1991, when his son Richard M. Daley was reelected for a second term as mayor, was a period of intense political competition in the city of Chicago, played out against a background of increasing minority representation among the population and the electorate. In 1970, two-thirds of the city's voting-age population was white, virtually all the rest black. By 1980, slightly under half (48 percent) was white, 39 percent black, and nearly 13 percent Hispanic.

The city's first black mayor, Harold Washington, mounted an unsuccessful challenge to Daley's successor in 1977 and was successful in 1983. He was the first to court the Hispanic vote and barely won the election with a majority of 51.6 percent but a substantially higher majority of black voters. He worked to increase his electoral support from other racial and ethnic groups in the city and raised his majority in the 1987 election to nearly 54 percent of the vote. But Washington died soon after his reelection, leaving a gap that showed how frail the black voting bloc was.

The black community in Chicago in fact spanned a wide range of groups by the 1970s and 1980s, divided by education, income, and residence. Washington was old enough to have grown up during the period of increasing divergence. He had also grown up with the Democratic machine, in which his father was a precinct captain. The combination put him in what turned out to be a unique position to paper over differences within the black community. These differences erupted immediately after his death, as leaders of different black factions struggled and failed to take over his position as leader of a single black community. This struggle yielded two irreconcilable black factions in 1989, guaranteeing the election of the second-generation Daley. Daley campaigned and used patronage to increase his following among Chicago blacks and was reelected in 1991 with 70 percent of the vote.

Unlike Adams's view of Philadelphia, author Pinderhughes views Chicago's current coalition behind Daley as relatively stable. "The new policy consensus is that a loose coalition has 'formed' led by the Irish, dominated by white ethnics, but incorporating representation from all sectors of the city, including African-Americans and Latinos. The politics of race are quite important in sustaining this alliance, although it is not the only factor." Interestingly, she attributes at least part of the failure to sustain a stable coalition around a black successor to Harold Washington to the black community's expectation that it "deserved to control the mayor's office through a black official, rather than that the community should consolidate around a candidate with a substantive policy agenda attractive to black, and other communities', interests." The result was to draw the different white ethnic groups together into a cohesive opposition force and "to make a liberal coalition comprising Washington's 1987 supporters . . . extremely unlikely."

LOS ANGELES

The changing coalitions over the years in Los Angeles can be seen even more clearly than in other cities, because of the long tenure of a single black mayor. Tom Bradley was the mayor from 1973 to 1993. During this period the demographic balance of the city changed drastically, as both non-Hispanic Whites and African-Americans declined as a share of the city's population, replaced by rapid growth in the Latino and Asian population.

Bradley had winning coalitions throughout this period. But the strength of his support varied. An analysis by council district tells the story. Voter turnout, by district, declined steadily from his first to his last campaign. The percentage of votes by which he won reached its highest level in 1985, when he won every district except one. In 1989, however, he only just avoided a runoff election, with only a little over 51 percent of the overall vote.

Bradley's governing coalition also changed substantially over his long period as mayor, which authors Jackson and Preston regard as important in explaining both his reduced majority in 1989 and the results of the subsequent election in 1993 and the current political situation in Los Angeles. They divide his tenure into three phases. In the first phase (1973–1982), Bradley's governing coalition reflected his electoral mandate, made up of Jews, blacks, and other liberals in the city. This represented a sharp departure from his predecessor's approach. In the next phase (1983–1989), according to this analysis, Bradley used his popularity to pursue a more candidate-based strategy and a wider coalition. "Developers and downtown business groups began to slowly dominate his agenda" as he tried to bring economic development to the city. This continued until his last period in office, when he assumed the role of power-broker in giving city hall access to business and commercial interests. Jackson and Preston imply that this was in part personal preference. But the increasingly conspicuous problems of Los Angeles, particularly in its poorer areas, could also have forced him, or any mayor, to court these new partners in an effort to turn the city around economically, particularly in the face of defections from his original electoral base.

The year 1993 saw a spectacular collapse of the traditional liberal coalition—a collapse that Bradley's long tenure could have simply postponed. Richard Riordan, a white Republican, won handily, rolling up large margins in the affluent San Fernando Valley district, and making inroads on his Democratic opponent in several of the traditionally liberal council districts. Incredibly, two out of every five voters who supported Bradley in 1989 voted for Riordan in 1993. Voter turnout among blacks and in the central city was low.

THE BACKDROP OF FISCAL STRAIN

Throughout the story of big-city politics and governance in the 1980s runs the refrain of political limitations imposed by fiscal pressure. Fundamentally, the job of city government is to deliver the services needed by city residents at reasonable tax rates and to balance the budget. To the extent that demographic changes reduce the tax base at the same time as they increase service needs, the options open to city governments are all politically distasteful. Mayors looking for reelection, for fiscal reasons alone, are likely to be harder and harder pressed to hold their public support and increasingly desperate in looking for ways to increase the economic viability of the city. From this perspective, it may not be surprising that the city stories told in this book feature increasing attention by the mayors to the need for economic development and courting of the interests that might make that happen.

The fiscal trends in big cities over the past two decades are documented and discussed in detail by Helen Ladd in chapter 9 of the book. Her thesis, in a nutshell, is that many big cities are in worse fiscal condition than in the late 1970s, and that the long national economic expansion of the 1980s may have diverted attention from what were, in fact, underlying fiscal problems throughout that decade.

Her fundamental point is made by means of a measure that she constructs of "standardized fiscal health." Cities have different demographic makeups, leading to different tax bases and service costs, as well as different degrees of support from state and federal governments. "This measure reveals the net effect of a city's economic, social, and demographic characteristics on its ability to deliver a standard level of public services at a standard tax burden on its residents."

According to analyses of 70 central cities undertaken by Ladd and John Yinger, the typical central city would have needed 11 percent additional revenue from noncity sources in 1982 to have been able to provide its 1972 service level at the 1972 tax burden. The deterioration in standardized fiscal health was most severe for large cities, those with more than 100,000 population, where the typical city would have needed 73 percent more outside revenue in 1982 to deliver the 1972 service level. "This finding implies that economic and social trends . . . worsened the balance between revenue-raising capacity and expenditure need in the typical big city." Rough estimates based on incomplete data indicate that standardized fiscal health of big cities improved over the 1980s but still failed to recover to the standard of 1972.

Did state and federal revenue sources provide the necessary additional revenues? Ladd addresses this question with an equally detailed analysis of the contribution to city's fiscal well-being of state and federal funds. She finds that, between 1972 and 1982, state assistance offset about half the effects of the increasing social and economic pressures on big cities. State assistance was also relatively well targeted, in the sense that the cities with the poorest fiscal health received the most aid. But that did not stop the fiscal health of big cities from declining over the period. Even with state assistance, the larger the city the greater the decline. Data since 1982 are, again, partial, but suggest that help from states has declined slightly on average.

How much did federal aid help in covering the remaining gap in the revenue-raising capacity of big cities? For the average city over the 1972–1982 period, federal aid fully offset the decline in fiscal health that was not accounted for by state assistance. But for the largest cities (over one million population), federal aid offset only about one-third of the decline. Since federal aid to cities declined substantially during the 1980s, the underlying fiscal position of the largest cities has undoubtedly worsened.

Did these big cities raise taxes to cope with the increasing financial pressure? Yes, with the highest tax burdens falling on the residents of cities with the poorest fiscal health. Did they also reduce services? Service quality appears to have increased slightly between 1972 and 1977, declined substantially between 1977 and 1982, and then recovered somewhat between 1982 and 1989. Abstracting from the economic cycle, however, one can see a tightening fiscal vise that for most big cities has greatly limited political options whoever occupies the mayor's office.

THE OUTLOOK FOR CITIZEN PARTICIPATION IN THE 1990s

Voting is only one way to express political demands. In chapter 8 Christopher Howard, Michael Lipsky, and Dale Rogers Marshall trace the history of citizen participation. They see enormous expansion in citizen participation since the War on Poverty and the Great Society of the 1960s. But they also see a process by which that participation has become routinized. At the same time they see the politics of race giving way to the politics of class and income. The combination progressively leaves out the more disadvantaged groups, because middle- and upper-income groups, irrespective of race and ethnic group, have more of the political resources necessary for routine modes of participation.

About future prospects for developing coalitions that give priority to "the challenge of poverty and the plight of American cities," they are not sanguine. They see strains of a new urban populism among neighborhood groups and community organizations. But these organizations remain largely outside the realm of electoral politics and are often dependent financially on government. Unless they change along both these dimensions, they are unlikely to achieve significant political change. It is also true that these organizations have yet to incorporate the urban poor.

The authors end with a warning. The urban poor may have gone through a period of increased political participation but the current trend, in the face of continued neglect, is to "sever their ties to the body politic. This calculus must be changed. . . . Urban poverty, drugs, and crime will not yield even to enlightened policy intervention unless the urban poor are able to mobilize to change destructive community patterns. It is for this reason that the entire society may be said to have a stake in increasing the scope and substance of citizen participation in American cities. Otherwise, we can fully expect disadvantaged citizens to again practice the politics of disruption."

Chapter Two

RACE AND CLASS IN PHILADELPHIA MAYORAL ELECTIONS

Carolyn T. Adams

To many observers in the mid-1980s, Philadelphia's electorate seemed destined to divide along racial lines. Having succeeded in 1983 in electing the first black mayor in the city's 300-year history, the Philadelphia Democratic party began losing white registered voters shortly after W. Wilson Goode took office (see figure 2.1). By the time Goode ran for renomination against a white Democratic challenger in the primary of May 1987, Democratic party registrations were about evenly split between blacks and whites. Headlines in the local media emphasized the racial split among Democratic voters: "Goode's Win Came in a Vote Along Racial Lines"; "Tally Indicates Race Was Primary Fulcrum"; and "A Campaign in Black and White." Some political forecasters even spoke of a time when blacks would completely dominate the Democratic party and all white Democrats would migrate to the Republicans, producing a racially based party system.

The defections among white Democrats continued during Wilson Goode's second term in office (1987–1991). All told, from 1983 to 1991, the party lost over one-quarter of its white base. During Goode's mayoralty the party went from a white majority to a black majority. Black registered Democrats outnumbered white registered Democrats by over 50,000 for the Spring 1991 primary, by which time whites comprised only 40 percent of the party's base.

At first glance, then, Philadelphia would appear to confirm the conclusion reached in Huckfeldt and Kohfeld's (1989) study of race in American national politics, that "the extent to which whites are willing to support the Democratic party is directly related to the reliance of the party on black voters. As the Democratic coalition becomes blacker, whites become less willing to participate" (1989:184). The analysis further asserts that because the unwilling-ness to remain in cross-race coalitions is especially pronounced among lower-class white voters, the factor of race is responsible for

Figure 2.1 REGISTERED DEMOCRATIC PARTY VOTERS IN PHILADELPHIA

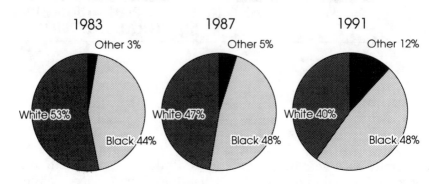

Source: Office of the City Commissioners, Voter Registration Division, Philadelphia.

disrupting lower-class coalitions that might otherwise be viable in U.S. politics (Huckfelt and Kohfeld 1989: 184).

The emphasis on the importance of race as an impediment to class politics may help to illuminate some of Philadelphia's recent political history, but it does not tell the whole story. For if one sees race as an element that fractures class coalitions, one must increasingly acknowledge class as an element that fractures racial coalitions. This chapter argues that the racial solidarity apparent in the early 1980s— particularly in the black electorate's overwhelming support for Wilson Goode's election—has been undermined by class polarization among the city's black citizens. In the end, a white candidate, Edward G. Rendell, won both the 1991 Democratic party nomination for mayor and the general election.

EMERGENCE OF BLACK MAJORITY IN CITY DEMOCRATIC PARTY

It is commonplace to observe that black empowerment in urban areas has resulted from the shifting numerical ratios of blacks to whites. But numerical ratios alone provide too simple an explanation for electoral behavior. True, the exodus of whites from Philadelphia, combined with the migration of blacks into the city since 1945, has created an increasingly black electorate (see tables 2.1 and 2.2). (Currently other minorities comprise less than 10 percent of Philadel-

Table 2.1 DEMOGRAPHIC PROFILE OF PHILADELPHIA, 1950–90

Year	White	Black	Other
1950	1,692,637	376,041	2,927
	(82%)	(18%)	(.2%)
1960	1,467,479	529,240	5,793
	(73%)	(26%)	(.3%)
1970	1,278,710	653,791	16,101
	(65%)	(34%)	(1%)
1980	983,084	638,878	66,248
	(58%)	(38%)	(4%)
1990	848,586	631,936	105,055
	(54%)	(40%)	(6%)

Source: *U.S. Census of Population, 1960: Volume 1, Characteristics of the Population;* *U.S. Census of Population, 1990: Characteristics of the Population.* Washington, D.C.: U.S. Department of Commerce.

Table 2.2 RACIAL COMPOSITION OF PHILADELPHIA ELECTORATE, 1979–91

Year	White (%)	Black (%)	Other (%)
1979	58	37	5
1983	58	39	3
1987	56	39	5
1991	52	36	12

Source: Office of the City Commissioners, Voter Registration Division, Philadelphia.

phia's population and exhibit far lower levels of political activism.) Yet if changing demographics were the only explanation, we would expect to have witnessed a gradual emergence of bloc voting and leadership formation in the city's black communities starting at the time suburbanization got under way. Instead, until well into the 1970s, black participation was channeled through a white-dominated party. Black candidates did not generally make election appeals based on race, nor did the black electorate vote on the basis of race. Instead, the city's black voters staunchly supported the Democratic party from the 1940s to the mid-1970s, registering and voting as Democrats, whether the party's candidates were white or black. In the first few decades following World War II, black electoral participation in Philadelphia declined, even as the size of the black population increased. From 1950 to 1960 the difference in registration rates between Philadelphia whites and blacks widened, with the percentage of blacks who registered declining from 44 percent to 41 percent, while the white rate increased from 52 percent to 55 percent. This was the third consecutive decade that blacks' registration rate had declined (Strange 1973: 122). Blacks were not only registered in smaller proportions than whites; they consistently turned out to vote in lower proportions as well.

The turning point for black participation in Philadelphia politics appears to have been the referendum of 1978. Although ostensibly about changing the provisions of the city charter, in reality this referendum was a vote of confidence on the two-term mayoralty of Frank Rizzo, the swaggering, law-and-order politician who had run for mayor in 1971 based on his record as the city's police chief. He had occupied City Hall for eight years; his administration was marked by an emphasis on fighting crime and pursuing downtown development, but little attention to education and social services. Rizzo's most publicized policy statement on neighborhoods was his declaration that stable neighborhoods were entitled to resist intrusion by government-subsidized housing. In practice, this meant he supported white working-class areas in their refusal to accept subsidized housing that might introduce black residents into their communities.

As Rizzo's second term drew to a close, he tried to amend the city charter's provision that no Philadelphia mayor could serve more than two consecutive terms. Not surprisingly, black Philadelphians were in the vanguard of the forces opposed to his aspirations for yet another term. They succeeded in registering over 62,000 additional black voters and defeating the proposed change. That campaign signaled the formation of a black voting bloc.

Shortly afterward, in 1979, a group of black Democratic ward leaders met to hear presentations from the main candidates running for mayor and city council and to endorse its own slate, independent from the Democratic party's official endorsements. One of their endorsements went to Charles Bowser, a black attorney campaigning for the mayoralty. Bowser lost the primary fight to William Green, but when Green took office he acknowledged the importance of the black voting bloc in the Democratic party by appointing a black public administrator, W. Wilson Goode, as managing director of the city. Both registration rates and turnout rates surged among black voters in the early 1980s. By May 1983, when Wilson Goode became the first black to win either party's nomination for mayor, 98 percent of the city's eligible black voters were registered to vote. That extraordinary record of participation gave blacks almost 44 percent of all Democratic party registrations. And in the general election of 1983, black voter turnout exceeded the citywide average for the first time in Philadelphia history. Moreover, the black community was more financially involved in Democratic politics than ever before. Local newspapers estimated that of the approximately $5 million Wilson Goode spent on his campaign, $2 million had been contributed by blacks (20 times the amount of black contributions to any previous mayoral candidate).

Wilson Goode's convincing victory in 1983 aroused enormous expectations among Democrats, both black and white. At last the Democrats appeared to have a candidate who could unify a party that had increasingly splintered during the 1960s and 1970s, along much the same lines as the national Democratic coalition. Liberal reformers, pro-growth business leaders, labor unions, traditional white working-class politicians, and independent black politicians— all elements of Philadelphia's Democratic party revival in the late 1940s and 1950s—found it more and more difficult to sustain the coalition, especially after federal aid to the city declined in the early 1970s. In large measure the benefits flowing from urban renewal and other federal programs had helped to reconcile disparate sets of inter-ests in the ways outlined by Mollenkopf in *The Contested City* (1983).

Wilson Goode's candidacy appealed to many of those disparate Democratic constituencies. He claimed the support not only of down-town businesses but also of neighborhood groups whose municipal services had improved during his term as managing director. White reformers saw Wilson Goode as a hard-working administrator with a record of honest, efficient management of the city's operating departments. Black Democrats lined up solidly behind this candidate who had worked effectively for inner-city neighborhoods as manag-ing director, and who symbolized greater opportunities for blacks. Goode's campaign even accommodated the party regulars in white working-class wards along the Delaware River and in South Philadel-phia. In return for the ward leaders' support, Goode offered to endorse some of their handpicked candidates for lower-level offices and pat-ronage jobs in his administration. Goode's coalition-building efforts paid off. His winning campaign in 1983 never took on an overtly racial tone (Ransom 1987: 256–89). Instead, he put forward a classic reform platform, pledging a more businesslike approach to managing municipal government and a strong emphasis on economic develop-ment projects like the port and the convention center. Goode prom-ised to deliver services more efficiently and to create jobs by attracting and retaining business. He reminded his audiences that there was no black or white way to deliver city programs.

Yet a mayoralty that began with great promise was crippled almost beyond recovery in May 1985 by the city's disastrous confrontation with a small extremist commune known as "MOVE." In a largely black neighborhood of West Philadelphia that had been threatened by violence from the commune's residents, police erected barricades around the MOVE house and ultimately dropped explosives on it, setting off a fire that killed all 11 MOVE members inside the house and destroyed two city blocks (Bowser 1989). In addition to destroying human lives and over 60 homes, the incident devastated Wilson Goode's hopes of being the politician who would put the city's fractured political majority back together. No longer did Goode enjoy the unqualified support of black Democrats, some of whom saw the city's decision to drop explosives on a residential area as a racist act. Business leaders were appalled at the lapse in managerial control that led to the incident; a blue-ribbon investigating panel accused the mayor of abandoning his command responsibilities in the emergency. And many white liberals were shocked at the use of such brutal force to quell a neighborhood disturbance. Although Wilson Goode was able to reestablish his control over municipal operations, he never regained the personal loyalty that might have allowed him to act as the peacemaker among quarreling party factions.

Facing his reelection campaign in 1987, Goode was in an uncomfortable position. The MOVE incident had cost him much of his white liberal support. And even more importantly, many white Democrats had shifted their registrations to the Republican Party before the 1987 primary in order to vote for Frank Rizzo. (Having been out of office for two terms, ex-mayor Rizzo was eligible to run again, but chose to run as a Republican this time.) So significant were these white defections from the party rolls that by the time Wilson Goode ran for reelection in 1987, registration figures showed black Democrats actually exceeded whites by 10,000 (see figure 2.1). Thus, Goode's electoral base had narrowed considerably, and it was clear that he would have to rely more completely on black voters than in his campaign four years earlier. Recognizing this fact, Goode's campaign organizers worked intensively in the city's black neighborhoods, even while the mayor continued to downplay race as a factor in the campaign. There was, in short, a discrepancy between the reality of Goode's electoral base (Goode won by drawing about 97 percent of the black vote), and the resolutely nonracial rhetoric of his campaign.

DIVISIONS WITHIN BLACK MAJORITY

Surprisingly, the black numerical majority within the party did not translate into a black candidacy in the mayoral contest of 1991. Instead, the spring primary produced a white nominee (Edward Rendell) to be the Democrat's standard bearer in the fall election for Mayor. In the primary of 1991, the city's black electorate split its vote among four contenders, two blacks and two whites.

The split occurred despite the best efforts of powerful local leaders to promote solidarity within the black electorate in order to maintain control of City Hall. They included the Black Clergy of Philadelphia and Vicinity, a group of over 300 of the city's 1,600 black churches that had proved highly effective in pushing Wilson Goode to victory in the early 1980s. The clergy at the head of this organization met for 18 months leading up to the May 1991 primary, struggling to agree on which candidate to endorse as a group. Eventually, separate subgroups endorsed two different black candidates.

The United Black Ward Leaders also attempted to narrow the field of black candidates in December 1990, when they sponsored a retreat at Lincoln University outside Philadelphia—an event they titled "Mending the Broken Circles." Both of the major black contenders for the nomination attended and listened to pleas for unity from other political leaders, but neither proved willing to step aside.

In March 1991, Jesse Jackson came to Philadelphia to urge the two front-running black candidates to "come together" because "both of them cannot win" (Diaz 1991). He warned that Philadelphians must avoid repeating the situation in Chicago in 1989, when competition between black candidates split black voters during the Democratic primary, enabling a white to win.

But these appeals for unity ultimately proved fruitless. Strategists for the two black front-runners directed their main campaign appeals at the city's black communities, where each assumed his main competition would come from his black rival rather than from the two whites who were also in the race for the nomination. Hence, the two black candidates targeted each other for their most bitter attacks. George Burrell accused his rival, Lucien Blackwell, of maintaining ties to organized crime because Blackwell's brother had been identified by the Pennsylvania Crime Commission as running a numbers racket in the city. For his part, Blackwell publicized Burrell's having defaulted on $16,000 in student loans, and questioned Burrell's recent tax returns, which showed suspiciously large business deductions.

Two weeks before the primary election, a poll showed the two black candidates running about even among black voters, with each of them garnering 29 percent and an unusually large number of blacks undecided. The poll showed that 60 percent of all those classified as undecided were black voters. On voting day, although blacks comprised about 48 percent of Democratic party registrations, the black candidates together received slightly less than 42 percent of Democratic votes. In a few predominantly black wards, the white winner got as much as 20 percent of the vote. One of the city's leading black newspaper columnists explained the outcome by observing that many black voters were "confused and dispirited" by the conflict between the two black rivals (Moore 1991).

PATTERN OF BLACK ELECTORAL SUPPORT FOR BLACK CANDIDATES

One way to examine recent electoral trends among Philadelphia's black voters is to review the racial composition of the vote for black candidates in four successive mayoral primaries: 1979, 1983, 1987, and 1991. In each of these years, the Democratic primary was a contest between black and white candidates. Hence, these primary elections offer a chance to observe black support for black candidates in a way that the general elections do not, because the general elections have not always included black candidates for mayor. (Philadelphia's Republican Party has never run a black candidate for mayor in either a primary or a general election.)

Table 2.3 displays the voting record in these four primary elections for the city's 15 most heavily black wards. In all these wards, 85 percent or more of registered Democrats are black. Note that the table shows the percentage of *all eligible* voters who supported the black candidates, not just the percentage of people voting who supported the black candidates. Thus, it incorporates the element of turnout to measure the relative success of different black candidates in mobilizing their constituents. Clearly 1983 was the pinnacle of black mobilization. That was the first election in which a black candidate, W. Wilson Goode, appeared to have a realistic chance of capturing the nomination. Both the primary and general elections brought into the political process a large number of first-time voters, many of whom were younger and poorer than previously registered voters. Activists hoped that once they had participated, they would continue

Table 2.3 PERCENTAGE OF REGISTERED DEMOCRATS VOTING FOR BLACK
CANDIDATES IN PHILADELPHIA'S MOST HEAVILY BLACK WARDS,
1979–91

Ward Number	1979 (%)	1983 (%)	1987 (%)	1991 (%)
3	58	64	60	37
4	56	63	59	35
6	50	61	53	30
10	56	70	61	39
11	48	57	52	33
16	47	62	53	31
17	52	65	54	35
28	49	59	53	35
29	47	61	49	30
32	44	61	50	32
44	53	60	56	33
47	34	55	40	24
50	51	68	60	38
51	50	62	54	32
60	50	63	58	35
Mean	50	62	54	33

Source: Office of the City Commissioners, Voter Registration Division, Philadelphia.

to vote. But in Goode's fight for renomination in 1987 his appeal
declined in every ward included in table 2.3, although he still managed to draw a majority of the voters to the polls to support him.
The uniform and very steep drop-off in the 1991 figures reflects the
fact that the total combined vote for both black candidates represented barely a third of the eligible voters in these 15 wards. What
accounted for this decline?

The black voters who failed to support the black candidates in the
elections of 1987 and 1991 were not defecting in large numbers to
other candidates; they were simply staying away from the polls.
Table 2.4 makes clear that the falloff in black support for the black
candidates after 1983 was due primarily to declining voter turnout.
The table shows turnout rates increasing in 1983 for Wilson Goode's
first election, but then sliding in his second election, and dropping
off precipitously in the 1991 election. The extent of black nonpartici-
pation in 1991 was especially surprising, given the traditional pattern
of higher turnouts in races when no incumbent is running. (This
falloff in voter turnout for black candidates after 1983 was accompanied by a parallel drop in rates of registration. From 1983 to 1991,
Democratic registrations declined by 15 percent in these predominantly black wards.)

Table 2.4 TURNOUT AMONG REGISTERED DEMOCRATS IN PHILADELPHIA'S
MOST HEAVILY BLACK WARDS, 1979–91

Ward Number	1979 (%)	1983 (%)	1987 (%)	1991 (%)
3	64	71	63	48
4	61	69	62	44
6	56	68	57	36
10	63	76	65	49
11	54	68	55	41
16	56	67	56	38
17	63	71	59	46
28	53	46	55	43
29	58	66	55	37
32	50	66	54	38
44	60	68	59	42
47	46	58	45	28
50	61	75	66	51
51	56	67	56	40
60	56	69	62	45
Mean	57	67	58	42

Source: Office of the City Commissioners, Voter Registration Division, Philadelphia.

WILSON GOODE'S RESPONSIVENESS TO BLACK CONSTITUENT CONCERNS

One common explanation for these declines in black electoral participation is that they reflect disappointment in the performance of the
city's first black mayor. Is such disappointment justified? How closely
did the city's first black mayor identify himself with the problems
and needs of his black constituents?

Wilson Goode's first and most visible public signal that he intended
to bring blacks into the mainstream of municipal government was
his cabinet appointments. When Goode himself had been appointed
managing director in 1980 under Mayor William Green, he became
the first black ever to hold a cabinet-level position in Philadelphia.
During his first term as mayor, Goode appointed three blacks to his
own six-member cabinet. During his two terms he also appointed
numerous black administrators to head key departments, commissions, and boards, including the city's first black police commissioner
in 1988.

Wilson Goode was also the city's most vocal advocate of a set-
aside law for municipal contracts, a key component of the political
agenda of the city's black political leaders. Relative to other major

Table 2.5 CONTRACTING WITH MINORITY BUSINESS ENTERPRISES:
PHILADELPHIA

	Services, Equipment, and Supplies	Public Works
FYª 1987	$13,100,000 (11.6%)	$21,000,000 (16.8%)
FY 1988	$17,100,000 (13.4%)	$14,500,000 (15.4%)
FY 1989	$16,700,000 (13.8%)	$27,800,000 (17.3%)
FY 1990	$15,300,000 (12.8%)	$15,200,000 (13.3%)
FY 1991ᵇ	$ 4,900,000 (4.8%)	$ 2,700,000 (4.9%)

Source: Minority Business Enterprise Council, Philadelphia.
a. FY, fiscal year.
b. Figures are for the first 10 months only.

U.S. cities, Philadelphia was late in enacting set-asides. Not until 1983 was the city's Minority Business Enterprise Council (MBEC) created to implement a new ordinance requiring that 15 percent of the city's contract work go directly to firms owned and operated by minorities, and that 10 percent of contracts go to female-owned firms. The MBEC's mission includes monitoring the awarding of contracts and working to familiarize minority firms with the city's bidding and procurement system, especially requirements pertaining to insurance, bonding, delivery schedules, and so forth.

In 1983, the year that Goode became mayor, Philadelphia awarded a total of only $17 million in contracts to minority business firms in the two main categories of contracts: services, equipment, and supplies; and public works. Table 2.5 shows that by the time Goode ran for reelection in 1987, minority contracts awarded in the two categories had climbed to $34 million, a doubling of performance in less than four years. The table also makes clear, however, that the city suffered a precipitous drop in minority contracting at the end of Mayor Goode's second term. After the U.S. Supreme Court struck down set-asides in the Richmond, Virginia, case of 1989 (*City of Richmond v. Croson*, 1095, Ct. 706), Mayor Goode opposed either modifying Philadelphia's rules or voluntarily suspending the city's set-asides, steps that numerous other cities took in the wake of the *Croson* decision. Even after a U.S. district judge voided Philadelphia's minority contracting law in April 1990, Goode signed an exec-

Table 2.6 BLACK REPRESENTATION IN PHILADELPHIA MUNICIPAL
WORK FORCE

	1975 (%)	1979 (%)	1983 (%)	1987 (%)	1990 (%)
Officials/administrators	20.7	20.1	19.8	20.5	22.5
Professionals	19.4	21.7	25.7	28.8	32.9
Technicians	33.8	31.2	33.0	35.8	35.2
Paraprofessionals	78.6	71.6	68.8	73.0	66.0
Protective	21.2	21.9	23.2	27.7	33.0
Office/clerical	49.2	48.1	48.6	52.6	56.5
Skilled craft	40.1	44.4	47.9	45.3	46.9
Service/maintenance	81.5	77.7	81.6	80.5	78.7

Source: City of Philadelphia, Civil Service Commission, *Annual Report to the Mayor*,
December 31, 1990.

utive order to continue set-asides on a contract-by-contract basis
until a new law could be passed. Nevertheless, the figures for fiscal
year (FY) 1991 reveal the drastic drop in performance resulting from
the Court's ruling. (Well after Goode had left office, the U.S. Court
of Appeals vindicated his interpretation of the law by ruling in October 1993 that Philadelphia's set-aside program was sufficiently different from Richmond's to be constitutional.)

During Goode's two terms, blacks gained increasing access to
municipal jobs, as shown in table 2.6. In five out of eight categories
of employment included in the table, the proportion of jobs held by
blacks increased between 1983 and 1990. This accomplishment is
particularly noteworthy because of the hiring constraints and even
hiring freezes that prevailed during much of Goode's mayoralty.

As tenacious as he was in defending minority participation in
contracts and municipal employment, Wilson Goode became an
equally persistent advocate of other municipal priorities—ones far
less appealing to his black constituents. For example, he placed heavy
emphasis on two massive downtown projects: a convention center
and a waterfront development known as Penn's Landing. Goode's
drive for economic development at times took precedence over other
goals of his administration, even affirmative action. So determined
was he to secure the state legislature's financial support for the convention center that, unlike the city council, he was willing to agree
to a legislative package that omitted any affirmative action guidelines
regarding the workers who would be employed for the construction
project—guidelines the city council regarded as necessary. Moreover,
the mayor balked at the city council's desire in 1985 to supplement
the minority contracting policy mentioned earlier by stipulating that

not just construction contracts, but construction employment as well, would be governed by affirmative action guidelines. He vigorously opposed the measure, which would have required that any construction project involving more than $1 million in city funds would have to give at least 25 percent of total employment to minorities and 5 percent to women workers. Aligning himself with the business community, most of the construction unions, and the building contractors, Mayor Goode argued that such a law would impose unfair regulation on the construction industry and discourage investment. On this issue the mayor's view prevailed; the bill never made it out of committee to the floor of the council (Beauregard 1989).

Mayor Goode also dismayed many black supporters by battling against the city's major public employee union, an organization with a predominantly black membership whose leaders had enthusiastically supported his candidacy in 1983. In July 1986 the mayor withstood a 20-day trash strike in order to demonstrate to those who were most concerned about the city's solvency that he was willing to resist the city workers' demands. Two weeks into the disruptive strike, which left mountains of garbage rotting in the summer sun, the president of the chamber of commerce praised Mayor Goode for his tough stand: "It's the fiscally responsible thing to do. . . . Sometimes you have to take strikes rather than give the store away" (Nussbaum 1986). Goode finally broke the strike by persuading the courts to issue a back-to-work order. Only a year later, in the midst of his reelection campaign, Goode commissioned a study on privatizing trash pickup and then endorsed its conclusion that Philadelphia should contract out two-thirds of its residential trash collection and reduce the remaining crews from three or four workers to only two workers. The proposal threatened to eliminate the jobs of about 1,500 sanitation workers, prompting a bitter protest from several of the city's labor leaders who had previously supported Goode.

The fiscal austerity that prevailed during much of Goode's eight-year term served as a backdrop to constant conflict between the mayor and city council. According to an opinion survey conducted by the Philadelphia City Planning Commission shortly before Goode took office, the overwhelming majority of black respondents cited housing programs as "the most important action needed to improve neighborhoods" (1982: 20). (Interestingly, white respondents ranked police protection as their highest priority.) The virtual disappearance of federal housing subsidies in the 1980s hampered Goode's capacity to respond to this top priority in black communities. Although he invested political capital in large-scale, widely publicized development ventures, Goode cut city services and discouraged the construction of new neighborhood facilities on the grounds that the city's limited operating funds could not provide staffing for new recreation centers, libraries, and swimming pools. A frustrated woman representing the Philadelphia Council of Neighborhood Organizations summarized the views of many community activists this way:

> It seems as though whatever is needed by the taxpayers—just the basic services that are needed, what they have a right to expect to receive for their tax dollars—there is never enough money to do this. . . . But the major projects—any development downtown or whatever—we always seem to be able to find the money. So, of course we are very, very disturbed with that. (Derr 1987)

Another community activist who chaired a North Philadelphia-based coalition of 16 neighborhood organizations explained the low turnout in many black neighborhoods in spring 1991 this way: "The same black voters who went out in droves and voted for Wilson Goode in '83 have not seen what it meant. . . . Our streets are just as dirty. To the average person in North Philly, the skyline doesn't mean shit" (Omjasisa Kentu, quoted in Holmes 1991).

The difference in the levels of funding committed to downtown projects versus neighborhood projects frequently brought the city's first black mayor into open conflict with members of the city council, who saw themselves as defenders of neighborhood interests (Adams 1988: chap. 5). Led by black council members whose political power was neighborhood-based, the council took a populist stand against cutting services or closing facilities. For example, when Mayor Goode closed two fire stations in West Philadelphia to save money in 1988, the council passed an ordinance to keep them open and then filed a lawsuit when the mayor refused to abide by their wishes. The inability of the mayor and council to reach agreement on the mayor's numerous proposals to raise taxes, cut spending, and streamline government through privatizing services helped to propel the city to the edge of bankruptcy in 1990–91.

CLASS POLARIZATION WITHIN BLACK ELECTORATE

It is a truism that black elected officials have attained power in America's cities at a time when their opportunities as leaders are severely constrained by shrinking resources. Urban political leaders of the 1980s did not dispose of massive federal aid, as had the mayors of earlier decades. The extent of the difference is evident in the mayoral terms of Frank Rizzo (1971–79) and Wilson Goode (1983–91). During Rizzo's final year in office, Philadelphia received $98 million through the federal Comprehensive Employment and Training Act (CETA) to hire 3,163 workers to clean the streets, repair potholes, clean recreation centers, and staff branch libraries. The city also received $48 million in federal revenue sharing. Federal aid to Philadelphia peaked at $255 million in 1981 and then began to decline, until in 1990 the federal contribution to the city's operation totaled only $183 million. Adjusted for inflation, that represented a decline of 50 percent during the 1980s. During Wilson Goode's two terms in the 1980s, revenue sharing as well as the CETA program were eliminated, so that the city government now has no federally funded jobs.

Nor did Philadelphia get adequate assistance from the state govern-ment. A study comparing Philadelphia with 16 other large cities across the United States showed that in 1988 Philadelphia ranked 10th in the amount of state aid per capita received for city government functions (Pennsylvania Economy League 1989). Philadelphia com-pared especially unfavorably with other northeastern cities (e.g., New York, Boston, Newark, Baltimore, and Pittsburgh). Philadelphia ranked last among the six in state aid per capita (Pennsylvania Econ-omy League 1989: 13). Furthermore, unlike many large cities, Phila-delphia could not appeal to county-level government for assistance in funding social services, health services, and so on, because Phila-delphia is a county unto itself.

However, I would argue that the resource problem—as significant as it is—is not the most fundamental constraint urban leaders face. Equally important is the reality that officials must use whatever resources are available to satisfy the demands of an increasingly fractured electorate. In Philadelphia two factors are driving this class polarization, which is occurring among both blacks and whites. One is the urban labor market, which is generating new jobs that are either highly paid or poorly paid, but few jobs in-between. The problem of "the disappearing middle" identified by Harrison and Bluestone (1988) can be demonstrated to have occurred in the Philadelphia economy during Wilson Goode's mayoralty (see table 2.7).

Another factor accounting for income disparities was discrepancies in the number of earners per family unit. Households led by a single adult, either working or nonworking, are far more likely to be in the low-income category than households with more than one earner

Table 2.7 PERCENTAGE OF JOBS AND OF EARNINGS IN DIFFERENT JOB
CATEGORIES IN PHILADELPHIA

	Percentage of Jobs		Percentage of Earnings	
Wage Level	1980	1987	1980	1987
High wage[a]	5	11	12	26
Medium wage[b]	83	75	84	70
Low wage[c]	12	14	4	4

Source: Adams et al. (1991: chap. 2).
a. Paying more than twice the median wage.
b. Paying half to twice the median wage.
c. Paying less than half the median wage.

(Adams et al. 1991: chap. 2). Philadelphia fits the pattern for the
nation as a whole (Harrison and Gorham 1992), which is that practi-
cally all the growth in the number of high-income black families
during the 1980s took place in households with multiple earners,
some of whom worked more than one job.

Since the publication of William Julius Wilson's *The Truly Disadvantaged* (1987), the subject of class polarization within the black
community in the United States has dominated many contemporary
discussions of race. Wilson described an emerging black middle class
that has gradually separated itself from a largely black urban "underclass," both by its social and geographical mobility. The polarization
of black family incomes during the 1980s, he argued, split American
blacks into two diverging communities. It may well be that the widening disparity in household incomes, which was clearly occurring in
Philadelphia, began to manifest itself in local politics.

The media in the city characterized the split within the black
political leadership as a generational conflict that pitted the city's
older established black ward leaders against a newer generation of
professional blacks with ties to business. At the center of this so-
called new generation of the 1980s was Congressman William Gray,
a Baptist preacher from North Philadelphia who, by virtue of his
post as chair of the House Democratic Caucus, became the most
influential black elected official in the U.S. Congress. Gray used the
power and money he achieved in Washington, D.C., to establish
himself as the sponsor of a new generation of political leadership in
his hometown. He handpicked reform candidates, both white and
black, for city council, for the state legislature, and for mayor, and
then bolstered their campaigns with money and personal support.
Enough of his protégées won in the 1980s to mark Gray as a powerbroker. When he abandoned that role in 1991, giving up his congres-

sional seat to become president of the United Negro College Fund, Gray left a half-dozen city and state officials in place who represented his legacy.

The divisions observed within the city's black electorate, however, were more than generational. They were not spawned only by new-comers challenging entrenched politicians, but by class divisions as well. As was reflected in the campaigns of the two black contenders for mayor in 1991, Philadelphia's black electorate appears increasingly split along class lines.

The two black rivals for mayor in 1991 symbolized the split. Lucien Blackwell was a rough-and-tumble politician who never finished high school and who rose through the ranks to become leader of a longshoremen's union. As a representative of the city's working- and lower-class black communities, he won endorsements from grass-roots neighborhood organizations and labor unions, including the American Federation of State, County and Municipal Employees (AFSCME) District Council 33, which represents the city's 12,000 uniformed municipal workers. During the primary campaign, he reported having raised $206,000 in campaign contributions, only about a third as much as his black rival, and only a fifth of what the winning white candidate raised (Paolantonio 1991). In his mayoral campaign, as in his earlier race for city council in 1987, Blackwell relied heavily on low-income campaign workers, including homeless people paid $25 each, to turn out the vote. His electoral strongholds were the working-class and low-income neighborhoods of West Philadelphia and North Philadelphia.

His black rival, George Burrell, was a lawyer with both a business degree and a law degree from an Ivy League institution. Burrell's campaign drew over $600,000 in contributions, including $135,000 from a New Jersey-based defense contractor and $25,000 from Congressman William Gray (Paolantonio 1991). Backed by both Gray and outgoing Mayor Goode, Burrell also carried the endorsement of AFSCME District Council 47, the union representing City Hall's 4,000 white-collar professional employees. Burrell even got long-distance support from David Dinkins, the mayor of New York. Dinkins threw a fund-raiser for Burrell in midtown Manhatten, introducing the Philadelphia candidate to his own loyal contributors and raising $60,000 for Burrell. Throughout the campaign Burrell was backed by, and spoke for, black middle-class professionals. He stressed such themes as fiscal responsibility and living within the city's means. Like the two white candidates in the race, Burrell supported privatization of many city services, whereas the union leader Blackwell opposed contracting out public services to private firms. As the more moderate black choice, Burrell argued, he would be more likely to win white support in the general election. The hostility between Burrell's and Blackwell's camps was evident early in the race. The day that George Burrell filed his candidate petition at City Hall, he was taunted by a group of street vendors supporting Blackwell and carrying a sign that highlighted the class antagonism in this rivalry: "George Burrell: an educated fool from a sophisticated school."

When the votes from the primary were tallied, Blackwell had out-polled Burrell by almost two to one, prevailing over his black rival in the vast majority of wards where black voters predominate. Burrell's stongest showing, not surprisingly, came in the highest-income black wards in the city, which hug the northern city limits adjacent to suburban Montgomery County (see figure 2.2). Table 2.8 shows that whereas Burrell did best in the highest-income wards, Blackwell did best in the lowest-income wards.

Philadelphia is not the only city in which class differences within the black community have become important in mayoral races. A similar contest occurred in Cleveland in 1989, when five candidates ran in a mayoral primary that narrowed ultimately to a runoff between two black contestants: a tough-talking 26-year veteran of city council who drew more support from low-income voters versus a young state legislator with a master's degree in public administration who captured a larger share of middle-income votes. (The younger candi-date, Michael White, ultimately proved the victor in both the primary and the general election). Like the Philadelphia case, the Cleveland example illustrates the point that it is increasingly difficult for a single black candidate to appeal to the disparate socioeconomic groups within the black community.

To answer the question "Was Wilson Goode responsive to the city's black community?" one needs to specify which black community. By elevating blacks to cabinet posts and insisting that minority firms participate in city contracts, Goode was encouraging blacks in busi-nesses and professions to identify with his administration. For exam-ple, even after the MOVE tragedy, Goode's reelection was enthusiasti-cally promoted by the United Black Business Association, a group of nearly 300 regional firms. When the mayor resisted the construc-tion of new community recreational facilities, libraries, and fire sta-tions, and remained firm against a protracted strike by municipal employees, he was responding to middle-income taxpayers, both black and white, who demanded that he hold down taxes. But it is doubtful whether these measures improved the lives of low-income

Figure 2.2 LOW-, MODERATE-, AND HIGH-INCOME PHILADELPHIA
NEIGHBORHOODS WITH OVER 75 PERCENT BLACK RESIDENTS

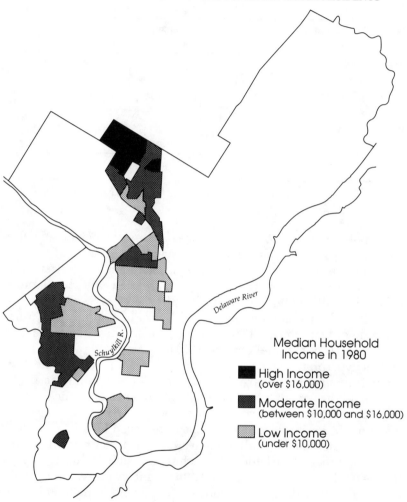

families who were struggling to protect their children in drug- and
crime-infested neighborhoods. Advocates for the city's disadvantaged citizens roundly criticized the mayor for failing to meet the
needs of the poor, the homeless, drug and alcohol abusers, AIDS
victims, abused children, and others. No mayor, regardless of
race, could simultaneously satisfy these diverging sets of political
interests.

Table 2.8 PERCENTAGE OF MAY 1991 VOTE FOR BLACK MAYORALTY
CANDIDATES IN PHILADELPHIA'S MOST HEAVILY BLACK WARDS,
GROUPED BY INCOME LEVELS

Median Household Income, 1980	Percentage for Lucian Blackwell	Percentage for George Burrell
Over $16,000 (Wards 10, 50)	38%	40%
$10,000 to $15,999 (Wards 3, 16, 17, 51, 60)	51%	27%
Under $10,000 (Wards 4, 6, 11, 28, 29, 32, 44, 47)	57%	25%

CENTRIFUGAL POLITICS

Black politicians have come to power at a moment when urban political structures are dissolving. Political scientists have spent much of
their time in recent decades unmasking the dominant power structures in cities, the growth coalitions, and so on. But the alarming
reality in Philadelphia, as in many other large U.S. cities, is that
there is no longer any dominant coalition. Philadelphia is a prime
example of what the authors of a recent book have labeled "hyperpluralism" (Thomas and Savitch 1991).

This hyperpluralism has been displayed in both the city's electoral
coalitions and its governing coalition. The Democratic Party,
although it has nominally controlled both the mayor's office and the
city council for over 40 years, has all but dissolved as an electoral
machine. In recent decades it has been replaced by a patchwork of
fiefdoms dominated by individual ward leaders, many of whom hold
positions as state legislators or city council members. In spring 1991
the recognized leader of the party for eight years, Wilson Goode,
could not persuade a single ward leader to vote to include his son
as one of the party's endorsed candidates for city council. The central
party organization within the city no longer even tries to control
the nomination of its candidate for mayor; in most recent mayoral
primaries, the party has refused to endorse any candidate. Moreover,
when the organization *does* achieve consensus on endorsements, it
has difficulty delivering the vote to its endorsed candidates because
it no longer holds a monopoly on instructing Democratic voters how
to cast their ballots. Admittedly, in every election the central party
organization distributes "sample ballots" door-to-door and at polling

places to remind voters which candidates have the party's endorsement. But individual ward leaders insist on the prerogative of printing their own customized sample ballots to endorse their own choices. The result is that in every election the city is blanketed with dozens of different versions of "official" party ballots, reflecting the shifting political alliances among ward leaders and candidates. Nor does the party exercise much control over patronage. Individual ward leaders often consult directly with municipal administrators to request appointments for their constituents, without even consulting the party leadership.

Predictably, the governing coalition that results from such an electoral structure is itself fragmented. There is no stable governing coalition linking the mayor to a group of reliable supporters in city council. Those who are elected to city council owed allegiance only to the particular ward leader or leaders who got them elected, not to any citywide coalition. Thus, party leaders have been too weak either to forge permanent alliances or to mediate the disputes arising among factions in a game of constantly shifting alliances. The result in recent years has often been a political standoff between the mayor, identified with economic development projects and austerity budgeting, and a city council dominated by populist politicians whose careers have depended on delivering services and jobs to their constituents. Unable to cooperate in making tough decisions to either raise taxes or cut services, in the late 1980s the mayor and council allowed the gap to widen between the city's revenues and its expenses. Deficits increased from $32 million in FY 1988 to a projected $284 million in FY 1992, with larger and larger deficits predicted for subsequent years, unless policies were changed.

The short-term solution to the financial crisis was the creation in June 1991 of a state-level authority, the Pennsylvania Intergovernmental Cooperation Authority (PICA), similar to the Municipal Assistance Corporation formed in 1975 to oversee New York City's bailout. The authority's five members were appointed by the governor and legislative leaders of Pennsylvania. Their official functions were to raise money for Philadelphia through the sale of bonds and to impose discipline on the city's budgeting process. These objectives were met. Between June 1992 and August 1992 the city completed $2 billion in bond sales to meet its cash needs. A 1 percent sales tax was imposed, and part of the city wage tax was diverted to the state to repay the new debt. In a highly publicized series of labor negotiations, Philadelphia's municipal labor unions agreed to reductions in the work force, cutbacks in wages, some reductions in automatic sick days and other leave time, and privatization of selected white-collar functions. A five-year financial plan was developed to move toward a structurally balanced city budget, without further tax increases.

For the time being, Mayor Edward Rendell's strategy of hardheaded municipal management, coupled with financial cooperation with the state, has proved highly successful in forging a governing political coalition. The administration thus far commands widespread voter support, and has greatly reduced the historical conflict between city council and the mayor's office. The city government ended FY 1993 with a small surplus, reversing a five-year trend of mounting budget deficits. That reversal was achieved by significantly renegotiating contracts with city workers to freeze some salaries and to cut the city's contribution to union health funds and other benefits.

Philadelphia's white mayor was able to cut municipal expenditures so dramatically only because he had forged an unprecedented degree of cooperation with the black leader of city council, John Street. Replacing years of deadlock between the mayor and council with a partnership approach to government, these two public officials appear to share power in virtually all important decisions. In return for access to decisions, as well as to the awarding of lucrative patronage contracts and making board appointments, the council president has delivered council votes endorsing crucial budgetary and policy proposals from the mayor. Not all Philadelphians are pleased with this newly forged alliance between the city's two leading public officials. For example, the head of a major municipal union has criticized the lock-step unity between the mayor and council president for excluding other interests: "I think they're both cut from the same cloth—political opportunism" (Purdy and Carvajal 1993).

Whether such a partnership is more than a temporary fix for the "hyper-plural" politics of Philadelphia remains to be seen. It may represent no more than a temporary truce among competing politicians imposed from outside by the state authority's constant calls for fiscal and political responsibility. Local political leaders must use the respite to build new coalitions that self-consciously cross classes, racial lines, and neighborhoods. In an earlier urban era, Philadelphia and many other cities designed such coalitions to bridge a multitude of ethnic and class distinctions. These were the political machines of the late 19th and early 20th century. They mediated intergroup conflicts and rivalries by strategically dispensing patronage and favors, fashioning electoral coalitions that remained stable in many cities for decades.

Yet the machines failed in one crucial respect: they failed to link electoral coalitions to governing coalitions in ways that achieved accountable government. Indeed, the survival capacity of the machines lay in their ability to insulate the governing coalition from the electoral coalition. Officeholders felt no need to respond to the needs of their constituents with policies and programs, since they could guarantee themselves reelection by handing out jobs to key supporters, their families, and friends. The challenge now in Philadelphia and in many other cities whose electorates are increasingly diverse will be to create a stable, dominant political coalition that both represents diverse communities of interest *and* ties electoral politics to governing platforms.

References

Adams, C. 1988. *The Politics of Capital Investment: The Case of Philadelphia.* Albany, N.Y.: State University of New York Press.

Adams, C., D. Bartelt, D. Elesh, I. Goldstein, N. Kleniewski, and W. Yancey. 1991. *Philadelphia: Neighborhoods, Division, and Conflict in a Post-industrial City.* Philadelphia: Temple University Press.

Beauregard, R. 1989. "Local Politics and the Employment Relation: Construction Jobs in Philadelphia." In *Economic Restructuring and Response,* edited by R. Beauregard (149–79). Beverly Hills, Calif.: Sage Publications.

Bowser, C. 1989. *Let the Bunker Burn: The Final Battle with MOVE.* Philadelphia: Camino Books.

Derr, T. 1987. "Win or Lose, You'll Still Be Breaking Rocks." *Focus Magazine* (Philadelphia), May 20: 19–25.

Diaz, I. 1991. "Jesse Jackson Makes No Mayoral Endorsement." *Philadelphia Inquirer,* March 28, p. B1.

Harrison, B., and B. Bluestone. 1988. *The Great U-Turn: Corporate Restructuring and the Polarizing of America.* New York: Basic Books.

Harrison, B., and L. Gorham. 1992. "What Happened to Black Wages in the 1980s?" In *The Metropolis in Black and White: Place, Power, and Polarization,* edited by George Galster and Edward Hill. New Brunswick, NJ: Center for Urban Policy Research, Rutgers University.

Holmes, S. 1991. "Blackwell-Rizzo Alliance?" *Philadelphia Tribune,* June 6, p. A8.

Huckfeldt, R., and C. Kohfeld. 1989. *Race and the Decline of Class in American Politics.* Urbana: University of Illinois Press.

Mollenkopf, John H. 1983. *The Contested City.* Princeton, N.J.: Princeton University Press.

Moore, A. 1991. "After the Election: A Tale of Two Cities." *Philadelphia Inquirer*, May 23, p. A27.

Nussbaum, P. 1986. "Talking Tough to Unions, Goode Strengthens Image." *Philadelphia Inquirer*, July 13, p. C1.

Paolantonio, S. A. 1991. "Mayoral Contributions Make History." *Philadelphia Inquirer*, May 11, p. B1.

Pennsylvania Economy League. 1989. *Revenue and Expenditure Comparisons: Philadelphia vs. Selected Major Cities.* Philadelphia: Author, June.

Philadelphia City Planning Commission. 1982. *Citizen Survey: City of Philadelphia.* Philadelphia: Author, April.

Purdy, M., and D. Carvajal. 1993. "Philadelphia's Odd Power Couple." *Philadelphia Inquirer*, April 25, p. A1.

Ransom, B. 1987. "Black Independent Electoral Politics in Philadelphia and the Election of Mayor W. Wilson Goode." In *The New Black Politics*, 2d ed., edited by M. B. Preston, L. J. Henderson, and P. Puryear. New York: Longman.

Strange, J. H. 1973. "Blacks and Philadelphia Politics: 1963–1966." In *Black Politics in Philadelphia*, edited by M. Ershkowitz and J. Likmunds (109–44). New York: Basic Books.

Thomas, J. C., and H. Savitch, eds. 1991. *Big City Politics in Transition.* Beverly Hills, Calif.: Sage Publications.

Wilson, William Julius. 1987. *The Truly Disadvantaged: The Inner City, the Underclass, and Public Policy.* Chicago: University of Chicago Press.

Chapter Three

RACIAL AND ETHNIC POLITICS IN CHICAGO MAYORAL ELECTIONS

Dianne M. Pinderhughes

This chapter analyzes nearly two decades of intense political competition in Chicago by examining the electoral participation of racial and ethnic groups in mayoral elections. The period begins with Richard J. Daley's final election as mayor, in 1975, and ends with the reelection of his son, Richard M. Daley, as mayor in 1991. Over much of this time span, it seemed that the traditional power coalition in Chicago would disintegrate, or at the least be profoundly redefined in the face of new ethnic challenges. Chicago's political history during this era represents a search for a new electoral and governing consensus, precipitated by the demise of the city's longtime leader and the city's changing demography.

To govern and manage the city of Chicago, political leaders need to control a number of points of power. First, any person who seeks to be mayor must develop and control an electoral coalition. This involves management of racial and ethnic politics, partisan politics, and also ideological issues, although ideology plus partisan politics are subordinate to the other components. Second, the mayor must find a way to deal with the Chicago City Council—the legislative body in a city government that, years of the Democratic machine and Richard J. Daley to the contrary, has a weak mayor system. Moreover, the city of Chicago is located entirely within Cook County, which is governed by its own Board of Commissioners, another power center. Finally, there is the Cook County Democratic Committee, the management arm of the local Democratic party, which at times is assumed to be synonymous with Chicago politics, but at least formally is independent of city government. Richard J. Daley was the first person to join the mayor's office and the party's central committee in a powerful political marriage. This arrangement, however, did not automatically continue for his successors.

In previous work, I have developed a political participation model that predicts a group's likelihood of winning political leadership in terms of external variables arising from outside the group's behavior, such as the structure and organization of elections; demographic factors; and internal variables, which have developed from the group's own specific history (Pinderhughes 1987). Those variables are not described here; however, I do use the broader conceptual framework to discuss the changes that occurred in Chicago over the period of study.

This chapter focuses on one aspect of political competition, the effort to establish electoral control of the mayor's office. By the mid-1970s, Chicago had entered a volatile political period. The leadership change caused by Richard J. Daley's death in 1976 greatly intensified competition for the mayor's office, which already had been strongly contested in the 1975 election. Demographic shifts in the electorate, including growth in the black, Mexican-American, and Puerto Rican populations, placed pressure on the Democratic party to redefine its constituency at the same time that it lost its highly skilled leader. In the 1960s and 1970s, Daley had shifted the party's electoral base away from blacks and toward white ethnics. He and his successors also limited the rewards for the black constituency to tangible, ward-based descriptive benefits. His successors' denial of even descriptive representation in the leadership of city agencies made possible a broad-based challenge to the machine (Preston 1982; Zikmund 1982).

With the election of Richard M. Daley to a four-year term as mayor in April 1991, Chicago appears to have reached the end of this unusually volatile period of political history. The period compares closely with the dramatic decades early in this century when competition in the city over ethnicity and race, economic differences, and party partisanship erupted in a tumultuous era of electoral politics. This earlier period was an electorally competitive one in which rival groups and their leaders offered both ideological and tangible incentives to mobilize voters. The period ended with the mayoral election of 1931, which marked the formation of the Chicago Democratic machine. The machine linked rival groups to a single, dominant organization, which routinely elected its slates, minimized electoral competition for office, and limited policy debate, while strengthening the tangible reward system for supporters.

With Richard J. Daley's demise, the machine's reach, and its ability to manage new crises, seemed to crumble. As a result, group-based conflict took on new vigor. African-Americans, whose population base had grown substantially, competed directly with whites, rather than with specific European ethnic groups. To mount a challenge to the political status quo, blacks converted their interlocking sets of political interest groups, community organizations, churches, social and fraternal groups, and professional organizations into vehicles for political socialization and electoral mobilization. However, the new coalition proved fragile. Its leader, Harold Washington, was the only person able to represent the many elements of the coalition, and was elected mayor in 1983. With his death in 1987, the coalition splintered into warring factions, opening the way for restoration of an updated machine operated by Richard J. Daley's son.

BALANCE OF POWER: DEMOGRAPHICS AND PARTISAN POLITICS

The demographic balance in an urban area is an important factor in shaping the opportunities to win election to office and to maintain control over the political process (Karnig and Welch 1980). Cities that have majority black populations, especially those over 65–70 percent black, are most likely to have elected black mayors—as in Detroit, Washington, D.C., Atlanta, and Gary (Indiana). Below 65 percent black, the coalition is much less secure and more likely to be subject to the vagaries of partisan politics and/or intragroup fission, as occurred in New Orleans after Mayor Ernest Morial's term expired, and as occurred in Chicago after Harold Washington's death. In cities with black populations above 40 percent and below 65 percent of the population, the black community finds it possible to win control of city hall if it can minimize conflict within the group. Where the black electorate is a minority or only a narrow majority, possibilities of internal conflict *may* be more easily controlled because the stakes are clearer. Even cities with minorities of 38 percent or less may elect a black mayor, as have Denver, Hartford, Los Angeles, Kansas City, Charlotte (North Carolina), and New York City, although the individuals elected have had to rely on a significantly broader multiracial coalition to win.

The structure of partisan politics in a city, especially the political character of the black community, further shapes opportunities for controlling the mayor's office. Where blacks are able to resist the development of political factions among their own voters, they are significantly more likely to be able to elect a black candidate, or to elect a black candidate whose positions are viewed with approval by a majority of black voters. In other words, debate over policy or competition for office between more than one black candidate makes election of a candidate who has the support of a majority of black voters significantly more difficult.

Chicago is no exception to the rule that demography is destiny. In the early 1970s, as Richard J. Daley's mayoral service was reaching the end of its second decade, there still was considerable competition among the European communities for leadership of the city. A Pole, Ben Adamowski, challenged the mayor in the 1963 mayoral primary. After Daley's death, Roman Pucinski was one of the serious competitors for the mayor's office in 1977 against Michael Bilandic, Daley's successor chosen by the city council. However, though Polish-Americans were the largest white ethnic bloc in the city, they were unsuccessful in organizing a political campaign to win political leadership. Several blacks also challenged the party's chosen candidate for the mayor's office—Richard Newhouse against Daley in 1975, and Harold Washington first in 1977 against Bilandic, and again successfully against Jane Byrne in 1983. Yet one of the smaller groups, the Irish, has dominated the mayor's office and the Democratic political machine for much of this century, and continues to do so.

The institutionalized nature of group life in Chicago translates demography into politics. The political system is organized around group-based representation and is especially sensitive to new groups. The building blocks of political life tend to rest on the geographic and political isolation of these groups. Although Chicago politics always has had a strong ethnic orientation, the city's population became dramatically more diverse between 1970 and 1990. Two-thirds of the city population was white in 1970. By 1980, the city's total population had contracted by 10 percent. The white population had fallen by two-fifths to 43.6 percent of the total, while the black population had grown to a 39.6 percent share. The largest change, however, involved the Latino population, which grew from 7.3 percent of the total in 1970 to 14 percent in 1980. By 1990 the city's population had fallen further. Both the white and black populations declined, though the share of the white population actually increased. The slight loss in the black share reflects the fact that outmigration of African-Americans to the suburbs accelerated. Again, the largest population gains centered on Latinos. Table 3.1 shows how the changes in overall population translated into numbers of those of voting age. By 1989 the black and white voting-age populations were quite comparable.

The preceding ethnic categorizations are much simpler than the actual population groups of the city. The white category, for example, includes a variety of European ethnic groups who for the most part

Table 3.1 RACIAL COMPOSITION OF CHICAGO'S VOTING-AGE POPULATION, 1940–80

	Numbers (in thousands)			Percentage of Total		
	White	Black	Hispanic	White	Black	Hispanic
1940	2,205	191		86.6	7.9	
1950	2,236	345		79.7	13.3	
1960	1,850	471		71.7	20.2	
1970	1,513	576		63.1	27.1	
1980	946	758	252	48.3	38.7	12.8
1989	945	875	253	44.5	41.3	12.0

Sources: Data for 1940–80 from Kleppner (1985: 67); data for 1989 from CUL/NIU *Atlas* (1990: 10).

Table 3.2 CHICAGO VOTER REGISTRATION BY RACE, APRIL 1989

Group	Total	Percentage
White	814,105	52.2
Black	646,509	41.4
Latino	89,416	5.7
Other	10,413	0.8
Total	1,560,485	100

Source: CUL/NIU *Atlas* (1990: 20).

are third- or fourth-generation citizens of the United States, among them Irish, Germans, Italians, Poles, Lithuanians, Czechs, Slovaks, and Croatians. Hispanics and Latinos in Chicago include, in order of their numerical significance, Mexican-Americans, Puerto Ricans, Cubans, and to a much lesser extent residents from Central and South America, the Caribbean, and Spain.

The pressure of the new demography has lessened political competition among the different European ethnic groups. These groups have associated themselves into a predominantly white, loosely affiliated coalition, though important differences remain among the component elements. Other groups such as Latinos and Asian-Pacifics have become a large enough part of the political environment to require representation or at least attention.

Largely because of the intensity of political competition in the 1980s, voter registration rates in Chicago have increased sharply. More than three-quarters of the city's voting-age population was registered to vote at the beginning of the 1980s. That proportion increased during the years of most acutely contested mayoral elections, reaching a peak of 79.9 percent and 78.9 percent in 1983 and 1984, respectively. Since then, the registration rate has declined—it was 73.6 percent in 1989 (Chicago Urban League/Northeastern Illinois University [henceforth, CUL/NIU] *Atlas* 1990). Of the 1.56 million registered voters in 1989, 52.2 percent were white, 41.4 percent were black, and 5.7 percent were Hispanic (see table 3.2). The underrepresentation of Hispanics reflects the fact that many Mexican-Americans, in particular, are not citizens or do not hold legal residence in the United States.

Chicago is often noted as one of the country's most segregated cities (Massey and Denton 1988, 1993). Its racial and ethnic groups reside in distinct locations, so neighborhoods and wards are easily identifiable for political purposes. Zikmund (1982), Kleppner (1985), and the CUL/NIU *Atlas* (1990) divide the neighborhoods into racial and ethnic political enclaves. These have shifted over the years as the black population has grown, the white population has shrunk, and the Puerto Rican and Mexican groups established distinct residential locations on the northwest and south sides, respectively, and grew in size. Detailed knowledge of racial and ethnic group location is used by the city's politicians in the decennial redistrictings of local, state, and national office boundaries to acknowledge growth in some groups, but more often to maintain the power of those designing the districts. Democratic party politics has been organized around the foundation of small political units or wards since early in the century. When other cities sought to undercut and eliminate ward-based political systems, Chicago reinforced and strengthened its structure by moving from a 35-seat city council to a 50-seat council after 1920. The size of the city's wards attracts the interest of small as well as large racial or ethnic groups. The average ward in the 1980s had only about 42,000 people in the voting-age population (CUL/NIU *Atlas* 1990). Smaller groups are usually able to control at least one or more wards. Larger groups simply accumulate more authority as their population expands. The wards become the electoral building blocks used to win the mayor's office, as well as other county, state, and national positions. The ability to control the wards in significant numbers, and to turn out the vote, is of continuing concern to the party. The demographic changes in the city, and the policy issues that arose from them, therefore challenged the machine at the most fundamental level.

GROUP ISSUES

Political Leadership and Community Self-Government in the Black Community

Harold Washington's election as mayor "solved" for a time the problem of political inclusion of the black community. His death, however, posed an acute leadership crisis for African-Americans. Eugene Sawyer, Danny Davis, Tim Evans, and Eugene Pincham represented different elements of the complex black community in the city and subsequently competed against whites as mayoral candidates. The "black community" was structurally integrated in the early 1980s by the community organizations, interest groups, and religious and social groups that formed the base of Washington's campaign and supported him for most of his first administration. The subordination of that community's differences, however, by no means eliminated them, and they reappeared with a vengeance after Washington's death (Starks 1991). Chicago Black United Communities (CBUC), People Organized for Welfare and Employment Rights (POWER), and Voice of the Ethnic Community (VOTE) (Woods 1987), as well as Sawyer, Davis, Evans, and Pincham—all represent the distinctive histories, generations, geographic areas, educational levels, types of links to the Chicago political establishment, economic status, and political ideologies found among blacks in Chicago. Developing a manageable political consensus and identifying an acceptable political representative for the city's blacks is particularly difficult since—although relatively homogeneous in relation to whites—they are by no means a cohesive group.

Washington's political history reflected the fact that he was old enough to have grown up with the multiple sectors of Chicago's black community. Spear's study of *Black Chicago* at the turn of the century described a population already self-conscious of a generationally distinct elite based on their freedom during slavery, direct economic links to whites, color, education, and tendency to support assimilation over self-help (Spear 1969). The black community of that era would be succeeded by a black population more than 36 times as great in size, and divided by education, social status, and neighborhood. For example, by the late 1980s, of the 749,692 black voters in wards dominated by blacks, one-third resided on the west side (CUL/NIU *Atlas* 1990). Southside black neighborhoods were the oldest in the city and the areas where black educational and social elites resided. Westside areas expanded most rapidly after World War II and were settled by southern migrants who had not had the resources to move previously. Harold Washington had also grown up with the machine, as his father was a precinct captain in it; he was one of the few African-American politicians who was able to transcend most of these divisions (Holli and Green 1989).

Hispanic and Latino Communities: Seeking Group Definition

Forging a cohesive political group in a city in which group identification is the fundamental basis of electoral power is the task of the Hispanic and Latino communities of Chicago. Although lack of agreement on a name for a group is not an indicator of electoral, ideological, or political divisions—as use of the terms *Negro, black, Afro-American, African-American*, and a host of other titles has shown—Hispanics/Latinos are in fact composed of many different groups. As of 1980, the *Chicago Reporter* (Vazquez 1982) noted that there were

499,322 Latinos in Chicago, including 310,428 Mexicans, 116,597
Puerto Ricans, 15,961 Cubans and 56,366 other Hispanics from Central and South America, the Caribbean, and Spain (Casuo and
Camacho 1985). Some, such as the Mexican-Americans, first began
immigrating around World War I, drawn by the same industrial
opportunities as southern blacks. They have continued to migrate,
so there is a diverse, multigenerational community with quite distinct
experiences in Mexico and in the United States. This long period
of immigration makes Mexican-Americans unique in this country.
Puerto Ricans began arriving after World War II. Many found entry-
level positions in service and light manufacturing industries. Immigration from Cuba and Central America introduced middle-class,
skilled professionals to the city's labor force in the 1960s, perhaps
the first time that immigrants arrived able to compete in other than
industrial or unskilled positions. More recently, low-skilled Central
Americans have joined the flow of poor immigrants from Mexico
(Casuo and Camacho 1985).

Thus, the Latino "community" is complex, comprising people from
many different countries, with distinctive generational variations
even among those from the same country, and groups of distinct
socioeconomic backgrounds. Hispanics also belong to different racial
and nationality groups, which affects the manner in which they are
perceived and responded to upon arriving in the city.

> Each Hispanic group holds deeply felt concerns and attitudes, not
> shared by the others. . . . Many Mexicans are concerned with
> immigration issues, which do not affect Puerto Ricans, because they are
> citizens, or Cubans because they are political refugees. . . . Cubans are
> viewed by others as arrogant and self-serving . . . "who never get
> involved in helping the community.". . . Immigrants from Cuba and
> South America, because many are affluent, are dismissed by some
> Mexicans and Puerto Ricans as not really Hispanic. (Casuo and
> Camacho 1985)

Early in the 20th century European groups such as the Poles, which
were considerably *less* differentiated than the Latino community of
Chicago, did not consolidate their political interests within one party
or support Polish candidates for ward offices, since Poles were not
concentrated in specific neighborhoods (Pinderhughes 1987). In the
second half of the century as the machine lost its electoral dominance,
Polish candidates were unsuccessful at using their demographic
advantage in their own behalf. For example, Zikmund reported that
in 1963 Ben Adamowski won only 12 of the 20 wards where the

Table 3.3 CHICAGO LATINO VOTING-AGE POPULATION AND VOTER
REGISTRATION, 1989

	Number	Turnout Percentage
Voting-age population	253,526	
Registered voters	89,416	35.3
Vote for mayor, primary election	31,472[a]	35.1
Vote for mayor, general election	40,052[a]	44.8

Source: CUL/NIU *Atlas* (1990).
a. Based on population concentrated in ward groups.

population was 10 percent or more Polish. In the 1977 mayoral primary Alderman Roman Pucinski won 8 wards, but all were north of
the loop; he won none of the 7 wards on the southwest side where
there was a significant Polish population (Zikmund 1982).

Because Latino groups are much more diverse than any single
European ethnic group, they face a complicated process of group
definition, socialization, partisan identification, and issue focus. At
present, they are unlikely to be able to act as a single political group.
The only likelihood of unification arises if the larger community
treats them as an undifferentiated group and limits them to highly
segregated neighborhoods. In short, they are unlikely to behave as a
group unless they are isolated for a long enough period to become a
new undifferentiated Hispanic group. Although Mexican-Americans
and Puerto Ricans live in concentrated neighborhoods, they are relatively separate ones; Cubans live all over the city.

These issues are especially intricate in Chicago because it is the
only major American city with a substantial number of Hispanics
from many different groups, although Mexican-Americans are the
largest and clearly the dominant proportion. Hispanics are the only
major sector of the population of the city that is increasing in numbers. In the mid-1970s, Hispanics were not recognized as a group of
any significance in electoral politics. Latino voters began to be cour-
ted beginning with Harold Washington's 1983 campaign for mayor,
as demographic changes made black and white voting groups more
evenly matched. Latinos will continue to be a significant factor in
mayoral contests despite the fact that their registration and turnout
are low relative to both whites and blacks (see table 3.3).

European-Americans

Poles, Italians, Germans, Irish, Czechs, Lithuanians, Bohemians, and
Slovaks comprise the heterogeneous European groups now residing

in Chicago. Most have been in the country for three generations or more. There were and are white ethnic neighborhoods in Chicago, but none are as concentrated as those of black residents today or early in the 20th century. Only small portions of Northern Europeans lived in ghettos, or areas of concentrated residence; most were constantly "integrated" with other ethnic groups. In contrast, more than 90 percent of blacks lived in areas more than 90 percent black. Chicago's "ethnic" neighborhoods are areas in which businesses, cultural institutions, and churches are located, but their population is not necessarily drawn from only one ethnic group, and the entire group does not live in contiguous clusters. Today Asian neigborhoods that parallel the European mixed communities have developed.

As a result of their ethnic diversification, European groups had greater variation in their internal variables such as leadership institutions, political socialization, partisan identification, and political issues. There were not necessarily specific patterns of Italian, Polish, or Czech partisan identification or political issues; where they did exist, they were not as highly developed because of the groups' geographic spread throughout the city and the lack of externally and consistently imposed discriminatory criteria. Because immigration from most of these countries has not continued at any intensity, and many of the ethnics have migrated to the suburbs, their numbers have fallen over the years and their communities have lost their original vitality. Social assimilation and intermarriage have also occurred among European ethnics, so that the groups are no longer as distinctive. Since their neighborhoods were never highly segregated, successive decades of residence have blurred their boundaries within larger white areas. Many of the European-Americans were Catholic and experienced hostility from the city's strongly nativist Protestants. However, this enmity has dissipated somewhat, so that the Catholic school system, including colleges that played important roles in socializing and protecting these groups, is much less significant. The city's archdiocese is closing parishes and schools, and public schools now educate many Catholics.

By the late 20th century, as the city's demographics shifted and blacks organized a group-based mayoral campaign, European-American groups responded in unified fashion, opposing the election of Harold Washington. For example, only 12.5 percent of voters in the white northwest and white southside wards voted for Harold Washington in the April 1983 general election, and only 5.6 percent of such voters voted for Washington in the 1983 primary. Among blacks in the south and westside areas, by contrast, 21.7 percent voted for Byrne and Daley in the primary, but only 6.3 percent in the general election (CUL/*Atlas* 1990).

This is not to say that European-Americans are an undifferentiated amalgam. Rather, it is to suggest that hierarchical relationships or differences in political power and/or skill may have developed among the European groups that are related to experience rather than group identity.

SEARCH FOR AN ELECTORAL AND GOVERNING COALITION

In multiracial, multiethnic settings, one group may be able to mediate among competing interests. For close to three-quarters of a century in Chicago, Irish politicians have played this mediating role. Put another way they are leaders, or perhaps more appropriately, managers of complex coalitions of groups. Much has been written about the realignments in the city's electorate, and the successive reorganizations of the Democratic machine in 1931, 1947, and 1955. I briefly describe here the efforts of other ethnic and racial groups to reconstruct a lasting coalition in the late 1970s and early 1980s after the decline of the coalition that had been formulated in the 1950s.

One of the striking aspects of Chicago politics is that although machine politics has consistently characterized its operation, machine leaders have never hesitated to reorganize their core constituencies. Richard J. Daley was first elected in 1955 with strong support from the black population. That continued until the mid-1960s, when important shifts away from the machine occurred among black voters. Charlie Chew won election to the state Senate, running as an independent against the machine, and middle-class black voters drifted away toward independent status. Daley then began to rely more strongly on support from white ethnic wards that had not supported him in his earlier administrations. The important fact, however, is that electoral balances, although they may have shifted from one group to another, always included some components of support from both black and white wards.

Even as black middle-class areas began to vote independently of the machine, and poor black areas shifted toward independent status as community organizations arranged voter registration drives and get-out-the-vote campaigns, the machine continued to turn out a significant proportion of voters on its behalf through the mid- and late 1970s. Zikmund (1982) has shown that black wards produced a

Table 3.4 MAYORAL VOTES RANKED BY WINNER'S TOTAL

Winner's Total Votes				Percentage of Total Votes Cast
740,137	1971	Richard J. Daley	G	70
671,189	1979	Jane Byrne	G	83.6
666,911	1983	Harold Washington	G	51.6
600,252	1987	Harold Washington	G	53.7
586,941	1987	Harold Washington	P	53.5
576,620	1989	Richard M. Daley	G	55.4
542,817	1975	Richard J. Daley	G	79.5
485,182	1989	Richard M. Daley	P	55.3
475,169	1977	Michael Bilandic	G	77.3
463,623	1975	Richard J. Daley	P	57.8
450,155	1991	Richard M. Daley	G	71.1
424,122	1983	Harold Washington	P	38.1
412,909	1979	Jane Byrne	P	51.0
407,730	1991	Richard M. Daley	P	32.2
342,301	1977	Michael Bilandic	P	49.3

Notes: G = general election; P = primary election.

mean of 47.2 percent of their votes for Daley in 1975, and 46.2 percent for Michael Bilandic in 1977. Daley had been challenged by Richard Newhouse, Edward Hanrahan, and Dick Singer in 1975, and Bilandic was opposed by Pucinski and Washington in 1977. This structural capacity to generate turnout and significant loyalty in many areas in the city is suggested in table 3.4, which ranks mayoral winners' total votes by size. From 1971 to 1991 the largest vote was turned out for Daley in the 1971 general election, in which he won 70 percent of the total (he was unopposed in the primary). His total dropped significantly in the 1975 primary, but he had three opponents and still won 57.8 percent of the primary vote and 79.5 percent of the general election vote (see table 3.4). According to Zikmund (1982), he won majorities of the vote of the machine core, southside white ethnics, northside white ethnics, and Polish northwest. He fell slightly below majority only in the black wards and in the reform/ lakefront areas.

Michael Bilandic was first elected mayor by the Chicago City Council in the weeks following Daley's death. He won the mayoral primary in 1977 with only a plurality of the vote, turning out the *lowest* number of votes of all those who won primaries and general elections between 1971 and 1991. In the general election he improved his total turnout and won with 77.3 percent of the vote, but this election revealed the first of many significant alterations in the composition of voting (see table 3.4). In comparison to Daley in 1975, Bilandic's mean proportion of support was stable in three areas of the city in 1977: the machine core, the reform/northshore wards, and the black wards. His mean proportion of support among southside white ethnics, however, dropped by 9.8 percent, among the Polish northwest wards by 20.7 percent, and by 4.4 percent in the northside ethnic wards (Zikmund 1982).

The challengers from 1975 through 1989 represented stronger or weaker component units within the machine. As stated, Daley, already challenged by the reform and black sectors of the machine, was nevertheless able to hold on to a substantial portion of the vote in these areas. Bilandic retained the same level of support in these areas, but lost support in the white ethnic areas to Pucinski. In other words, conflict over leadership arose among whites. Washington increased the total turnout and the proportion of the votes won from black areas over Newhouse's showing in the 1975 mayoral primary, but won less than a mean (7 percent) of the vote in each of the other ward areas. Pucinski won more than half of the vote in 1977 in the Polish northwest side and 41.6 percent in the reform/northshore areas, but no more than 30.5 percent in the rest (Zikmund 1982).

The representatives of the major groups in the years between 1977 and 1989 typically mobilized votes in only one, or at the most two, of these ward groups: the machine core, the southwest side white ethnics, northside white ethnics, Polish northwest, black southside and westside wards, and the reform lakefront wards. Put more simply, they were able to generate interest among some of the white ethnic groups, or some sectors of the black population, but rarely were able to cross racial lines or generate interest across a number of ethnic sectors, which by the end of the era also included the Hispanic population.

Few of the candidates seemed able to comprehend the heterogeneous composition of the electorate and to be able to plot electoral strategy based on that demographic reality. In 1979 Jane Byrne won 11 out of 12 black wards, all of the reform/northshore wards, split the Polish areas, and took less than one-third of the vote in the remaining white ethnic and racially mixed machine areas. She garnered the second highest number of votes won in a mayoral contest as well as the highest proportion, with 83.6 percent of the votes in the general election, as shown in table 3.4. She proceeded as mayor to alienate her strongest base of support in an effort to lure support from the white areas of the city, at a point when demographic changes suggested this would probably not have been worth the investment. In 1983 Byrne and Daley then competed with each other for the white ethnic and machine vote, abandoning the black vote to Washington, and allowing Daley to cumulate through voter registration and voter mobilization efforts 79.4 percent of the vote in southside black wards, 73 percent of the vote on the west side, and some proportions of support in the remaining areas. In the 1987 election only Jane Byrne challenged Washington from the traditional machine competitors; in the general election Edward Vrdolyak ran as an independent along with Republican Donald Haider.

Washington won a thin plurality of 38.1 percent in the 1983 primary and a razor-thin majority of 51.6 percent in the general election (see table 3.4); he then worked at increasing his electoral support and his city council votes from among other racial and ethnic groups in the city from 1983 through 1987. By his 1987 election Washington had solidified his electoral and governing coalition to the extent that he won 53.5 percent of the votes cast in the primary and 53.7 percent in the general election (table 3.4). His voting majority in the city council shifted dramatically upward, from a bare majority to 40 or more votes in designating committee appointments.

After Washington's death in 1987, the city council's second effort at electing a mayor who would take firm control was also unsuccessful. As the candidate of a coalition led by white northside and machine city council members, (black) Alderman Eugene Sawyer was viewed with great suspicion by the black community, which set up a competition between disparate elements of and within it. The focus on the succession question in the black community, between candidates Tim Evans and Eugene Sawyer, and the tendency to limit debate to the participation of and mobilization of the black ward groups, held down the total turnout, and split the black vote between the February 1989 primary and the April 1989 general election. This guaranteed Richard M. Daley's election. Once in office, Daley reinvigorated the traditional roles of the varying sectors of the white community, and began incrementally to increase his support in the black communities.

Daley increased support just by being in office and by having effective connections with the state legislature. The inability to consolidate support around a single candidate in the 1989 primary and general election, which led to Daley's victory, gave him an enormously important advantage in preparation for the 1991 election: access to the vast resources of city government. Even with patronage limitations imposed during the Washington era, the city could offer a greater deal in financial rewards. Nearly 50 years of Democratic machine rule from 1931 through the late 1970s proved that material incentives skillfully used could substitute for a greater emphasis on more generally constructed substantive public policy, and could demobilize the parts of the black community that could, when united with white voters, elect a charismatic leader like Big Bill Thompson or Harold Washington. That is, the loyalty of even a small proportion of the black population to the Democratic "machine" and a relatively demobilized black population could, along with moderate levels of support from other racial and ethnic groups, help guarantee the winning electoral coalition for the machine candidate.

White ethnic conflict was reduced because, by 1991, most of the disparate European ethnic subunits within the machine had sponsored a candidate for office and had failed at their efforts. In 1977 Roman Pucinski of the Polish northwest side had run a losing campaign against Michael Bilandic, winning only on the northwest side. In 1979 Bilandic had lost to Jane Byrne with the mixed support of white ethnics, the machine core, the southside white ethnics, splitting the reform/North Shore wards, and losing the black wards decisively. In the 1983 primary, Daley won the southside white ethnics, and Byrne the northside white ethnics, thereby leaving the reform areas and the black vote entirely to Washington. In the general election, Bernard Epton lost to Harold Washington, winning the white ethnic areas on the northside and southside, winning the inner lakefront, and splitting the lakeshore and Latino areas.

In 1987 Byrne lost a head-to-head runoff to Washington in the primary, winning the white northwest and white southside, losing the black wards, but splitting lakeshore and Latino areas. In the general election two whites ran against Washington. Donald Haider, a Northwestern University faculty member, won the Republican nomination but less than 5 percent of the vote in the general election. Alderman Eddie Vrdolyak ran as an independent on the Solidarity ticket, basically duplicating Byrne's areas of vote strengths and weaknesses, but winning 39,159 *fewer* votes, while Washington increased his support from the primary to the general election by about 14,000 votes.

In 1989 Daley ran unopposed in the primary but faced Vrdolyak as the Republican nominee in the general election. However, unlike their behavior in 1983 when Byrne and Daley were candidates, the whites concentrated their votes on one of the white candidates, the Democratic nominee Daley, giving Vrdolyak 35,964, or fewer votes than they had given Haider in 1987. In 1991 Byrne, along with Danny Davis and Jones, challenged Daley in the primary, but she won only 38,112 votes. In the 1991 general election, Daley faced a weak chal-

Table 3.5 1991 MAYORAL PRIMARY AND GENERAL ELECTION

Primary results	Daley (%)	Davis (%)	Jones (%)	Byrne (%)	Total
Black wards	15.8	77.0	—	5.89	198,667
City total	63.0	30.7	.33	5.8	646,795

General election	Daley (%)	Pincham (%)	Gottlieb (%)	Total
Black wards	23.7	75.1	1.1	202,051
City total	25.2	71.0	3.6	623,148

Notes: Data are for wards 2, 3, 4, 5, 6, 7, 8, 9, 15, 16, 17, 20, 21, 24, 27, 29, 34, and 37. Wards were 80 percent or more black based on CUL/NIU *Atlas* (1990: 13).

lenge of 159,608 from Judge Eugene Pincham, running on the Harold Washington party ticket. So by 1991 Byrne, representing the north-side Irish, Vrdolyak the southwest-side white ethnics, Pucinski the northwest-side white ethnics, and Don Haider the white reform lakeshore had all taken a chance at the office and had failed.

Daley won in 1989 and 1991 for the same reason Washington won in 1983; Sawyer and Evans split the black vote and did not compete for the white vote. The effect was to hold down turnout and divide the support available among two challengers. Sawyer won only 383,535 votes in the 1989 primary as some sectors of black organizations prepared to promote Evans in the general election. Sawyer split his support from Latinos evenly with Daley and won only 10 percent of his votes from whites. Evans increased his vote over Sawyer's to 427,954, but Daley had increased his support in the general election to 576,620 from 485,182 in the primary. Black voter loyalty also began to falter by 1989, and the contributions of black wards to white candidates began to edge upward. In the 1991 primary Daley won 15.8 percent of the vote in the predominantly black wards, and 23.7 percent of that vote in the general election (see table 3.5).

After the losing efforts of Sawyer, the former mayor, and Alderman Evans, who claimed the Washington legacy, Alderman Danny Davis's candidacy in 1991 in the primary and Judge Eugene Pincham's campaign in the general election represented attempts by third- and fourth-line black candidates about whom there was significantly less consensus and enthusiasm than there had been for either Evans or Sawyer. That, combined with the fact that Richard M. Daley had been mayor for two years and had begun to distribute resources in the judicious fashion possible in a city with a strong machine tradition, had a depressing effect on overall black voter turnout. Davis won 198,815 in the 1991 primary and Pincham only 159,608 in the 1991 general election, or between 46.8 percent and 37.6 percent, respectively, of Washington's *lowest* vote turnout, in the 1983 primary.

In 1985 I argued that attractive black candidates, substantive policies, and get-out-the-vote campaigns would produce large and loyal turnouts among black voters. The community organizations that had mobilized on behalf of Harold Washington in the early 1980s mobilized again, but whereas there had been considerable agreement on Harold Washington as a mayoral candidate, there was a less-broad-based consensus on Davis or Pincham. The community organizations agreed on Davis, but clearly there was not the same intensity of support in the larger black population. The small but increasing percentages of the black vote won by Daley in black areas had more to do with the structure of electoral competition and the decreasing mobilization of the black electorate than with voters' expectations that Daley would provide substantive policy reforms. As Zikmund put it:

> Hypothetically, if all the blocs were to unite against an isolated
> machine core, the regular Democratic organization would go down to
> defeat. . . . [But] the machine, largely because of its organizational
> capacity, won 40 percent of the votes in all of the city's voting
> blocs. . . . Put somewhat differently, the machine was everyone's second
> choice. The machine, largely because of its organizational capacity, won
> 43 percent of the votes in all of the city's voting blocs (1982: 48).

By the late 1980s several things had happened that will structure political outcomes for some time to come. The black community lost its goal-specific focus—support for and of a leader whom most voters found attractive—and it began to engage in intragroup conflict over goals and leadership and to express this conflict at the polls. Simultaneously, European ethnic communities, after the 1983 primary and the 1987 general election, began to reduce conflict among European ethnic candidates—in the 1989 general election Vrdolyak won only 3.2 percent of the total vote. They also competed for the support of Hispanic voters.

WHAT OF THE FUTURE?

Governance of the city can be considered a problem with a variety of leadership solutions: one component involves leadership personnel representing various political coalitions; a second component emphasizes policy choices, including both specific areas of policy focus (i.e., education, housing, economic development, infrastructure) as well as specific types of approaches to those policies (i.e., broader distribution of resources; emphasis on fiscal conservatism). From the mid-1970s to the early 1990s, voters were presented with a variety of political solutions to these issues. Basically, Daley's death offered the city the opportunity to consider a number of alternative approaches, or what might be characterized as differing solutions to the leadership/governance puzzle.

Some of the political solutions put forward were untenable—for instance, those represented by Bilandic and Evans. Others held, for a time, but could not survive the death of their architects, namely Richard J. Daley and Washington. Finally, others seemed tenable, but could not survive coalition drift or unstable coalitions, namely those of Byrne and Sawyer. Balancing the competing interests in political leadership of diverse groups that also interconnect with economic status makes managing the city's political and economic life a complex challenge. The Democratic machine gradually increased racial and ethnic descriptive representation and will continue to do so to maintain ties to the disparate groups that constitute its electoral constituency. That has proved an effective way to increase voter loyalty.

The new policy consensus is that a loose coalition has "formed," led by the Irish, dominated by white ethnics, but incorporating representation from all sectors of the city, including African-Americans and Latinos. The politics of race are important in sustaining this alliance, although race is not the only factor. This means that there probably is no policy consensus across groups, but that specific needs and concerns are being met. Since Richard M. Daley won about 90 percent of the white vote in 1989 and 95 percent of his coalition was white (CUL/NIU *Atlas* 1990), whites presumably felt that their interests were best, or at least safely, represented by this specific individual. All whites have not supported all white candidates, but most have offered their support only to a white candidate over the last decade. Black voters have been somewhat more pluralistic, offering their strong support to Byrne in 1979 and a minority of their votes to Daley in 1991.

I would hypothesize that the major political conflicts of the last 12 to 15 years have now concluded with Daley's reelection in 1991. The African-American and Mexican-American communities now have greater representation in the city council and state legislature, as well as in some isolated management positions in the city. This means that there is no massive increase in political power for the black community in comparison to the years before 1975, but also no sense of total exclusion.

The strongest residue from the Washington years was the expectation that the black community deserved to control the mayor's office through a black official, rather than that the community should consolidate support around a candidate with a substantive policy agenda attractive to black, and other communities', interests, while also forging a winning coalition. Black political leaders consistently chose black candidates, even if successively weaker, to carry the flag. The outcome was to strengthen their white ethnic opponents and to make a liberal coalition—comprising Washington's 1987 supporters, some of them machine politicians from the Daley-Bilandic-Byrne era—unlikely.

Appendix 3.A

PARTY ORGANIZATION AND SPENDING PATTERNS

Rowan Miranda has examined evidence for the fit between the strong party organization (SPO) theory and the citizen preference models. Briefly, in the former, SPOs rein in spending because "they are less responsive to [pro-spending] interest groups." In the latter, "citizen preference models hypothesize that spending policies will reflect the policy preferences of the core constituency of the mayor" (Miranda 1991). Miranda's findings are not clear, though his description of the Washington administration as having "'redistributed' funds from city agencies to community groups, many of whom would be important in future elections," is a plausible explanation for some of the spending increases shown in the accompanying figures 3.A.1 and 3.A.2. Miranda (1991) stated: "The number of community groups and delegate agencies receiving funding increased by more than 500 percent between 1983 and 1987. . . . Mayor Washington expanded programs

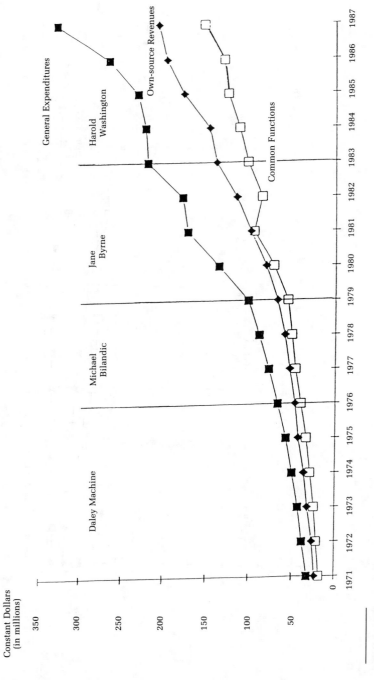

Figure 3.A.1 CITY OF CHICAGO REVENUE AND EXPENDITURE TRENDS 1971–87

Source: Miranda (1991: 14).

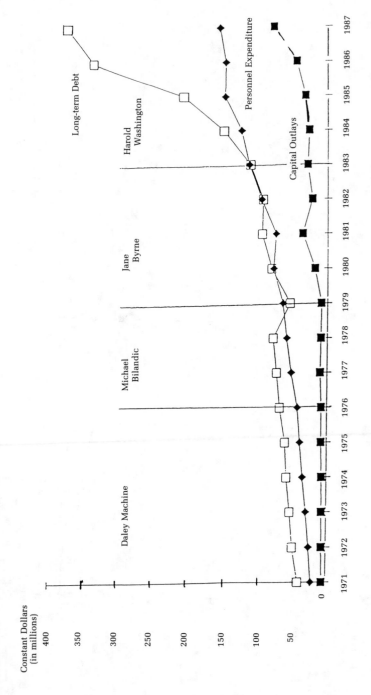

Figure 3.A.2 CITY OF CHICAGO FISCAL POLICY OUTPUTS 1971–87

Source: Miranda (1991: 15)

in other areas [low- to moderate-income residents] also, further solidi-
fying his support." This latter finding could be construed to fit within
the citizen preference theory. Miranda's study implies that the incentives in the Daley administrations, whether through SPO, citizen
preference, or a combination of the two, supported conservative fiscal
policies. Other interpretations, including the concentration of spending in neighborhoods loyal to the machine and/or in areas of ethnic
similarity, and the rationing of personnel appointments, rather than
a focus on capital construction or social welfare, might account for
the low level of spending during Richard J. Daley's years in office.

Richard J. Daley held the offices of mayor and chair of the party;
this was the strongest form of party organization in its history, and
it certainly gave Daley considerably greater discretion than mayors
who governed before or after him. Since only Daley has held both
these offices, but the machine has existed for a much longer time
period, the link between conservative budgeting and a strong party
organization is not clear. This hypothesis will need further investigation as the characteristics of the organization and the patterns of
spending are further specified and examined.

References

Browning, Rufus P., Dale Rogers Marshall, and David H. Tabb. 1984. *Protest
    Is Not Enough, The Struggle of Blacks and Hispanics for Equality
    in Urban Politics.* Berkeley: University of California Press.
Casuo, Jorge, and Eduardo Camacho. 1985. "Hispanics in Chicago, Conclu-
    sion." *Chicago Reporter,* 14(4, April): 1–4.
CUL/NIU *Atlas.* 1990. *Chicago Politics.* Chicago: Author.
Davidson, Chandler, ed. 1984. *Minority Vote Dilution.* Washington, D.C.:
    Howard University Press.
Fremon, David K. 1988. *Chicago Politics Ward by Ward.* Bloomington: Indi-
    ana University Press.
Gove, Samuel K., and Louis H. Masotti, eds. 1982. *After Daley: Chicago
    Politics in Transition.* Urbana: University of Illinois Press.
Green, Paul. 1988. "Paul Green's Chicago." In *Illinois Issues.* Springfield,
    Ill.: *Illinois Issues,* Sangamon State University.
Grimshaw, William. 1982. "The Daley Legacy and Declining Politics of Party,
    Race, and Public Unions." In *After Daley Chicago Politics in Transi-
    tion,* edited by Samuel K. Gove and Louis H. Masotti. Urbana: Uni-
    versity of Illinois Press.

Gurin, Patricia, Shirley Hatchett, and James S. Jackson. 1989. *Hope and Independence, Blacks' Response to Electoral and Party Politics.* New York: Russell Sage Foundation.

Holli, Melvin G., and Paul M. Green. 1989. *Bashing Chicago Traditions, Harold Washington's Last Campaign: Chicago 1987.* Grand Rapids, Mich: William B. Eerdman's Publishing Co.

Holli, Melvin G., and Peter d'A. Jones, eds. 1984. *Ethnic Chicago*, rev. and expanded ed. Grand Rapids, Mich.: William B. Eerdman's Publishing Co.

Karnig, Albert, and Susan Welch. 1980. *Black Representation and Urban Policy.* Chicago: University of Chicago Press.

Kleppner, Paul. 1985. *Chicago Divided: The Making of a Black Mayor.* DeKalb: Northern Illinois University Press, 1985.

Massey, Douglas S., and Nancy A. Denton. 1988. "Suburbanization and Segregation in U.S. Metropolitan Areas." *American Journal of Sociology* 94(3, November): 592–626.

———. 1993. *American Apartheid: Segregation and the Making of the Underclass.* Cambridge, Mass.: Harvard University Press.

Miranda, Rowan A. 1991. "Post-Machine Regimes and the Growth of Government: A Fiscal History of the City of Chicago, 1970–1990." Paper presented at the Annual Meeting of the Midwest Political Science Association, April 18–20, Chicago.

Peterman, William, and Qi Sanshi. 1991. "Lending Discrimination in Metropolitan Chicago: Continuing Connection between Race, Racial Change, and Mortgage Credit." In *Credit by Color: Mortgage Market Discrimination in Chicagoland* (21–49). Chicago: Chicago Area Fair Housing Alliance, January.

Pinderhughes, Dianne M. 1985. "Legal Strategies for Voting Rights: Political Science and the Law." *Howard Law Journal*, 28(2): 515–40.

———. 1987. *Race and Ethnicity in Chicago Politics: A Reexamination of Pluralist Theory.* Urbana: University of Illinois Press.

———. 1988a. "Race and Ethnicity in Chicago Politics." Address to the Human Relations Task Force, Chicago Community Trust, October 21, Chicago.

———. 1988b. "The Black Community in Chicago." Paper presented to the Social Science History Association, November 4–5, Chicago.

Pitkin, Hanna. 1967. *The Concept of Representation.* Berkeley: University of California Press.

Preston, Michael B. 1982. "Black Politics in the Post-Daley Era." In *After Daley: Chicago Politics in Transition*, edited by Samuel K. Gove and Louis H. Masotti (88–117). Urbana: University of Illinois Press.

Spear, Allan H. 1969. *Black Chicago: The Making of a Negro Ghetto, 1890–1920.* Chicago: University of Chicago Press.

Starks, Robert T. 1982. "Reapportionment and Black Politics: The Case of Chicago." In *Redistricting: An Exercise in Prophecy*, edited by Anna

J. Merritt (53–64). Urbana: Institute of Government and Public Affairs and the Department of Journalism, University of Illinois.

————. 1991. "Community Organizations, Neighborhood Associations, and Urban Politics: The Case of the Harold Washington Crusade and Election in Chicago in 1983." Paper presented to The Urban Institute–Urban Opportunity Program Conference on Big City Governance and Fiscal Choices, June 6–7, Los Angeles.

Travis, Dempsey J. 1987. *An Autobiography of Black Politics.* Chicago: Urban Research Press.

Turner, Margery, Michael Fix, and Raymond Struyk. 1991. *Opportunities Denied, Opportunities Diminished: Racial Discrimination in Hiring.* UI Report 81-9. Washington, D.C.: Urban Institute Press.

Vazquez, Enid. 1982. "Reporter Accepts Both *Hispanic* or *Latino.* Diverse Community Split on Generic Name." *Chicago Reporter* 11(10, October): 8–16.

Woods, Daryl D. 1987. "The Chicago Crusade." In *Strategies for Mobilizing Black Voters: Four Case Studies,* edited by Thomas E. Cavanagh (11–36). Washington, D.C.: Joint Center for Political Studies.

Zikmund, Joseph, II. 1982. "Mayoral Voting and Ethnic Politics in the Daley-Bilandic-Byrne Era." In *After Daley: Chicago Politics in Transition,* edited by Samuel K. Gove and Louis H. Masotti (27–56). Urbana: University of Illinois Press.

Chapter Four

RACIAL AND ETHNIC VOTING PATTERNS IN MIAMI

Genie N. L. Stowers and Ronald K. Vogel

Miami is distinguished from most U.S. cities by the swiftness and depth of change it has undergone in the last three decades. In 1960, Miami was known chiefly as a tourist destination. Less than 3 percent of the population was Hispanic (City of Miami 1988: I-6). In 1990, over 60 percent of the city's population was Hispanic (U.S. Bureau of the Census [henceforth, Census Bureau] 1990). This dramatic shift in the city's demographics is one indicator of how the Latin population, specifically Cubans, has come to dominate Miami politics. Now, there are only "minority" groups in Miami, whether non-Latin whites (Anglos), Hispanics (Cubans, Puerto Ricans, Nicaraguans, Mexicans, and others), or blacks (African-Americans, Haitians, and others). The degree of social diversity is astonishing in a medium-sized city—the population of Miami in 1990 was 358,548 persons (Census Bureau 1990). At the same time, the level of racial and ethnic conflict within the city is reflective of problems experienced by large cities.

The city of Miami has a council-manager form of government. Five commissioners, one being the mayor, are elected at-large in nonpartisan races. The manager is appointed by the commission and is responsible for appointing the department heads, including the police chief. In theory, the commission is to refrain from interfering in the city's administration, and the managers are to stay out of politics. Yet, the government of Miami illustrates the fallacy of the politics-administration dichotomy. The city's administration is rife with politics, and commissioners are not reluctant to tell the city manager and staff what to do. Recent mayors, including Maurice Ferre and Xavier Suarez, have attempted to run the city as strong mayors.[1] Yet, the form of government and election system have come under attack as factors limiting the city's ability to solve its own problems.

An analysis of Miami's situation is complicated by the "metropolitan" form of government of Dade County (Lotz 1984; Sofen 1966).

"Metro-Dade" has about 1.94 million persons (Census Bureau 1990). The Metro-Dade government, established in 1958, created a two-tier system of government with the county government providing "system maintenance" services and city governments providing "life-style" services (Harrigan 1989). However, the two-tier system has not been maintained, as over half the population now lives in unincorporated Dade County, meaning that all of their services are provided by the Metro government.

The problems facing the population of the city of Miami are not wholly the responsibility of the city government. A number of services are provided by the Metro government, and there is no clear division of responsibility as to who should address the problems of poorer residents. This was evident in the response to the 1980 riots in Liberty City. Liberty City, which is not a city at all, is divided, with half of it lying in unincorporated Dade County and the other half in the city of Miami (Porter and Dunn 1984; U.S. Commission on Civil Rights 1982). As another example, in response to the devastation wreaked by Hurricane Andrew in 1992, the rebuilding effort, especially in low-income neighborhoods, ran into a maze of overlapping regulatory and planning authorities divided between the county and city governments.

This chapter tells the story of local electoral politics and policy in Miami over the past three decades. The story is somewhat different from those of Philadelphia and Chicago told in the previous two chapters. Miami saw major demographic changes in population, voter registration, and voter turnout. But unlike in the other two cities, a minority group—Cuban Americans—was able to build and hold onto a position of political dominance in Miami. The period saw some employment gains for all minority groups. There was little overall change in policy toward poor and disadvantaged residents, however, because the minority group in control is essentially middle class and conservative in its politics, as was the non-Hispanic white majority in power at the beginning of the period.

DEMOGRAPHIC PROFILE OF MIAMI

Between 1960 and 1990, Hispanics rose from being a statistically insignificant group in Miami—less than 3 percent of the total population—to over 60 percent of the population (see figure 4.1 and table 4.1). By 1970, the non-Hispanic white population, known as Anglos, was no

Figure 4.1 RACE AND ETHNICITY IN CITY OF MIAMI, 1960–90

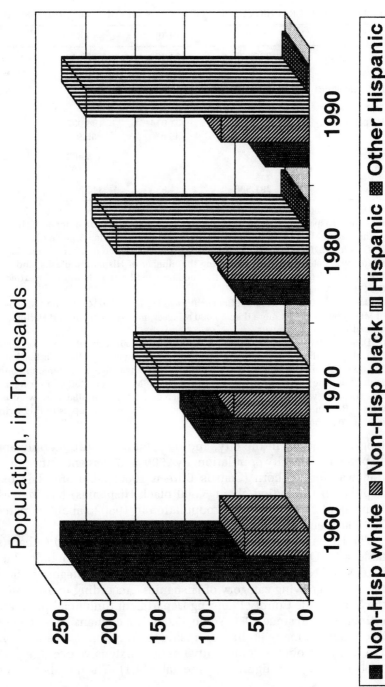

Table 4.1 DEMOGRAPHIC PROFILE OF CITY OF MIAMI: 1960, 1970, 1980, 1990

	1960[a]	1970[b]	1980[c]	1990[d]
Non-Hispanic white	225,888 77.4%	104,463 31.1%	67,249 18.9%	43,752 12.2%
Non-Hispanic black	65,213 22.4%	76,156 22.7%	82,098 25.1%	88,319 24.6%
Hispanic	N.A.[e] (>9,000)	151,914 45.4%	194,037 55.9%	223,964 62.4%
Other Non-Hispanic			3,482 1%	2,513 .7%
Total	291,688	334,859	346,865	358,548

a. Data for 1960 come from the Census Bureau (1960). The Census category "white" includes "Hispanics." For 1960, this is not a problem, since the number of Hispanics in the city of Miami was not statistically significant (less than 3 percent).
b. Data for 1970 come from the Census Bureau (1970). The number of non-Hispanic whites was determined by subtracting the number of Hispanics, blacks, and others from the total population. This is the method used by the Planning Department of the City of Miami.
c. Data for 1980 come from the Census Bureau (1980: tables 14, 15, and 16). The city of Miami believes that more than 50,000 refugees, mostly Hispanic and Haitian, were missed in the 1980 Census.
d. Data for 1990 come from the Census Bureau (1990). City of Miami projections indicate that there were actually 105,000 blacks (including Hispanic blacks) and 235,000 Hispanics in Miami in 1990 and that the Census figures undercounted these minorities. The Division of Planning in the city of Miami reported a lower figure for non-Hispanic whites, 18,114, or about 5 percent. They indicated they were using Census Bureau data, but the discrepancy could not be cleared up as of this writing.
e. N.A., data not available.

longer a majority in the city, and by 1990 it constituted only about 12 percent of the city population. By 1980, 53.7 percent of the population was foreign-born (Census Bureau 1980; table 56). The black population (including about 5,000 black Hispanics) has increased from about 22 percent of the population in 1960 to about 26 percent in 1990 (Census Bureau 1990).

The Hispanic population of Miami is over 60 percent Cuban (see table 4.2). Other significant Hispanic populations include Puerto Ricans and Nicaraguans, but the "other Hispanic" category is clearly the fastest growing category of Hispanics. According to estimates of the Metro-Dade County Planning Department (unofficial population estimate, 1989) since 1980, some 65,000 Nicaraguans have moved to Dade County, many ending up inside the city limits (see table 4.3). White flight from the community has been extensive over the period 1960 to 1990 (see figure 4.1 and table 4.1). The number of non-

Table 4.2 HISPANIC POPULATION PROFILE OF CITY OF MIAMI, 1980
AND 1990

Type of Spanish Origin	1980	1990	Percentage Difference
Mexican	1,496 (.7%)	1,923 (.9%)	+28.5
Puerto Rican	12,320 (6.3%)	12,004 (5.4%)	−2.6
Cuban	147,313 (75.9%)	139,367 (62.2%)	−5.4
Other Hispanic	32,908 (16.9%)	70,670 (31.6%)	+114.8
Total Hispanic	194,037	223,964	+15.4

Sources: Census Bureau (1980: table 16); and City of Miami (1993).

Table 4.3 HISPANIC POPULATION OF METRO-DADE COUNTY, 1980 AND 1990

	1980	1990	Percentage Change
Cuban	407,000 (70%)	563,979 (59.2%)	+38.6
Other Hispanic	90,000 (15.5%)	165,663 (17.4%)	+84.1
Nicaraguan	7,000 (1.2%)	74,244 (7.8%)	+960.6
Puerto Rican	45,000 (7.7%)	72,827 (7.6%)	+61.8
Colombian	19,000 (3.3%)	53,582 (5.6%)	+182.0
Mexican	13,000 (2.2%)	23,112 (2.4%)	+77.8
Total Hispanic	581,000	953,407	+64.1

Sources: Data for 1980 are 1991 estimates from Metro-Dade County Planning Department; 1990 figures are from *Dade County Facts*, Metro-Dade County Planning Department (1993) and are based upon 1990 U.S. Census data.

Hispanic whites has declined spectacularly, not only as a percentage of the city's population (from 77.4 percent in 1960 to 12.2 percent in 1990) but in absolute terms as well (from 225,888 to 43,752). The white flight has had a significant effect on the electoral fortunes of candidates and has made it more difficult for the traditional business elite to maintain its power (Vogel and Stowers 1991). A major prob-

Table 4.4 BLACK POPULATION OF METRO-DADE COUNTY, 1990

	Country of Origin	Percentage
United States	266,000	64.1
Haiti	85,000	20.5
Jamaica	20,000	4.8
Bahamas	7,500	1.8
Trinidad	3,500	.8
Other West Indies	16,000	3.9
Other	17,000	4.1
Total	415,000	100.0

Source: Population estimates of Metro-Dade County Planning Department, 1991.

lem from the city's standpoint is that white flight is also associated more broadly with "middle class flight" (City of Miami 1988: I-5–I-6).

In addition to the astonishing growth of the Latin community and the equally pronounced decline of the non-Latin white population, important changes have occurred in the black community (see table 4.4). According to an estimate by the Metro-Dade County Planning Department (1991), there were 85,000 Haitians in Dade County in 1990 compared to only 18,000 in 1980. Many of these Haitians live within the corporate boundaries of the city of Miami. In 1980, about 89.6 percent of the county's black population was classified as American (Metro-Dade County Planning Department, unofficial population estimate, 1989). In 1990, only about 64 percent were American (Metro-Dade County Planning Department 1991). Much of this change results from Haitian immigration. The various black populations retain their separate identities and cultures and have not coalesced into a single black community.

POLITICAL PARTICIPATION BY RACIAL AND ETHNIC MINORITIES

The political structure of Miami has been in continual transition over the last 30 years. In the late 1950s, Miami was a small, sleepy southern town distinguished by its beaches and its white male power structure. No one anticipated the drastic change that would accompany the arrival of Cuban political refugees fleeing Fidel Castro's revolution. Beginning their political exile in 1959, they arrived for what was assumed to be a temporary stay (McCoy and Gonzalez 1985).

But the Cubans remained and, retaining their professional identity and interest in politics, they built a strong and vibrant economic community on the foundation of numerous small businesses (Wilson and Portes 1980). They were then able to convert this economic power into the dominant political power in Miami. The growth in Cuban political power in Miami, signaled by the appointment of a Cuban-American to a vacant seat on the city commission in 1972, rapidly advanced, culminating in the election of the first Cuban-American as mayor in 1985.

The African-American community, on the other hand, did not fare as well politically or economically during this period. Although an African-American was appointed to the city commission in 1966, and subsequently reelected in 1967, African-Americans were unable to gain the same level of political power, limited by their small numbers in an at-large election system and their lack of economic power. The Cuban exiles arrived at a time when African-American communities around the South were organizing effective civil rights movements. Elsewhere, political battles were fought between the white and African-American communities. In Miami, that situation was complicated by the arrival of another minority group with middle-class status and a high level of political interest. Further, the Cuban exiles received considerable federal aid in resettling and recertifying into their original professional specialties (Pedraza-Bailey 1985).

A tripartite, "three-legged-stool" political situation was created, with three different racial/ethnic communities competing with one another for political representation and public policies. The arrival of a new wave of refugees from Haiti added an additional language and culture to the area. The 1980s has also seen the arrival of many other Latinos from Central and South America, further aggravating relations within and among Miami's different communities. Rivalries have became increasingly competitive, focused around shifting, unstable electoral coalitions and governing coalitions that were nothing short of nonexistent. Racial disturbances and riots are no longer out of the ordinary in Miami.

Patterns in Voter Registration

The patterns of local political power can first be observed in the changing patterns of voter registration over time. Table 4.5 indicates the changing nature of the electoral system in Miami as Hispanics have replaced non-Latin whites as the dominant group in the city.

Table 4.5 RACIAL AND ETHNIC COMPOSITION, CITY OF MIAMI AND METRO-
DADE COUNTY VOTER REGISTRATION, 1973–89

Year	Non-Latin White (%) Miami	Non-Latin White (%) Dade	Hispanic (%) Miami	Hispanic (%) Dade	African-American (%) Miami	African-American (%) Dade
1973	N.A.	80.3	N.A.	6.3	N.A.	13.3
1975	49.9	77.0	19.8	8.4	30.3	14.7
1977	43.8	71.7	26.3	12.9	29.9	15.3
1979	40.0	68.1	30.4	15.9	29.6	16.0
1981	34.2	64.1	35.7	19.0	29.7	17.0
1983	29.8	61.9	37.6	19.7	32.6	18.4
1985	29.5	57.4	40.7	24.2	29.8	18.4
1987	27.4	55.3	43.1	26.6	29.5	18.2
1989	27.1	53.0	42.3	27.8	30.7	19.1

Source: Derived from Metro-Dade County Elections Department data.
Note: N.A., data not available.

In 1975, non-Latin whites comprised 49.9 percent of the registered
voters in Miami, and African-Americans comprised 30.3 percent of
the city's voters (the latter level was maintained through 1989). On
the other hand, Hispanic-Americans were only 19.8 percent of the
registered electorate in 1975. By 1989, the pattern for non-Latin
whites and Hispanics had shifted sharply. As a group, non-Latin
whites comprised only 27.1 percent of all registered voters, while
Hispanic-Americans had taken their place as the dominant group,
encompassing 42.3 percent of the registered electorate of the city.

Although the same political shifts were apparent in Dade County,
non-Latin whites have still been able to maintain a numerical majority. It is clear that the non-Latin white advantage in Dade County
will dissipate within a few years and that the county will become a
polity without a majority. African-Americans were only 19.1 percent
of the county's electorate in 1989, whereas Hispanics were only 27.8
percent of the electorate in that year (table 4.5).

Patterns in Voter Turnout

One result of electoral competition has been the increased salience
of local elections, often due to the manipulation and emphasis on
racial and ethnic issues in the campaigns. Important indicators of
the vigor of these elections are the turnout patterns for the whole
community as well as for individual ethnic and racial groups (see
table 4.6). Table 4.6 shows that, with Hispanic-Americans leading
the way, Miami voter turnout in local mayoral elections has gradually

Table 4.6 PERCENTAGE TURNOUT BY GROUP FOR MAYORAL RACES,
CITY OF MIAMI, 1969–89

Year	Total Turnout (%)	African-American (%)	Hispanic-American (%)	Non-Latin White (%)
1969	21.0	16.5	21.7	22.4
1971	25.7	22.0	27.7	25.6
1973	30.6	23.1	37.0	29.6
1975	22.9	14.1	30.5	20.1
1977	26.9	15.9	37.6	21.1
1979	29.7	18.9	40.0	23.5
1981	45.0	39.3	52.7	36.7
1983	49.2	41.2	56.7	43.2
1985	46.9	39.5	53.3	41.2
1987	48.9	N.A.	N.A.	N.A.
1989	34.3	N.A.	N.A.	N.A.

Sources: Stowers (1987, 1990); and Metro-Dade County Elections Department.
Note: N.A., data not available.

increased. Total community turnout increased from 21.0 percent in
1969 to a high of 48.9 percent in 1987, before dropping to 34.3 percent
in 1989.

In all years except 1969, Hispanic-Americans exhibited higher levels of voter turnout (up to 53.2 percent in 1985) than either non-Latin
whites (41.2 percent in 1985) or African-Americans (39.5 percent in
1985) (table 4.6). This is, of course, counter to findings about voter
participation rates of earlier ethnic immigrant groups as well as other
contemporary groups, and even other Hispanic groups.

The combined impact of high levels of voter registration and voter
turnout explains the significant influence that Hispanic-Americans
have had on the political process in Miami. By virtue of numbers
and the extreme social and demographic changes experienced in
the city, minority control of the city commission was accomplished
without the advantage of single-member district elections. From 1972
until the 1993 election, the commission was a majority "minority"
commission, highlighted by the election of a Puerto Rican, Maurice
Ferre, in 1973, which resulted in a Hispanic majority on the commission in 1979. The first Cuban-American mayor, Xavier Suarez, was
elected in 1985, leading to a Cuban-American majority (three members) on the commission.

Suarez was subsequently reelected—once in a rematch with former
Mayor Maurice Ferre—until he decided not to run for reelection in
1993. In what many interpreted as a backlash against the ethnically
divisive mayoral campaign of Cuban-American City Commissioner

Miriam Alonso, the pattern of this influence was altered in the 1993 election when former mayor (1967–1970) Steven Clark, a non-Latin white, was elected mayor over Alonso. Clark picked up the support of younger Cuban-American voters as well as African-American, white non-Hispanic, and "other" Hispanic voters to become the first non-Hispanic mayor of Miami since 1973 (*Miami Herald* 1993). Thus, after the 1993 election, the ethnic and racial makeup of the commission changed from majority Hispanic-American (Cuban) to having only two commissioners of Hispanic descent, one African-American, and two non-Latin whites (including the new mayor).

RACIAL AND ETHNIC IMPACT ON URBAN POLICY

Browning, Marshall, and Tabb (1990) have suggested that the growth of minority political power will have a positive impact upon some types of urban policies. The remainder of this chapter examines several such policies—ballot issues (bond issues and referenda), minority public employement, and police review boards.[2]

Electoral Ballot Issues

Bond issues and referenda are major vehicles for citizen expression as well as important ways to measure citizen preferences for urban policies. In a conflicted community such as Miami, they serve both a functional role in establishing public policy and a symbolic role in allowing groups to air their concerns and make a public statement. Table 4.7 outlines a number of these ballot issues in Miami, the year they were on the ballot, the percentage total vote, and a breakdown of each vote by population group. The issues are categorized as social or group issues, economic development issues, and taxation issues. The time period over which these issues range is from 1972 until 1985.[3]

GROUP PREFERENCES

As table 4.7 indicates, clear patterns of differences in policy preferences emerge among the three population groups in Miami. Hispanic-Americans tend to be more fiscally and socially conservative on spending issues than either African-Americans or non-Latin whites.

Table 4.7 GROUP VOTING PREFERENCES ON BALLOT ISSUES IN MIAMI, 1972–85

	Year	Percentage Overall Vote	Group Vote Preferences (%)		
			African-American	Hispanic-American	Non-Latin White
Social/Group Issues					
Low/moderate income housing bonds (+)	1976	56.6	69.9	50.3	53.7
Lottery proceeds to low/moderate housing (+)	1983	29.6	39.5	19.6	34.2
City funds to conferences with communist representation (+)	1982	26.0	33.9	17.0	35.7
Economic Development Issues					
Parks/recreation bonds (+)	1974	42.3	45.9	38.8	43.7
Orange Bowl improvement bonds (+)	1977	34.8	36.3	29.5	41.6
Storm sewer bonds (+)	1978	62.1	58.8	62.4	65.2
Fire/rescue bonds (+)	1981	66.2	69.2	63.6	67.8
Parks/recreation bonds (+)	1985	46.1	55.8	44.7	42.5
Taxation Issues					
County tourist room tax (+)	1978	56.1	55.5	56.0	56.9
County property tax cut ["tax revolt" measure] (+)	1979	32.6	14.6	43.7	32.8
Millage increase (+)	1985	87.5	84.1	90.3	85.0

Source: Stowers (1987).
Note: Plus sign (+) means voters were asked to approve the proposal.

However, their voting patterns do bear some resemblance to those of the non-Latin white population.

Hispanic precincts voted, by only a slight majority, to approve bonds to build housing for low- and moderate-income citizens and provided the least support of the subgroups (19.6 percent) for a lottery whose proceeds would go to the same purpose (see table 4.7). On an issue closer to their interest, they voted overwhelmingly against a proposal to allow city funds to go to conferences with representatives from communist countries attending. On two of these issues (city funds and lottery), the African-American and non-Latin white communities exhibited strikingly similar voting patterns. On the bond issue, however, Hispanic-American and non-Latin white groups voted alike.

Fewer group differences are observed for the economic development ballot issues.[4] Only two significant differences emerge between the groups. Hispanic-American precincts provided significantly less support for the Orange Bowl improvement bonds (1977) than other groups and significantly less support for the parks/recreation bonds in 1985 than did African-Americans. Although all three groups still voted to defeat the Orange Bowl measure, African-American precincts voted to approve the parks bonds (1985), which failed, while the other two groups voted to defeat them.

The taxation issues demonstrate only one significant difference between the groups. All groups voted to approve Metropolitan Dade County's tourist room tax (an attempt to place the tax burden on outsiders and so, less on themselves) and to approve a 1985 millage increase. However, the county property tax cut, which was defeated, was overwhelmingly rejected by voters in African-American precincts but received significantly more support in both non-Latin white and Hispanic-American precincts (see table 4.7). This ballot issue, part of the "tax revolt," was extremely unusual. Placed on the ballot by petition, the petition's writers mistakenly asked for a 99.5 percent tax cut rather than the 50 percent they intended. The county refused to take the issue off the ballot, but the resulting confusion made it difficult to interpret the defeat of the measure.

Minority Employment

Since the days of immigrant political machines, governmental responsiveness to immigrant ethnic groups and racial minorities has come in the form of public employment. In machine times, political

Table 4.8 EMPLOYMENT OF CITY OF MIAMI AND METRO-DADE COUNTY BY ETHNICITY AND RACE, SELECTED YEARS, 1977–90

Year	Percentage Non-Latin White		Percentage African-American		Percentage Hispanic-American	
	Miami	Dade	Miami	Dade	Miami	Dade
1977	50.2	N.A.	29.7	N.A.	19.9	N.A.
1979	N.A.	50.4	N.A.	30.4	N.A.	18.6
1980	N.A.	48.0	N.A.	31.7	N.A.	19.5
1985	N.A.	39.5	N.A.	34.5	N.A.	24.6
1989	30.6	34.8	29.9	34.6	38.7	29.0
1990	29.8	34.2	30.6	34.5	38.8	29.7

Sources: Metro-Dade County *Affirmative Action Annual Reports,* various years; and City of Miami (1978) and personnel statistics.
Notes: The category "Other," which never exceeds 1.4 percent, is excluded from the table; N.A., data not available.

patronage was the backbone of political machines. Today, government employment continues to be important for minorities and serves as an indicator of group access to the political system. In Miami and Dade County, government jobs provide over one-half the "management and professional" jobs held by African-Americans (Lowe 1983: 1A).

In 1977, the city of Miami entered into a consent decree with the U.S. Justice Department over the issue of the hiring of minorities and women. This decree was filed on behalf of women and Latin and African-American male employees and future employees of the city, and was to be in effect for five years. The decree included specific minority and female employment goals for traditionally Anglo male jobs (City of Miami 1978). For instance, a goal of 56 percent minorities and women was established for the traditionally Anglo male positions of police officer, public service aide, firefighter, and traditionally male positions in the Building and Finance departments. For the traditionally African-American entry-level maintenance positions, the goal was 35 percent non-African-American persons hired each year. Skilled, technical, and entry-level administrative positions had hiring goals of 50 percent minorities and women each year. Upper-level administrative positions had hiring goals of 20 percent women and minorities per year (City of Miami 1978).

The effect of this consent decree is seen clearly in table 4.8, which provides comparisons of non-Latin white, Hispanic, and African-American employment by both the city of Miami and Metropolitan Dade County. The inclusion of county data permits a crucial comparison of the relationship between demographic change, electoral political power, and subsequent government employment. Significantly, no employment data broken down by race, ethnicity, and gender were even available before the date of the consent decree, in 1977.

The proportion of the non-Latin white employment in the city of Miami shows a drop from 50.2 percent in 1977 to 29.8 percent in 1990 (see table 4.8—surprisingly similar to the trend seen in non-Latin white registration patterns). Non-Latin white employment in Metro Dade County also dropped during this period, from 50.4 percent of total employment in 1979 to 34.2 percent in 1990. Although these are both significant declines, no major differences emerge in levels of non-Latin white employment between the two governmental bodies.

Like voter registration patterns, the proportion of African-American employment in both the city and county governments has remained relatively stable over time. In 1977, African-Americans comprised 29.7 percent of city employees and 30.4 percent of county employees in 1979 (the first figures available); 12 years later, the proportion had increased only slightly (see table 4.8).

Significant differences in group employment between the city and county appear to emerge for Hispanic employees by 1989.[5] Although beginning at virtually the same levels of Hispanic employment (19.9 percent Hispanic for the city in 1977 and 18.6 percent for the county in 1979), by 1989 a difference of 9.7 percentage points less for the county had emerged (table 4.8). This had declined slightly, to 9.1 percentage points, by 1990. Clearly, the city of Miami has shifted faster toward Hispanic employment than has Metropolitan Dade County.

Although the consent decree was unquestionably the trigger for this change, there were other factors behind the impetus for the decree itself. Unlike the county, the African-American and Hispanic communities together already constituted 55 percent of the electorate in the city of Miami in 1977. In addition, the Cuban-American community had already begun to exhibit its high rates of voter turnout in 1973; these high levels maintained themselves through 1977. This increased voter registration and voter turnout added credibility to the perception of increased minority interest in politics and the community at large.

Already, race and ethnicity were important factors in the city's election campaigns. Miami elected a Puerto Rican as mayor during the regular election in November of 1973 and reelected the Cuban-American and African-American members on the commission.

Also for the first time during the 1973 races, the salience of the election and of developing political interest was apparent in the large number of candidates who ran for office. Seven candidates ran for mayor (including 1 Cuban-American and 1 African-American), 12 candidates ran for the seat occupied by the Cuban-American on the commission (including 5 Cuban-Americans), and 6 ran for the seat won by the African-American (including 2 African-Americans and 1 Cuban-American). Obviously, both communities, but particularly the Cuban-American community, were showing high levels of interest and political development.

Miami enjoyed a relatively quiet campaign in 1975. The 1977 election campaigns were far from quiet, however. Eight of the 10 candidates for the 3 seats up for election were either Hispanic-American or African-American. Further, Hispanics came close to achieving a majority on the commission that year, by nearly defeating the incumbent African-American member. Until the primary election, the 3 minority members on the commission (the Puerto Rican Ferre, the Cuban-American Reboso, and African-American Theodore Gibson) had actually campaigned together as a block. However, when it appeared that another would be in a runoff against Gibson, the coalition broke apart. However, Gibson won reelection.

This was the political context into which the consent decree was entered. Unlike the political situation in Metropolitan Dade County, minorities already had attained a majority in voter registration, showed increased levels of voter turnout, and held a majority on the City Commission.

Voter registration in Metro Dade County was still overwhelmingly (71.7 percent) non-Latin white by 1977. Fewer Hispanics or African-Americans lived in the county, and their political clout was significantly lower. The first (and only) Cuban-American representative on the County Commission was not appointed until 1981 and was subsequently reelected. Until 1992, there was also only one African-American on the County Commission, also initially appointed and subsequently reelected.

Only in 1993, after a successful six-year-old Voting Rights Act suit against Metropolitan Dade County, did the political situation on the Metro-Dade County Commission change for racial and ethnic groups. As a result of the lawsuit's resolution, district elections were established, the number of commission seats was expanded (to 13 seats from 9), and special elections were held in 1992. The result was a Metro-Dade County Commission with 4 African-American (30.8 percent) and 6 Hispanic-American (46.2 percent) members, for a total of 77 percent racial or ethnic minority representation on the commission (up from 22.2 percent prior to the lawsuit).

Thus, the existing and potential political power of the minority communities in Metro-Dade County was significantly less than in the city of Miami until 1993; the results of this major shift in political power remain to be seen. The earlier differences between the city and the county account for the push toward the consent decree in the city of Miami and the relative lack of attention paid by the county to such factors.

Police-Community Relations

In 1975, 75.3 percent of the sworn police officers in Miami were non-Latin whites, 11.3 percent were African-American, and 13.2 percent were Hispanic. By 1991, the percentage of non-Latin white sworn officers had dropped to just 33.5 percent of the force, while African-Americans had increased their proportion to 20.9 percent of the force and Hispanic officers accounted for 45.2 percent of the force. The absolute number of non-Latin white officers had been nearly halved, whereas the number of African-American officers had more than doubled and the number of Hispanic officers had more than quadrupled (see table 4.9). (City of Miami Police Department, Personnel Unit, 1991.)

Yet, the African-American community has complained that progress in hiring African-American police officers has been too slow, that non-Latin whites still account for too great a share of the promotions, that police hiring policies are harmful to African-American applicants, and that African-Americans were suspended or terminated at higher rates than non-Latin whites (*Metro-Miami Action Plan* 1989: 23).

The Miami police force has been criticized by the African-American community for many years. Indeed, many of the racial incidents and riots that have occurred in the city over the last decade were directly or indirectly related to acts of police brutality toward African-Americans (Porter and Dunn 1984). The most recent such occurrence provoked the Overtown riot in January 1989. As Miami prepared to host the Superbowl, a Miami police officer shot and killed an African-American motorcyclist, instigating a riot in the African-American community of Overtown. This was Miami's fourth serious racial disturbance in the 1980s. Once again Miami's racial and ethnic tensions were the focus of unwanted national and even international attention (City of Miami 1989).

Table 4.9 SWORN POLICE OFFICERS, CITY OF MIAMI BY ETHNICITY AND RACE, 1979–91

Year	Total	Percentage Non-Latin White	Percentage African-American	Percentage Hispanic-American
1979	675	68.0	13.5	18.4
1980	688	58.7	16.6	24.6
1981	859	49.9	17.6	32.2
1982	1,046	44.0	16.8	39.0
1983	1,045	43.7	17.1	38.9
1984	1,047	43.4	16.2	40.2
1985	1,040	42.3	16.7	40.8
1986	1,020	41.7	17.0	41.2
1987	1,047	40.6	17.2	41.9
1988	1,043	38.8	17.6	43.2
1989	1,095	36.8	18.9	44.0
1990	1,080	34.9	20.1	44.6
1991	1,069	33.5	20.9	45.2

Source: Figures supplied by City of Miami Police Department, Personnel Unit, 1991.
Notes: Numer of police are reported for month of October for years 1979–85 and the month of September for years 1986–91. The category "Other" is excluded from the table.

Following the riot, a panel was established by the city commission to examine the riot's causes and to assess the overall state of police-community relations. The panel's findings were published in two reports, one focusing on police-community relations, the other on economic issues. The panel concluded that "the root causes of the civil disturbance . . . are found in deep-seated and long-standing social, economic, and political inequities" (City of Miami 1989: 9). The panel further noted that the "incidents leading to these violent manifestations have reinforced the Black community's belief that a dual system of justice prevails in the Miami/Dade area and that a system in which Blacks receive unequal treatment at the hands of law enforcement personnel continues to exist" (p. 12).

A major finding of the panel was the need for a citizen review board to investigate and monitor complaints of police brutality (City of Miami 1989: 2).[6] Other criticisms focused on the use of polygraph tests to screen out African-American police applicants in apparent violation of the consent decree, a high "washout" rate of African-American police officer candidates, the "overdelegation of the Police Chief's authority" in hiring decisions, and the failure of the police department to reach its "21 percent affirmative action goal established for Black sworn personnel" (pp. 2–3).

The report also stated that "there is a strong perception that a pattern of racial injustice exists within the Miami Police Department which adversely impacts Black police officers" and that "there are serious problems between the Black community and the Miami Police Department with regard to both trust and communication" (City of Miami 1989: 13). Although the police department was close to its 21 percent goal for sworn African-American police officers, the tensions among and between members of the force and the community had not abated.

Indeed, when the final report was submitted in December 1990, the panel noted, "The City of Miami has not pursued the implementation of the recommendations with the level of intensity or aggressiveness which is required to correct the many inappropriate actions/procedures noted by the Panel" (City of Miami 1990: 44). Alpert and Dunham (1988: 39) pointed out that the "management, supervision, and control of the Miami Police Departments lacks direction," and asserted that this is related to the ethnic and racial divisions within the city commission itself. Although Miami has had an African-American police chief since 1985, the larger political context within which he has operated has not greatly changed.

CONCLUSION

Minorities in Miami have certainly gained ground since the 1960s with respect to representation in local government and city employment. Initially, representation came about through appointment to the city commission and subsequent reelection. It is less clear what other policies of local government have changed in response to increased minority power.

The Cuban-American community in Miami has become the dominant group in city politics and government. Because of their numbers and economic status, Cuban-Americans have been able to use local government to benefit their community. However, aside from enhancing employment opportunities and gaining city contracts, the Cuban community is not interested in using local government to pursue redistributive policies. This is a function of the community's conservative values, which do not oppose the traditional business elite in Miami.

The non-Latin white population has opted out of the city of Miami. It maintains its influence through its economic power and business organizations and the biases associated with reform government. However, the traditional business elite seems more interested in seeing a strong-mayor form of government established for the city in which a strong leader will emerge as mayor and forge an enduring "governing coalition" with the various minority groups. At present, the mayor does not have the authority to negotiate significant issues with the business community. Further, elected officials lack stable electoral coalitions. In a community of minorities, elected offices cannot be won without support from outside one's own ethnic or racial group.

The African-American community has not fared so well as other minorities. Although African-Americans have also gained representation, they are overwhelmed by the size of the Cuban-American population and the growing number of other Hispanics. The Cuban-American experience is not replicable in the African-American community, since Cuban-American economic advancement was the result of its retained middle-class status and massive federal assistance. Political gains followed economic gains. The African-American community's strategy for upward mobility was to gain political power. Yet, in Miami, this avenue of advancement was closed in the 1960s and 1970s by Cuban advancement in politics. Blacks have benefited from some programs that were put in place for minorities; they could hardly be excluded from affirmative action employment. But the black community will never gain enough political power to pursue redistributive policies through city government.

Local government provides minorities with a vehicle to pursue group interests as reflected in employment and other city policies. In addition, control of city government provides groups with the ability to take positions on issues important to them, even if the positions are only symbolic. But control of city government cannot in itself alter many of the critical policies affecting residents' quality of life.

Notes

1. It remains to be seen how Mayor Steven Clark, elected in 1993, will attempt to run the city. Clark is a former mayor of Miami (1967–70) who subsequently served on the Metro-Dade County Commission for 20 years.

2. Not reported here are analyses of approved budget totals for parks, police, fire, public works, planning, social welfare, and total expenditures (1937–87). No signifi-

cant trends that could be attributed to ethnic or racial group influence were detected, either through aggregate budgetary analysis (percentages and trends) or statistical analyses (generalized least squares estimation). Although budgetary outcomes are significant indicators of urban policy, the incrementalism built into budget levels and the enormous constraints upon budgetary decision making reduce the possibility of detecting any shifts due to changes in group power through analysis at this aggregate level.

3. The percentages in table 4.7 were developed utilizing city election data at the precinct level. The figures reflect votes for the group of African-American-dominated precincts, Hispanic-American-dominated precincts, and non-Latin-white-dominated precincts. Thus, they are best interpreted as *group* voting patterns. The threat of committing an ecological fallacy, ever-present in this type of analysis, is reduced by clear and precise attention to this interpretation of group patterns, not individual patterns.

4. One issue supported by the public was the 1977 straw ballot on improvements to the Orange Bowl. The actual bond issue, however, was defeated only months later.

5. However, the date of the appearance of these differences is unclear owing to the lack of adequate data for every year for each governmental entity.

6. An Office of Professional Compliance was established in the city manager's office to investigate charges of police brutality following the 1989 death of an African-American motorcyclist. This office was later transferred to the police department to ensure access to personnel records otherwise unavailable and to afford a more direct and ongoing impact on police department policies. Creation of a citizen advisory board to work with the office is currently under consideration.

References

Alpert, Geoffrey, and Roger G. Dunham. 1988. *Policing Multi-Ethnic Neigh-borhoods: The Miami Study and Findings for Law Enforcement in the United States.* NY: Greenwood Press.

Batista, Laureano. 1969. "Political Sociology of the Cuban Exile." Master's thesis, University of Miami.

Boswell, Thomas D., and James R. Curtis. 1983. *The Cuban-American Experience: Culture, Images, and Perspectives.* Totowa, N.J.: Rowman & Allanheld.

Boswell, Thomas D., and Manuel Rivero. n.d. *Demographic Characteristics of Pre-Mariel Cubans Living in the United States: 1980.* Miami: Research Institute for Cuban Studies, University of Miami.

Browning, Rufus P., Dale Rogers Marshall, and David H. Tabb, eds. 1990. *Racial Politics in American Cities.* White Plains, N.Y.: Longman Publishing Group.

Castro, M. 1990. *Ethnic Audit.* Miami: Greater Miami United Census Bureau. *See* U.S. Bureau of the Census.

City of Miami. 1978. *City of Miami Affirmative Action Plan.* Miami: City of Miami Personnel Department.

————. 1988. *City of Miami Comprehensive Plan Phase I. Data and Analysis.* Miami: City of Miami Division of Planning.

————. 1993. *City of Miami Selected Demographic and Socio-Economic Variables, 1970–1990.* Miami: City of Miami Planning Department.

City of Miami, Overtown Independent Review Panel. 1989. "Findings and Recommendations Concerning Police-Community Relations: An Interim Report." July.

————. 1990. "Final Report Concerning Economic Issues Relative to the Overtown Civil Disturbance." December.

Harrigan, John. 1989. *Political Change in the Metropolis.* 4th ed. Glenview, Ill.: Scott, Foresman & Co.

Lineberry, Robert, and Edmund Fowler. 1967. "Reformism and Public Policies in American Cities." *American Political Science Review* 61: 701–17.

Lotz, Aileen. 1984. *Metropolitan Dade County: Two-Tier Government in Action.* Boston: Allyn & Bacon.

Lowe, Bob. 1983. "Good Jobs and Salaries for Blacks Still an Elusive Dream in Miami." *Miami Herald*, p. 1A.

McCoy, Clyde B., and Diana H. Gonzalez. 1985. *Cuban Immigration and Immigrants in Florida and the United States: Implications for Immigration Policy.* Gainesville: University of Florida Bureau for Economic and Business Research.

Metro-Dade County Planning Department, Research Division. 1985. "Demographic Profile, Dade County, Florida: 1960–1980." Miami: Author. Photocopy.

————. 1990. *Dade County Facts.* Miami: Author. Photocopy.

————. 1993. *Dade County Facts.* Miami: Author. May.

————. n.d. "Social and Economic Profile Undated." Miami: Author. Photocopy.

Metro-Miami Action Plan. 1989. Annual Report. Miami: Author.

Miami Herald. 1993. "Ex-Mayor Trounces Alonso." November 10: 1A, 20A.

Mohl, Raymond. 1989. "Ethnic Politics in Miami, 1960–1986." In *Shades of the Sunbelt*, edited by Randall M. Miller and George E. Pozzetta (143–60). Boca Raton: Florida Atlantic University Press.

Pedraza-Bailey, Sylvia. 1985. *Political and Economic Migrants in America: Cubans and Mexicans.* Austin: University of Texas Press.

Porter, Bruce, and Marvin Dunn. 1984. *The Miami Riot of 1980.* Lexington, Mass.: Lexington Books.

Portes, Alejandro, and Robert L. Bach. 1985. *Latin Journey.* Berkeley, Calif.: University of California Press.

Portes, Alejandro, and Rafael Mozo. 1985. "The Political Adaptation Process of Cubans and Other Ethnic Minorities in the United States: A Preliminary Analysis." *International Migration Review* 19(1): 35–63.

Research Institute for Cuba and the Caribbean. 1967. *The Cuban Immigration, 1959–65 and Its Impact on Miami-Dade County, Florida.* Coral

Gables, Fla.: Center for Advanced International Studies, University of Miami.

Sofen, Edward. 1966. *The Miami Metropolitan Experiment.* Garden City, N.Y.: Anchor Books.

Stepick, Alex, and Portes, Alejandro. 1986. "Flight into Despair: A Profile Of Recent Haitian Refugees in South Florida." *International Migration Review* 20(2): 329–50.

Stowers, Genie N. L. 1987. "Cuban Political Development and Impact on Urban Policy: The Crucial Case of Cubans in Miami." Ph.D. diss., Florida State University, Tallahassee.

————. 1988. "Ethnic and Racial Candidates in the Transition to Urban Political Power." Paper presented at the American Political Science Association Annual Convention, Sept. 1–4, Washington, D.C.

————. 1990. Cuban Political Participation and Class Status. *Ethnic Groups* 8(2): 73–90.

Thompson, Sylvia Ann. 1984. "Community Leadership in Greater Miami, Florida: What Role for Blacks and Cuban Americans?" Ph.D. diss., Southern Illinois University.

U.S. Bureau of the Census. 1960. *Census of Population.* Washington, D.C.: U.S. Government Printing Office.

————. 1970. *Census of Population.* Washington, D.C.: U.S. Government Printing Office.

————. 1980. *General Population Characteristics.* Washington, D.C.: U.S. Government Printing Office.

————. 1990. *Census of Population and Housing* (PL 94-171 Redistricting Data). Washington, D.C.: U.S. Government Printing Office.

U.S. Commission on Civil Rights. 1982. *Confronting Racial Isolation in Miami.* Washington, D.C.: Author.

Vogel, Ronald K., and Genie N. L. Stowers. 1991. "Miami: Minority Empowerment and Regime Change." In *Big City Politics in Transition,* edited by H. V. Savitch and John Clayton Thomas. Beverly Hills, Calif.: Sage Publications.

Warren, Christopher, John G. Corbett, and John F. Stack, Jr. 1990. "Hispanic Ascendancy and Tripartite Politics in Miami." In *Racial Politics in American Cities,* edited by Rufus P. Browning, Dale Rogers Marshall, and David H. Tabb. (155–78). White Plains, N.Y.: Longman Publishing Books.

Wilson, Kenneth, and W. Allen Martin. 1982. "Ethic Enclaves: A Comparison of the Cuban and Black Economies in Miami." *American Journal of Sociology* 88: 135–60.

Wilson, Kenneth, and Alejandro Portes. 1980. "Immigrant Enclaves: An Analysis of the Labor Market Experiences of Cubans in Miami." *American Journal of Sociology* 86: 295–319.

Chapter Five

RACE AND ETHNICITY IN LOS ANGELES POLITICS

Byran O. Jackson and Michael B. Preston

If we view cities as organizations serving diverse clienteles and mayors as leaders of these organizations, we come to appreciate the importance of mayoral leadership in community politics. Furthermore, we can recognize the role of mayors in molding municipal organizations to their changing environments. To the degree that social goals in cities evolve with their environments, leadership must also change to address these conditions (see George 1968; Pressman 1972).

From 1973 to 1993, the city of Los Angeles—the focus of this chapter—experienced formidable ethnic and socioeconomic change. Its long-time mayor during this period, Tom Bradley, an African-American, was elected with a winning coalition of blacks, Jews, and other liberal whites. This coalition would be sustained, with additional support of Hispanics, throughout Bradley's tenure. Bradley brought to bear a variety of electoral strategies and patterns of governance in responding to two decades of demographic, political, and economic change. As described here, these strategies and styles of governance had, and have, important implications for minority empowerment in Los Angeles.

Even though the formal powers granted to Los Angeles's mayor are weak relative to mayoral power in New York or Chicago (the nation's two other largest cities), the mayor is still expected to play the lead role in setting the city's policy agenda. This point was clearly illustrated in 1992 in efforts to oust Police Chief Daryl Gates resulting from the Rodney King beating. Although Mayor Bradley did not have formal powers to fire the chief, there was a clear demand from the African-American community that all of the mayor's informal resources be used to force Gates's resignation.

On a broader level, the growth of ethnic populations in Los Angeles consisting largely of Asians and Latinos, changes in the city's socioeconomic makeup, and related increases in its social problems have

Table 5.1 COMPARISON OF 1980 AND 1990 DEMOGRAPHIC
CHARACTERISTICS IN LOS ANGELES

	1980		1990	
	Population	Percentage	Population	Percentage
White	1,816,761	61.2[a]	1,841,182	52.8[a]
Black	505,210	17.0[a]	487,674	14.0[a]
Indian	16,595	0.6	16,379	0.5
Asian and Pacific	196,017	6.6	341,807	9.8
Other	432,267	14.6	798,356	22.9
Total	2,966,850		3,485,398	
Hispanic	816,076	27.5	1,391,411	40.1
White	397,348		541,578	
Black	9,487		33,385	
Other	409,241		822,448	

a. The percentage represents both Hispanic and non-Hispanic whites, blacks, and so on. Non-Hispanic whites represented 48 percent of the total population in 1980 and 37 percent in 1990. Non-Hispanic blacks constituted 16.71 percent of the total city population in 1980 and 13.03 percent in 1990.

forced the city into a period of adjustment. The 1993 mayoral election, which ended the Bradley regime and ushered in the administration of Richard Riordan, may have played a pivotal role in determining the future direction of the city. It restored to power a coalition concerned about crime and job growth, a group led by middle-class whites but also supported by 43 percent of Latinos. Whether there will be a role within this coalition for African-Americans, only 14 percent of whom voted for Riordan, remains to be seen. This analysis examines the city's electoral changes in light of its ethnic and demographic changes. We also evaluate three regime types that we argue ruled Los Angeles during Tom Bradley's five terms in office and consider the regimes' impact on minority incorporation into political power. Finally, we briefly discuss the significance of the 1993 mayoral election.

RACIAL AND ETHNIC CHANGE IN LOS ANGELES

Asian and Hispanic groups have experienced the largest population increases in the United States over the last decade. California led the nation in the growth of Latino and Asian immigrants, with Latinos now comprising 25.8 percent of the state's population, Asians 9.6 percent, and blacks 12 percent. Table 5.1 reveals major population changes by race and ethnicity for the city of Los Angeles alone over the 1980–90 decade. The overall percentage of white residents dropped from about 61 percent to about 53 percent, while the proportion of non-Hispanic whites declined from 48 percent to 37 percent. The overall black population also declined, from 17 percent to 14 percent. On the other hand, the proportion of Asians in the total population climbed from about 7 percent to almost 10 percent. The largest increase in Los Angeles occurred in the Latino population, which jumped from almost 28 percent of the total to 40 percent.

A major question arising from these changes is: How do they translate politically? Both Asian and Hispanic groups have begun to lobby at the state and local levels in California for an increase in representation of their numbers in governmental institutions. Changes in the composition of council districts has also increased Latino representation in the Los Angeles City Council.

Nevertheless, it is important to note that despite significant changes in the racial and ethnic populations in Los Angeles, these changes are not likely to be fully reflected in the electoral arena for some time to come. Latino political participation remains relatively low because of citizenship issues and other factors (Jackson 1991). The citizenship problem also slows the translation of Asians into voters, as does the dispersed nature of Asian residential patterns.

Although the city of Los Angeles is known as a Democratic stronghold (see figure 5.1), there are sizable concentrations of Republican voters located largely in the San Fernando Valley council districts. These votes provided the major source of support for Richard Riordan's 1993 mayoral victory. The dark, solid portion of the map indicates where the strongest concentrations (76–100 percent) of Democratic voters are located; these are predominantly black areas. The dark crosshatch portion represents the next highest concentration (51–75 percent) and includes the heavily Jewish westside and predominantly Latino eastside portions of the city. These concentrations have potentially important ramifications for the relative political clout of blacks, Latinos, Jews, and Anglos in the city. Since a large number of African-Americans are registered and tend to vote as a bloc on certain issues and for certain candidates (see Jackson 1991), they sometimes are able to wield electoral power disproportionate to their numbers.

On the other hand, Latinos, while constituting a large share of the general population, constitute a much smaller share of voters. For this reason, they have so far been unable to translate their increase in numbers into commensurate electoral power. Latinos in the past

Figure 5.1 PERCENT DEMOCRATIC PARTY REGISTRATION BY COUNCIL
DISTRICT IN CITY OF LOS ANGELES

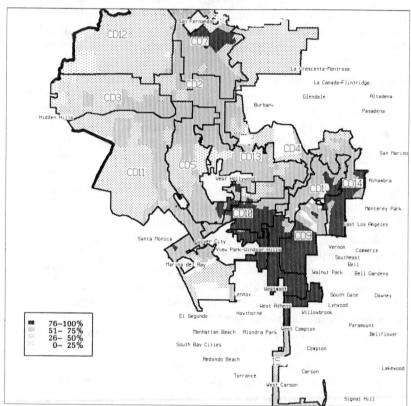

were strongly Democratic in partisan registration. However, in the
1993 mayoral election, substantial numbers voted for the Republican
candidate. In the future, as the number of registered Latino voters
increases and Latino support is sought by both major parties, Latinos
may become the critical "swing" group in Los Angeles elections.

VOTER TURNOUT BY CITY COUNCIL DISTRICTS

The 8th, 9th, and 10th council districts represented predominantly
black council districts over the years 1969–89. The 5th district is
heavily concentrated with Jews and other white liberals (Sonenshein 1991). Although district 9 was at one point contested by both

Figure 5.2 TURNOUT IN LOS ANGELES MAYORAL ELECTIONS BY COUNCIL
DISTRICT, 1969–89

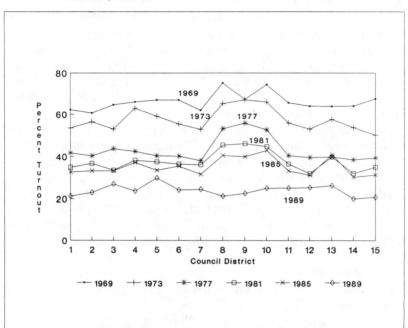

blacks and Latinos, this issue was settled with the 1963 appointment
and later election of the late Gilbert Lindsay, an African-American,
as a representative for the district. The black residents of districts 8, 9,
and 10, as well as the Jews and white liberals in district 5, consistently
turned out in large numbers in support of Mayor Bradley's early
candidacies for mayor. The 1969 mayoral primary and the subsequent
general election, in which Bradley first challenged incumbent Sam
Yorty, drew most of the registered voters in the city to the polls (see
figure 5.2). Black mobilization during this period either exceeded or
was comparable to voter turnout in other districts. This vote certainly
seemed to signify the high hopes that blacks had for political change
in the city.

Examining the periods between 1977 and 1985, we find that
although the turnout rate in mayoral races dropped appreciably (see
figure 5.2), Bradley still won office with 51 or more percent of the
vote in the primary, avoiding a runoff. As pointed out later here,
Bradley's popularity with the voters was at its highest from 1969 to
1977. In the 1989 election, turnout declined significantly for all

groups, and Mayor Bradley barely escaped a runoff while competing against two weak opponents.

Table 5.2 provides a breakdown of voting in mayoral elections by council district from 1969 to 1989. In the 1969 mayoral primary, Bradley carried the three predominantly black council districts by wide margins. He held this support during the 1969 general election while picking up districts 5 and 15, which are largely Jewish/liberal Anglo districts. Nevertheless, winning 5 of 15 districts was not enough to defeat Yorty in 1969.

A similar pattern prevailed in the 1973 primary with black voters voting overwhelmingly for Bradley. The strong black support given Bradley in the 1973 general election, coupled with solid victories in four Anglo/Jewish districts (including districts 5 and 15), provided Bradley with his first mayoral victory. Table 5.2 shows that the electoral support across council districts increased to the point of avoiding a runoff election in subsequent contests (1977–89), reaching its highest level in 1985, when Bradley carried every district except district 12.

The 1989 mayoral election shows a shift in support for Bradley. The mayor barely avoided a runoff, with slightly more than 51 percent of the vote. Black voters in districts 8, 9, and 10 prevented this potential embarrassment by overwhelmingly voting in his favor despite the candidacy of black councilman Nate Holden. Although there is some disagreement over the extent of Latino support for Bradley's early candidacies for mayor (Hahn and Almay 1971; Hahn, Klingman, and Pachon 1976), our data indicate that the Latino support after 1981 was moderately strong.

In sum, a review of voting data shows some of the elements that were valuable in maintaining mayor Bradley's electoral coalition. A cohesive black voting bloc with a substantial turnout rate, coupled with support from Jewish and other liberal voters, including Latinos, formed the core of the mayor's winning electoral coalition. However, the following section of the chapter demonstrates the difference between the electoral and governing coalitions formed during Mayor Bradley's tenure in office.

MAYORAL LEADERSHIP: 1973–91

There has been substantial controversy over whether the election of black mayors has led to increases in social, political, and economic

Table 5.2 VOTES CAST FOR MAYOR BY COUNCIL DISTRICT IN LOS ANGELES MAYORAL ELECTIONS, 1969–89

Council District	1969 Primary			1969 General			1973 Primary			1973 General		
	Total Votes	Bradley (%)	Yorty (%)	Total Votes	Bradley (%)	Yorty (%)	Total Votes	Bradley (%)	Yorty (%)	Total Votes	Bradley (%)	Yorty (%)
1	47,513	28.1	31.7	57,558	30.2	68.6	35,405	24.6	36.0	39,053	42.6	56.1
2	53,305	33.9	26.6	61,757	40.6	58.2	60,465	25.5	32.7	69,231	49.9	48.8
3	50,193	28.5	27.2	59,481	33.7	65.3	47,805	23.9	35.0	56,550	45.3	53.2
4	45,247	27.2	38.8	52,864	31.1	67.2	43,535	20.4	43.3	48,495	38.5	59.7
5	55,132	44.0	21.5	63,385	50.7	47.8	65,312	30.1	23.4	74,456	57.7	40.6
6	49,527	37.8	25.4	57,330	44.5	54.2	45,696	42.3	25.6	54,800	59.4	39.2
7	46,941	29.7	28.8	55,982	34.1	64.6	46,088	23.7	34.0	52,518	46.4	52.2
8	56,306	81.0	7.7	64,724	86.2	12.2	40,783	78.6	5.3	49,324	91.1	7.4
9	42,645	62.6	16.8	49,625	69.2	28.7	35,461	73.7	8.3	41,580	87.2	10.9
10	48,110	69.0	15.0	54,291	72.8	25.6	40,458	64.8	15.2	47,603	77.0	20.9
11	51,743	37.9	23.8	59,908	47.0	51.7	61,622	31.3	27.3	72,342	55.7	42.9
12	51,435	25.6	28.2	61,475	30.6	68.3	50,003	23.2	36.4	58,643	44.0	55.0
13	45,466	30.8	34.1	53,264	36.6	61.8	45,318	22.7	37.8	51,471	43.3	54.9
14	45,740	23.0	39.1	54,385	28.3	70.2	26,967	19.3	35.7	30,705	44.2	54.0
15	42,120	48.7	20.7	50,145	54.1	44.0	29,637	33.3	25.8	34,470	52.8	45.4

Table 5.2 (continued)

Council District	1977 Primary			1981 Primary			1985 Primary			1989 Primary			
	Total Votes	Bradley (%)	Robbins (%)	Total Votes	Bradley (%)	Yorty (%)	Total Votes	Bradley (%)	Ferraro (%)	Total Votes	Bradley (%)	Holder (%)	Ward (%)
1	26,786	44.3	40.4	25,837	48.7	43.3	27,702	55.4	40.3	6,145	48.7	23.3	13.7
2	41,573	50.0	32.2	38,614	56.3	37.5	34,978	58.4	37.2	19,596	39.4	33.6	19.3
3	39,055	44.7	39.6	32,763	47.5	45.8	34,466	56.2	45.5	25,072	39.6	33.1	19.1
4	27,251	49.2	29.6	24,382	53.3	39.2	20,498	51.0	44.2	16,678	44.3	30.3	16.5
5	43,539	61.8	24.2	40,440	69.1	24.2	40,918	71.6	24.2	33,411	51.5	26.5	13.7
6	31,963	64.9	22.2	31,778	69.6	25.4	39,968	72.7	23.0	23,849	52.8	27.7	11.9
7	31,045	43.1	42.1	30,795	49.9	42.6	27,178	55.2	40.3	16,646	45.2	27.5	16.8
8	33,466	90.3	2.7	33,020	91.9	3.2	39,927	92.4	2.4	17,254	73.8	16.9	1.4
9	28,183	86.5	4.2	25,169	88.5	5.1	25,271	88.8	4.2	12,740	70.3	17.0	1.8
10	30,829	83.5	0.3	27,624	85.6	9.4	28,949	86.5	9.1	18,279	63.2	25.3	4.8
11	44,449	55.5	28.6	40,944	59.9	34.4	42,811	59.8	35.7	25,382	45.3	29.2	17.8
12	38,440	40.1	43.6	34,237	44.1	49.5	36,120	46.3	43.4	24,833	39.0	34.1	19.3
13	28,368	50.0	30.2	29,007	56.1	35.8	31,525	60.3	34.6	17,740	46.7	27.6	16.3
14	17,118	55.1	27.9	15,228	53.3	37.3	18,437	58.4	37.0	10,569	45.6	25.7	17.0
15	22,628	56.7	28.6	22,886	61.3	30.8	25,737	65.1	30.0	15,293	51.3	23.2	15.3

opportunities for minority communities. Browning, Marshall, and Tabb (1984, 1990) have offered evidence suggesting that the political incorporation of racial and ethnic minorities has led in certain circumstances to policy outcomes beneficial to minority communities. They suggest that where minorities are members of a dominant liberal coalition, they are more likely to receive substantive benefits for their participation. Starks and Preston (1990) found this to be true in Chicago during the Harold Washington era, and Perry (1990) reported this to be the case in Birmingham and New Orleans.

On the other hand, other scholars have argued that the benefits have not been commensurate with the contributions of these communities (e.g., Jackson 1991). Mayor Bradley's tenure offers an opportunity to answer the question raised about who benefited most. Moreover, it provides a unique opportunity to explore the linkage between electoral coalition formation and governance.

An important question that must be answered regarding this analysis is: How does one measure benefits? The literature in this area has examined city employment, appointments to major boards and commissions, economic and community development in minority areas, and the quality of service delivery to minority communities as indicators of who benefits from political participation. Although we have not collected enough data on Los Angeles to provide a definitive measure of all these areas relative to the African-American community, we offer the following highlights of Bradley's job performance in delivering benefits to his black constituency over his 20-year tenure.

Municipal Employment

Table 5.3 provides a brief comparison of changes in municipal minority employment between the years 1973 and 1990. The table shows that the percentage of whites in the city's work force decreased between 1973 and 1990, yet in both periods whites were overrepresented in the work force relative to their percentage in the city's total population. In 1973, whites were 64 percent of the work force compared to being only 61 percent of the total population. In 1990, non-Hispanic whites comprised 37 percent of the total population while holding 46 percent of municipal jobs. (Note, however, that by 1993 non-Hispanic whites represented 70 percent of actual voters.)

Blacks in both years were even more strongly overrepresented in the city municipal work force relative to their population size. In 1973 blacks composed almost 22 percent of the overall work force

Table 5.3 REPRESENTATION OF POPULATION GROUPS IN LOS ANGELES CITY GOVERNMENT BY JOB CLASSIFICATION, 1973–90

Occupational Classification	Percentage Asian		Percentage Black		Percentage Hispanic		Percentage White	
	1973	1990	1973	1990	1973	1990	1973	1990
Overall work force	4.0	7.4	21.9	26.7	9.3	19.5	64.1	46.4
Officials and administrators	1.3	7.4	1.3	10.6	2.6	6.9	94.7	72.3
Professionals	8.0	14.9	5.0	12.1	4.6	11.0	81.4	55.7
Technicians	5.8	8.8	7.8	8.8	6.4	12.8	79.4	64.9
Protective services	.5	3.0	9.5	23.3	7.8	24.5	81.5	47.8
Paraprofessionals	2.9	10.1	24.9	26.8	14.3	26.1	57.4	31.8
Office/clerical	7.1	16.0	24.3	31.2	11.8	20.4	56.2	24.9
Skilled craft	2.5	7.3	24.2	18.1	9.5	18.2	63.2	53.7
Service maintenance	1.7	3.1	57.6	42.4	14.4	29.0	25.7	24.0

Source: From Work Force Analysis Report, City of Los Angeles Employment Development Department. Comparative analysis of data from city of Los Angeles, Numerical Progress, 1973–1991. (See also Sonenshein 1993, pp. 152–155).

but only 12 percent of the city's total population (table 5.3). In 1990 blacks constituted 26.7 percent of the work force compared to 13 percent of the non-Hispanic black population.

The underrepresentation of Latinos in the city's work force serves to explain the overrepresentation of whites and blacks. Latinos comprised 22 percent of the city's population in 1973, but held only 9.3 percent of the city jobs (table 5.3). In 1990, they were 40 percent of the population but held only 19.5 percent of the municipal jobs. One must consider, however, a number of other potential factors that negatively affect Latino municipal employment, including the earlier-mentioned question of citizenship as well as discrimination (Sonenshein 1993: pp. 151–155).

Table 5.3 shows that Asians are fairly well represented in the overall city work force compared to their population numbers. Asian representation in the work force increased from 4 percent to 7 percent between 1973 and 1990. (In 1990 they comprised about 10 percent of the city's population—see table 5.1).

Whereas blacks may be overrepresented in the city's overall work force, as of 1990 both blacks and Latinos were grossly underrepresented in the top three levels of the city's bureaucracy (officials and administrators, professionals, and technicians) (table 5.3). For example, in the officials and administrators category, whites comprised 72.3 percent of the total in 1990, compared to 10.6 percent for blacks and 6.9 percent for Latinos. A similar gap exists for blacks and Latinos in the two other top job categories, with Asians overrepresented in the professionals category, comprising almost 15 percent of the total.

In sum, the data do not show significant overall gains in black municipal employment under Mayor Bradley's leadership between 1973 and 1990. Based on the relative success of Asians in professional jobs compared to that of African-Americans and Latinos, one could argue that advancement in these positions is highly correlated with education. However, the relatively limited success of Asians, African-Americans, and Latinos compared to that of Anglos in official/administrator-type jobs suggests that discrimination may also be a barrier to advancement for all ethnic groups. The data are insufficient to make a qualitative assessment of the mayor's efforts in promoting affirmative action in hiring. Thus, the results may reflect constraints and limitations on mayoral power.

Appointments to Boards and Commissions

One of the mayor's chief powers in Los Angeles is the appointment and removal of certain city officials and commissioners, subject to confirmation by the city council. The commissioners help oversee the major departments of city government. Most of these appointments pay small sums of money but may be viewed as a way for minorities to have some influence in city government and to help ensure equitable delivery of city services.

Table 5.4 gives the ethnic breakdown of mayoral appointments in 1991 to boards and commissions in Los Angeles. Whites composed 50 percent or more of the members on half of the boards and commissions. Moreover, they held a plurality on many of the remaining boards and commissions. One notable exception was the police commission, which was dominated by African-Americans and had an African-American as its acting chair. The black majority on the police commission was only achieved in 1991, but obviously was of special importance in the wake of the Rodney King affair and the national search for a new police chief. Whereas the minority appointments overall appear to demonstrate an attempt on the mayor's part to promote fair representation, control of most of these boards and commissions remained in the hands of Anglos.

In the current era, the importance of the mayor's hand in the makeup of city commissions has been underscored by the initial appointments of Richard Riordan. His appointees have been strongly skewed toward the well-to-do, white neighborhoods from which he drew his voter support. For example, of the first 167 newly named commissioners, one-third came from just two of the city council districts—heavily Anglo, wealthy areas covering the hillsides from West Los Angeles and Pacific Palisades to Encino. Fewer than 6 percent of appointees came from two council districts of equal population in South Central Los Angeles (*Los Angeles Times* 1993).

Economic and Community Development in Minority Communities

One major area of urban policymaking affecting Los Angeles citizens, especially in the wake of the South Central riots and California's economic recession, is community and economic development. However, some observers (e.g., Paul Peterson 1981) argue that this area is the one where citizens have the least access and control. The antigrowth movement that has become popular in many U.S. cities, especially those on the West Coast such as San Francisco, Los Angeles, and San Diego, offers a challenge to this view. Nevertheless, in Los Angeles real estate developers and investors are major contributors to the campaign coffers of mayoral and city council candidates. Over the years, Mayor Bradley was viewed as a pro-growth mayor.

Table 5.4 ETHNIC BREAKDOWN OF MAYORAL APPOINTMENTS TO
LOS ANGELES BOARDS AND COMMISSIONS, 1991

Commission/Board	Total	Black (%)	Latino (%)	Asian (%)	White (%)
Affordable Housing	7.00	14.29	28.57	0.00	57.14
Airport	5.00	20.00	20.00	0.00	60.00
Animal Regulation	5.00	20.00	0.00	20.00	60.00
Building Advisor Appeals Board	5.00	40.00	0.00	40.00	60.00
Building and Safety	5.00	20.00	0.00	40.00	20.00
Child Care Advisory	5.00	40.00	20.00	40.00	40.00
City Ethnics	2.00	0.00	50.00	0.00	50.00
Civil Service	4.00	25.00	25.00	25.00	25.00
Community Redevelopment	6.00	16.67	16.67	0.00	16.67
Cultural Affairs	7.00	14.29	14.29	14.29	57.14
Cultural Heritage	5.00	20.00	20.00	40.00	0.00
Disability	9.00	33.33	11.11	11.11	44.44
Employee Relations	5.00	20.00	0.00	0.00	80.00
Employee Retirement System	3.00	33.33	33.33	0.00	0.00
Environmental Affairs	5.00	20.00	20.00	20.00	40.00
Fire	5.00	20.00	20.00	0.00	60.00
Fire and Police Safety Pension	5.00	20.00	20.00	40.00	20.00
Handicap Access	5.00	0.00	0.00	0.00	100.00
Harbor	5.00	20.00	0.00	20.00	60.00
Housing Authority	7.00	28.57	28.57	0.00	42.86
Human Relations	8.00	25.00	25.00	0.00	25.00
Library	5.00	20.00	0.00	0.00	80.00
Los Angeles Convention and Exhibition	7.00	14.29	14.29	28.57	42.86
Metro Water District	7.00	28.57	28.57	0.00	42.86
Municipal Auditorium	5.00	20.00	0.00	20.00	60.00
Native American Indian	5.00	0.00	0.00	0.00	0.00
Planning	5.00	0.00	20.00	0.00	80.00
Police	4.00	50.00	0.00	0.00	25.00
Productivity	6.00	16.67	0.00	0.00	83.33
Public Works	5.00	20.00	40.00	20.00	20.00
Recreation and Parks	5.00	20.00	20.00	0.00	60.00
Relocation Appeals	3.00	33.33	0.00	33.33	33.33
Rent Adjustment	7.00	14.29	14.29	14.29	57.14
Social Services	5.00	20.00	0.00	40.00	40.00
Status of Women	7.00	14.29	28.57	14.29	42.86
Telecommunications	5.00	20.00	0.00	20.00	60.00
Transportation	6.00	16.67	0.00	33.33	50.00
Water and Power	5.00	0.00	20.00	0.00	80.00
Zoning Appeals	5.00	40.00	0.00	0.00	60.00

Although at one point this view was an asset to his mayoral career, it increasingly became a liability. Blacks' position on the growth issue has had ironic results in the city. Survey polls show that blacks were the strongest supporters of Mayor Bradley's pro-economic development policies, yet their communities benefited least from the efforts to encourage economic development and growth in the city. Antigrowth forces shun the development of shopping centers, office high-rises, and food chains in their neighborhoods, whereas these entities are welcomed in the blighted and desolate communities of South Central and Watts.

The disinvestment of business, services, and job opportunities in the black community in Los Angeles is linked to gang violence, drug traffic, graffiti, trash, and other problems that have come to plague the community, as well as the generalized fear left by the 1992 riots. Earlier, in 1991, Bradley responded to his critics on economic and community development for the African-American community by unveiling a revitalization plan for the inner-city area. The program would have targeted poverty, crime, and dilapidated housing in neighborhoods of South Central Los Angeles by providing low-interest city loans to homeowners, improved trash collection services, a new police substation, replacement of through streets with cul-de-sacs to discourage drug trafficking and street crime, 100 units of low-cost housing to be built by the city, and the refurbishment of 200 existing homes using inner-city workers and donated paint.

EVOLUTION OF BRADLEY REGIME AND ITS IMPACT ON POLICYMAKING

In terms of Mayor Bradley's impact on policy, his tenure in office may be examined in three distinct phases that we have identified as the coalition phase (1973–82), the candidate-centered phase (1983–88), and the powerbroker phase (1989–93).

Progressive Coalition Phase (1973–82)

The coalition era, which lasted roughly from 1973, when Bradley first took office as mayor, until well into 1982, when he made his first bid for governor, can be characterized as the ideologically based coalition period. The major participants, as pointed out by Sonenshein (1989), were Jews, blacks, and other liberals in the city. Given the decentralized nature of Los Angeles politics, this coalition was able to overcome a more conservative coalition led by Sam Yorty in

1973, and to capture city hall. Although one could question the true beneficiaries of this coalition, it represented a major departure from the Yorty years.

This era ushered in a place for racial minorities, women, white liberals, and eventually downtown business interests. Bradley's top political advisor was Jewish, with a Latino appointed as the second deputy mayor. Two blacks were appointed as executive assistants to the mayor. In addition, Bradley placed minorities on commissions, increased minority hiring at city hall, and increased accountability of the bureaucracy to minority concerns (Sonenshein 1993: 140–62).

Candidate-Centered Phase: Symbolic Politics (1983–1988)

Toward the end of his tenure, Mayor Bradley was described by many news accounts as the Teflon mayor. No matter what problems plagued the city, few of these were ever associated with Bradley's leadership, at least not until the end of his regime. The second period began after Bradley's failed gubernatorial attempt in 1982 and represented a shift from an ideologically based strategy to a more candidate-centered strategy. During this period, Bradley won office by landslides and his popularity soared. No longer did he rely solely on his original political base for support. While symbolically addressing the concerns of his old constituency, he also began to take on new coalition partners. Developers and downtown business groups began to slowly dominate his agenda. The 1984 Olympics in Los Angeles symbolized Bradley's dream of making Los Angeles a "world class" city and a center of trade on the Pacific Rim. The beneficiaries during this period were largely developers, unions, businesses, and others who were part of the growth machine.

During this phase, Bradley relied less on his ideological (liberal) allies and moved to expand his base to include more business interests and thereby received more resources for his mayoral and gubernatorial races. Also during this period Bradley was at the peak of his popularity. Indeed, in 1985, he was reelected with 68 percent of the vote (Sonenshein 1993: 191). On the basis of his popularity, he ran for governor in 1982 and 1986; he lost both races. His political and economic policies during this phase seemed designed to win more political allies while giving symbolic assurances to minorities that he had not forgotten them. Thus, candidate Bradley was able to keep his multiracial coalition together while at the same time expanding its boundaries.

Powerbroker Phase (1989–1993)

By 1989, Mayor Bradley's regime had slipped into a final phase. At this point, many problems, such as traffic congestion, excessive business and commercial growth, gang warfare, and homelessness, began to receive media attention and negative reactions from the general public. The South Central riots of 1992 only highlighted this situation.

Although there are many competing explanations of Bradley's behavior during this period (i.e., too old to do the job, not interested), later financial scandals would suggest that Bradley had become preoccupied with the role of powerbroker. Such a role involved providing access to city hall for business, commercial interests, and so on (Sonenshein 1993: 206–7). In this capacity, Bradley was no different from other mayors seeking to fuel what Logan and others call the "growth machine" (Logan and Molotch 1987). This style of leadership is definitely in contrast to his original term in office.

These three electoral strategies and patterns of governance have important implications for minority politics in the city. In terms of minority political empowerment, ideologically based coalition strategies show the greatest promise for empowerment of and social change for minorities (Browning et al. 1984). The candidate-centered strategy, while offering some access for minority groups, ranks low on accountability and control by coalition partners. Finally, the powerbroker strategy resembles the Paul Peterson (1981) model of economic development policymaking in the city and offers the least amount of access and control by minority groups.

1993 MAYORAL ELECTION AND COLLAPSE OF LIBERAL COALITION

In 1973, Mayor Bradley was able to assemble a winning coalition consisting of blacks, Jews, and other liberal whites. In later elections, he added the Hispanic vote. The 1993 mayoral election, however, marked the disintegration and ultimate defeat of this coalition.

Richard Riordan, the Republican candidate, was able to outpoll Michael Woo, the Democrat, in several of the traditionally liberal areas of the westside. He carried the wealthier, Anglo-dominated districts, especially the San Fernando Valley. Turnout in these areas was very high. Polling revealed that voters favored Riordan—first, because he was outside the traditional political establishment and, second, because he came across as a tough manager who would be tough on crime. All in all, two out of every five voters who supported Mayor Bradley in 1989 voted for Riordan in 1993.

The liberal coalition also suffered from relatively low voter turnout among blacks and in central city neighborhoods. Although Woo received 85.9 percent of the vote in South Central Los Angeles and Crenshaw, only one-third of the voters in this district went to the polls. Overall, blacks accounted for only 12 percent of the votes cast in the general election, down from 18 percent in the April primary. Most of the difference could be attributed to the very high Anglo turnout in the general election.

CONCLUSION

Los Angeles is now a "world class" city and is expected to provide leadership for the Pacific Rim as we move into the 21st century. It is also a city undergoing tremendous demographic, political, and economic changes. How it handles these changes will say much about its future. Los Angeles is still a "port of entry" for new immigrant groups; its ability to absorb them and adapt old institutions to meet new needs will be severely tested in the years ahead. As these groups achieve citizenship and more education, their impacts on political institutions will be felt as well. In brief, Los Angeles's leadership will need to be sensitive to new challenges while it works to solve the old problems that remain, including the desire of the white middle class to imprint its priorities on the political system.

From a political standpoint, the growth of the Asian and Latino communities has both short- and long-range implications. The increases in the Latino population will expand its potential political clout, but only as Latinos become citizens and are persuaded to register and vote.

Our analysis reveals that it was the blacks, Jews, liberal whites and, more recently, Latinos who kept Mayor Bradley in office for over 20 years. It is also clear, however, that most of the registered voters are on the westside, in the San Fernando Valley, and in South Central Los Angeles. The old Bradley coalition could not be held together in the 1993 election, and it may not be possible to resurrect it in the future.

Our findings also indicate that although minorities have received some benefits from political participation, they are not commensurate with the level of political support from these groups during the Bradley era. Major gains for minorities have not been registered in municipal employment or appointments to boards and commissions. And in the arena of economic and community development, clearly more investment has gone to downtown and the westside interests than to South Central Los Angeles or the eastside. The reasons for these outcomes lie in the labor and business markets, as well as in politics. At this point, the future of minority political empowerment in the city is clouded. Initial evidence from the Riordan administration suggests that both development investment and commission appointments are now shifting toward the regions where Riordan received greatest voter support.

References

Bobo, Lawrence and Frank D. Gilliam, Jr. 1990. "Race, Sociopolitical Participation, and Black Empowerment." *American Political Science Review* 84 (2, June): 377–93.

Browning, Rufus P., Dale Rogers Marshall, and David H. Tabb. 1984. *Protest Is Not Enough: The Struggle of Blacks and Hispanics.* Berkeley: University of California Press.

———. 1990. *Racial Politics in American Cities.* White Plains, N.Y.: Longman Publishing Group.

Davis, Mike. 1990. *City of Quartz: Excavating the Future in Los Angeles.* New York: Verso.

DeLeon, Richard. 1991. "The Progressive Urban Regime: Ethnic Coalitions in San Francisco." In *Racial and Ethnic Politics in California,* edited by Byran Jackson and Michael B. Preston. Berkeley, Calif.: Institute of Governmental Studies Press.

Falcon, Angelo. 1988. "Black and Latino Politics in New York City: Race and Ethnicity in a Changing Urban Context." In *Latinos and the Political System,* edited by Chris Garcia. Notre Dame, Ind.: University of Notre Dame Press.

George, Alexander L. 1968. "Political Leadership and Social Change in American Cities." *Daedalus* (Fall): 1194–1217.

Hahn, Harlan, and Timothy Almy. 1971. "Ethnic Politics and Racial Issues: Voting in Los Angeles." *Western Political Quarterly* 24: 719–30.

Hahn, Harlan, David Klingman, and Harry Pachon. 1976. "Cleavages, Coalitions, and the Black Candidate: The Los Angeles Mayoralty Elections of 1969 and 1973." *Western Political Quarterly* 29: 507–20.

Henry, C. P. 1980. "Black-Chicano Coalitions: Possibilities and Problems." *Western Journal of Black Studies* 4 (Winter): 222–32.

Hero, Rodney. 1989. "Multi-racial Coalitions in City Elections Involving Minority Candidates: Some Evidence from Denver." *Urban Affairs Quarterly* 25 (2, December): 342–51.

Holloway, Harry. 1968. "Negro Political Strategy: Coalitions or Independent Power Politics?" *Social Science Quarterly* 49: 534–47.

————. "Inner City Still Mostly on Outside at City Hall." 1993. *Los Angeles Times* 1, Metro (September 9).

Jackson, Byran O. 1991. "Racial and Ethnic Voting Cleavages in Los Angeles Politics." In *Racial and Ethnic Politics in California,* edited by Byran Jackson and Michael B. Preston. Berkeley, Calif.: Institute of Governmental Studies Press.

Judd, Dennis. 1986. "Electoral Coalitions, Minority Mayors, and the Contradictions in the Municipal Policy Agenda." In *Cities in Stress: A New Look at the Urban Crisis,* vol. 30, edited by M. Grottdiener (145–70). *Urban Affairs Annual Reviews.* Beverly Hills, Calif.: Sage Publications.

"The Killing of South Central: The Untold Story of Malign Neglect." 1988. *L.A. Weekly* 4 (11, December 30–January 5).

Kingdon, John W. 1984. *Agendas, Alternatives, and Public Policies.* Boston: Little Brown & Co.

Logan, John R., and Harvey L. Molotch. 1987. *Urban Fortunes: The Political Economy of Place.* Berkeley, Calif.: University of California Press. Also see: Molotch, Harvey, "The City as a Growth Machine: Toward a Political Economy of Place." *American Journal of Sociology* 82 (2): 309–32.

McClain, Paula D., and Albert Karnig. 1990. "Black and Hispanic Socioeconomic and Political Competition." *American Political Science Review* 83 (1, March): 165–92.

Mlandenka, Kenneth. 1989. "Black and Hispanics in Urban Politics." *American Political Science Review* 83 (1, March): 165–92.

Molotch, Harvey. 1976. "The City as a Growth Machine: Toward a Political Economy of Place." *American Journal of Sociology* 82 (2, September): 309–32.

Muñoz, Carlos, Jr., and Charles P. Henry. 1990. "Coalition Politics in San Antonio and Denver: The Cisneros and Peña Mayoral Campaigns." In *Racial Politics in American Cities,* edited by Rufus P. Browning, Dale Rogers Marshall, and David H. Tabb. White Plains, N.Y.: Longman Publishing Group.

Oliver, Melvin, and James Johnson. 1984. "Inter-Ethnic Conflict in an Urban Ghetto: The Case of Blacks and Latinos in Los Angeles." *Research in Social Movements, Conflict, and Change* 6: 57–94.

————. 1990. "What Price Poverty?" *UCLA Magazine* 2 (3).

Perry, Huey L. 1990. "The Evolution and Impact of Biracial Coalitions and Black Mayors in Birmingham and New Orleans. In *Racial Politics in American Cities,* edited by Rufus P. Browning, Dale Rogers Marshall, and David H. Tabb. White Plains, New York: Longman Publishing Group.

Peterson, Paul. 1981. *City Limits.* Chicago: University of Chicago Press.

Pressman, Jeffrey L. 1972. "Preconditions of Mayoral Leadership." *American Political Science Review* 66 (2, June): 511–25.

Sears, David O., and John B. McConahay. 1973. *The Politics of Violence: The New Urban Blacks and the Watts Riot.* Boston: Houghton Mifflin Co.

Sonenshein, Raphael J. 1993. *Politics in Black and White: Race and Power in Los Angeles.* New Jersey: Princeton.

———. 1990. "Biracial Coalition Politics in Los Angeles." In *Racial Politics in American Cities,* edited by Rufus P. Browning, Dale Rogers Marshall, and David H. Tabb. White Plains, N.Y.: Longman Publishing Group.

———. 1989. "The Dynamics of Biracial Coalitions: Crossover Politics in Los Angeles." *Western Political Quarterly* 42 (June): 333–53.

———. 1991. "Jewish Participation in California Politics." In *Racial and Ethnic Politics in California,* edited by Byran Jackson and Michael B. Preston. Berkeley, Calif.: Institute of Governmental Studies Press.

Starks, Robert T., and Michael B. Preston. 1990. "Harold Washington and the Politics of Reform in Chicago: 1983–1987." In *Racial Politics in American Cities,* edited by Rufus P. Browning, Dale Rogers Marshall, and David H. Tabb. White Plains, N.Y.: Longman Publishing Group.

Stone, Clarence. 1980. "Systemic Power in Community Decision Making: A Restatement of Stratification Theory." *American Political Science Review* 74 (December): 978–90.

Warren, Christopher L., John G. Corbett, and John F. Stack, Jr. 1990. "Hispanic Ascendancy and Tripartite Politics in Miami." In *Racial Politics in American Cities,* edited by Rufus P. Browning, Dale Rogers Marshall, and David H. Tabb. White Plains, N.Y.: Longman Publishing Group.

Chapter Six

MEXICAN AMERICANS AND THE PROMISE OF DEMOCRACY: SAN ANTONIO MAYORAL ELECTIONS

Carlos Muñoz, Jr.

As the ninth largest city in the United States, San Antonio, Texas, exhibits problems characteristic of other major urban centers, but it differs from other big cities in being the nation's only large Mexican American city. Whereas Los Angeles has the largest population of people of Mexican descent in the country and Chicago has more Latinos, San Antonio is the only big city with a Mexican American majority population. According to the 1990 Census, Mexican Americans comprise 54 percent of the city's population.

After a long history of political powerlessness, Mexican Americans in San Antonio have achieved significant political representation. Mexican American representation at various levels of government within the city limits reached a total of 78 elected officials in 1990, including 2 congressmen, 1 state senator, 7 state representatives, 4 county officials, 4 city council members, 15 judicial and law enforcement officials, 5 community college board members, 37 school board members, and 3 special district board members (National Association of Latino Elected and Appointed Officials [NALEO] 1990). In no other big city are Mexican Americans so well represented at the local, state, and federal levels.

The city's "Mexicanness" has been extensively promoted and commercialized, especially by white civic and business leaders seeking to place tourism at the top of the city's economic agenda. San Antonio has been proclaimed a tantalizing international and low-cost vacation spot, where Mexican ambience exists alongside a "gleaming new high-tech $200 million . . . shopping mall." San Antonio, it is said, has become a city of "lots of laughs," with plenty of Mexican American comedians and mariachis to entertain tourists, and yet where "all the good Texas drawls in town belong to Latinos" (Zwick 1991: L3). Mexican Americans are depicted as well-to-do. A travel writer for the *Los Angeles Times* reported: "Once, while drinking a Lone Star beer along the River Walk in front of the Hilton, I heard a man say his pappy made his money in the awl bidness. I turned around to see who was speaking, and I found a perfect double for Fernando Valenzuela" (Zwick 1991).

This tourist image of San Antonio departs from the socioeconomic reality of the city as a whole and, in particular, of the majority Mexican American population. San Antonio may be what Zwick has called the "Mexican American cultural capital" of the United States, but it is far from being a city of "lots of laughs" for the majority of Mexican Americans. Given the depressed conditions in San Antonio's barrios, it is difficult to believe that the wealthy "Fernando Valenzuela" could exist but in the writer's imagination.

The political incorporation of Mexican Americans in city government coupled with the city's tourist image as a mecca for Mexican American culture has promoted a false perception: namely, that democracy for Mexican Americans in San Antonio is no longer a dream deferred, and that this population has made significant economic progress. A recent study of poverty in San Antonio by Partnership for Hope (1991), a San Antonio community agency funded by the Rockefeller Foundation, offers stark empirical evidence that most Mexican Americans have not experienced socioeconomic progress during the previous decade of incorporation into the local political system.

Among Partnership for Hope's (1991) findings are that the majority of San Antonio's Mexican American population (i.e., 64 percent), are members of the largely unskilled, blue-collar working class. Most of them fit the category of working poor. Twenty-one percent of them work in the cheap labor "service" occupational sector. Although 36 percent of the population have jobs in the white-collar labor force, only 10 percent of them are in the professional/managerial sector. Mexican Americans have consistently had the highest unemployment rates in the city and have shared with African Americans the highest percentages of substandard housing. In terms of annual income, 21 percent of Mexican Americans earned less than $5,000 (in 1990) and therefore were officially poor. Another 22 percent earned between $5,000 and $10,000. Only 4 percent had annual incomes of $35,000 or more (Partnership for Hope 1991).

A high number of San Antonio's Mexican Americans have inadequate health care and inadequate social welfare services. They have the highest infant mortality rate of any population segment in the city; the highest percentage (73 percent) of families receiving Aid to Families with Dependent Children (AFDC); Mexican American mothers receive less prenatal care than do whites or African-

Americans; and most Mexican Americans do not have health insurance. In terms of education, 71 percent of Mexican American youth do not graduate from high school, 29 percent of the 60 percent Mexican American students in school are poor, and 71 percent of them attend largely segregated schools (Partnership for Hope 1991).

The Partnership for Hope study makes clear the reality that Mexican American political incorporation has not resulted in the economic betterment of the Mexican American community as a whole. The reasons for this can be explained by the past and present domination of local politics by white economic elites.

HISTORICAL OVERVIEW

From the 1880s until approximately the 1940s, white political machines in San Antonio maintained power primarily through the patronage system, whereby Mexican American workers were given low-pay jobs in return for their votes. The patronage system lasted until World War II, when military bases in San Antonio opened up jobs controlled by the federal civil service system and not the political machines. Another factor in the demise of the patronage system was the transition of San Antonio's economy from an agricultural to an urban-based economy. But poll taxes, complicated voter registration requirements, and lack of opportunities in education, the professions, and so forth, continued to keep Mexican Americans "in their place."

In 1954, the last political machine, the Good Government League (GGL), was created by local white business elites, and it successfully controlled city politics for over two decades. The GGL worked closely with a small and select group of Mexican American small businessmen for the purpose of running their candidates at election time. One or two at most were elected to the city council, which was always dominated by a white majority. Mexican Americans were systematically excluded by the GGL political machine from meaningful participation in the electoral process (Muñoz and Henry 1990).

Control of the electoral process by the GGL was largely maintained through a system of at-large elections. In spite of the majority Mexican American population, whites always outnumbered them in the ranks of the registered voters and, most importantly, whites always had higher turnouts at the polls (Brischetto and de la Garza 1985).

In the early 1960s, the GGL was directly challenged by the Bexar County Democratic Coalition of Mexican Americans, African Americans, white liberal, and union activists (Muñoz and Henry 1990). But the first distinct Mexican American organized challenge to the GGL came from the Mexican American Youth Organization (MAYO) during the late 1960s and early 1970s. MAYO was largely a student organization and part of the Chicano Power Movement (Muñoz 1989). It eventually evolved into the La Raza Unida Party, a Chicano political party that first took power in Crystal City, Texas, in 1970 (Garcia 1990). Mexican American candidates supported by MAYO ran against GGL candidates under the banner of the Committee for Barrio Betterment (CBB), but they were never able to win elections. However, MAYO's presence in San Antonio politics contributed to the increasing militancy and political awareness of Mexican Americans in response to their political inequality.

By 1974, MAYO and the La Raza Unida Party had been replaced by another group, Communities Organized for Public Service (COPS), which was able to mobilize Mexican Americans against city hall and the GGL. Created by followers of activist Saul Alinsky and funded by the Catholic Church of San Antonio, COPS departed from the radical civil rights/protest orientations of the former organizations and defined itself as a "coalition of pressure groups dedicated to the pursuit of concrete improvements in the everyday standard of living" (Booth 1983). Compared to the other groups, COPS grew out of the discontent "among many lower-middle class homeowners and other residents of the largely poor west side with their substandard public services" (Booth 1983).

Nonprofit and therefore nonpartisan, COPS never directly engaged in electoral politics but indirectly participated in grass-roots mobilization via voter registration drives in the Mexican American community. In the process, COPS became a political force in city politics, challenging city council policies designed to benefit the white business elite and the white populated northside of the city.

DECLINE OF GGL AND RISE OF HENRY CISNEROS

The GGL began to lose its grip on city government in 1971 owing to several factors, including internal splits among white business elites; a scandal in which GGL city council members were accused of taking "bribes" from the chamber of commerce, Southwestern Bell, and the local utility company; and, finally, the GGL's failure to develop new leadership from within its ranks (Flores N.D.). The result was that in 1973, the GGL mayoral candidate lost the election for the first time. Nevertheless, the GGL's sway over city politics continued until 1977, when the city electoral process was changed from an at-large to a single-member district system as a result of lawsuits instigated by the Mexican American Legal Defense Fund (MALDEF) under the Voting Rights Act. This transformation finally permitted an increase in the number of Mexican Americans in the city council: specifically, 4 out of 10 councilmatic districts were created in predominantly Mexican American sections of the city.

As was the case throughout the United States, civil rights legislation enabled more minority representation in San Antonio, but it did not result in direct access to or incorporation of these groups into the city's economic power structure. White business elites shifted from a strategy of systematic exclusion of Mexican Americans from the political process to a strategy of cooptation. Mexican American political elites were recruited, encouraged to run for political office, and supported with endorsements and campaign contributions.

Henry Cisneros was one of the city councilmen who played a central role in the overhaul of the city's electoral process. Elected to the city council in 1975 as the GGL's Mexican American candidate, Cisneros had been named to the GGL slate owing to his conservative family connections to the political machine (Diehl and Jarboe 1985). After losing the mayor's race in 1973, the GGL leadership had been searching for new power bases and was willing to accept newcomers such as Cisneros who did not totally conform to the GGL's style.

Cisneros was elected to the city council prior to the switch to a single-member district system. He won with 52 percent of the total vote, receiving more votes from whites than from Mexican Americans. Once on the council, however, he proved himself adept at working with both GGL interest groups and COPS. He allied himself with COPS on several key issues related to improvements in communities represented by the organization. In the 1977 election, Cisneros was reelected to the council as a candidate in the largely Mexican American District Number 1 with 92 percent of the total vote. But by the time he ran for mayor in 1981, his alliance with COPS no longer existed. His conservative political bent was manifested when, as a city councilman, he sided with management during a workers' city garbage strike organized by the San Antonio Refuse Collectors Association. Cisneros supported the firing of the striking workers.

1981 MAYORAL ELECTION AND CISNEROS' TENURE

Prior to the election of Henry Cisneros in 1981, it had been 140 years since a Mexican American had served as mayor of San Antonio. Cisneros' victory was therefore perceived as a historic breakthrough for Mexican Americans, not only in San Antonio but throughout the United States, since he also became the first Mexican American to serve as mayor of a major urban metropolis. His election was indeed, to some extent, the culmination of a long process of Mexican American efforts to participate more directly in the local political system from which they had been systematically excluded.

When he announced his candidacy for mayor of San Antonio, Cisneros had established himself in both the Mexican American community and in the white business community. As a city councilman, he had preached and practiced a politics of compromise and consensus. He made clear that he did not see the role of Mexican American politicians as "dealing exclusively with social programs, voting rights, and police brutality but instead, concentrating their energies on economic development in the private sector" (Diehl and Jarboe 1985). He in essence became part of the white economic power structure, receiving most of his financial support from local key entrepreneurs and the corporate elite.

From the start of his campaign, Cisneros focused on getting the white votes he needed to be elected. Indeed, his wide support from white business elites proved significant in his victory over his opponent, white millionaire John Steen. Cisneros raised $247,000 for his campaign and was able to effectively counter Steen's strategy to label him antibusiness. Cisneros successfully convinced white voters that he was, in fact, strongly pro-growth and pro-economic development.

Henry Cisneros was elected mayor with 61.8 percent of the vote, receiving nearly 100 percent of the Mexican American vote and 45 percent of the white vote. At age 33, he became the youngest mayor in the history of the city, and he won as a direct result of what appears to be the most diverse electoral coalition in the city's history. Cisneros had the support of Mexican Americans, African Americans, whites, conservatives and liberals, environmentalists and expansionists (Muñoz and Henry 1986, 1990). But the support of those diverse political interest groups was not, in retrospect, a viable coalition committed to pursuing issues of common interest to African Americans and Mexican Americans. Soon after his election, Cisneros made clear his administration's priority to pursue the common interests of the developers and business elites who had largely funded and supported his mayoral campaign.

Cisneros nevertheless became a popular mayor, successfully winning reelection to three succeeding terms. In his final reelection bid, in 1987, he won handily by a margin of 67 percent to his challenger's 31 percent. He maintained his popularity primarily because, as a weak mayor in a strong city-council-with-city-manager system, he did not have to be overly concerned with being directly accountable to San Antonio voters. He enjoyed consistently favorable press coverage at the local, state, and national political levels. Even his opponents in the Mexican American COPS organization praised him for steering the city "away from deep racial and economic rifts" and, in particular, for promoting a "politics of inclusion" (LaFranchi 1988).

Although a "powerless" mayor, Cisneros did an excellent job of public relations for San Antonio and is credited with many of the city's improvements over the eight years he served as mayor (Cantu 1987). Although, with the decline of oil production, Texas as a whole was undergoing economic crisis during Cisneros' tenure, San Antonio enjoyed relative prosperity, experiencing "the largest volume of construction in the city's history" (ibid.). Packaged under the title, "Target '90: Goals for San Antonio," the construction projects included street improvements, a new downtown luxury hotel, a Sea World theme park, and the earlier-mentioned shopping mall. Cisneros' supporters ignored the high cost of these projects, which were reflected in substantial local tax increases. San Antonio also prospered owing to Cisneros' promotion of the city as the tourist and hospitality capital of Texas. The city earned a reputation as a "model of peaceful race relations."

In short, Cisneros enjoyed a relatively stable four terms, although he underwent more consistent public criticism during his final term. His successful tenure was due to his ability to maintain his good standing with both white business elites and the Mexican American community.

CISNEROS AND MEXICAN AMERICAN EMPOWERMENT

As indicated earlier, Cisneros' mayoralty did not lead to Mexican American political and economic empowerment, for several reasons. As mayor, Cisneros served as the at-large member of the 11-member council and therefore represented the fifth Mexican American vote in the council, one vote short of the majority. His presence theoretically increased Mexican American representation on the council, but it did not in practice translate into Mexican American control of the council. Although his supporters give him credit for making Mexican Americans key players in city government, he never made Mexican American community interests a priority, and during his tenure, the west and south sides of the city, with heavy populations of Mexican Americans, remained depressed. Outside the Mexican American community, Cisneros promoted neither his Mexican American identity nor the specific interests of that community. He acted as a mayor who happened to be Mexican American.

He did promote his *identity* within the Mexican American community in San Antonio and throughout the nation however. For Latinos nationwide, Cisneros personified their arrival at the center stage of American politics. (He would later become the first Latino politician to be seriously considered as a vice-presidential candidate for the Democratic Party and subsequently was appointed secretary of the U.S. Department of Housing and Urban Development.) His charisma not only made him the nation's most popular Latino political leader but also a key player in state and national political affairs. Outside of San Antonio, his image was that of a liberal Democrat. Within the city limits, he promoted more conservative politics that supported developers and the business sector.

If Cisneros had attempted to act as a Mexican American mayor, he would have had a difficult time directly promoting the interests of the Mexican American community or of surviving as mayor beyond one term. As indicated earlier, San Antonio's mayor has no real structural power to make changes. City government is a weak mayor/ strong city council system with a city manager. The majority of the council and the city manager were pro-business and pro-economic development before and during the Cisneros mayorship. As political scientist Henry Flores (1988) has stated:

> Business interests have dominated the economic development political process from 1955 to the present, the era in which the most intense and rapid growth has occurred . . . growth or investment patterns occur only in those geographical areas possessing higher land values, and in which residents enjoy higher incomes than in other parts of the city.

In summary, as mayor, Henry Cisneros became the key promoter of San Antonio's business interests and successfully campaigned for city policies and programs sought by developers and pro-growth forces. His "Target '90" projects were not targeted on the economic development of the Mexican American west and south sides of the city. Meanwhile, the white, northern areas of the city experienced increased real estate values and overall improvement.

1989 MAYORAL ELECTION

The 1989 mayoral election marked the return of a white politician to office in the person of Lila Cockrell. Cockrell had been a prominent member of the Good Government League as a city council member and had served three two-year terms (1975–81) as mayor of San Antonio prior to Cisneros' election. An enormously popular mayor with a successful public service record, Cockrell had left office in 1981 owing to her husband's serious illness. In her reelection bid, in 1989, she was opposed by six relatively unknown candidates and won by 60 percent of the total vote. Only 18 percent of the registered voters went to the polls, and there were no controversial issues. During her two years in office, Mayor Cockrell continued to support the pro-growth programs and policies of Cisneros, as promoted by white business elite.

1991 MAYORAL ELECTION

Two years later, in light of continued hard times, San Antonio's voters decided it was time for a change. On May 4, 1991, they voted to put a stop to the massive economic development programs of Cisneros and Cockrell. The major issue of the campaign was a huge city project—promoted by the business elite and endorsed by Mayor Cockrell—to build a $180 million dam and reservoir on the Medina River on the south side of San Antonio. Called the "Applewhite" project, the proposal had been launched by the Cisneros city council in 1988, and more than $23 million had been spent for land acquisition, legal fees, and construction costs, all without voter approval.

Eleven candidates ran for mayor, including the incumbent Cockrell. Of the 33 percent of San Antonio's registered voters who went to the polls, most of their votes were divided among three candidates: 10-year-veteran city councilwoman Maria Berriozabal, a Mexican American, who received 31 percent of the vote; Nelson Wolff, a two-term councilman who received 26.2 percent; and Cockrell, who was ousted as mayor with only 20.7 percent of the vote. Since neither Berriozabal nor Wolff won 50 percent of the vote, a runoff election was held the end of May.

Berriozabal's dramatic first-place showing stunned the political pundits and others who had predicted she had no chance of winning the election. Her first-place finish appeared to position her as the Mexican American successor to Cisneros and to her becoming the first Mexican American woman or Latina in the nation to be elected as mayor of a big city. Unfortunately, she did not receive the 50 percent of the vote necessary to avoid a runoff.

Berriozabal was strongly supported by the Mexican American community but not to the extent Cisneros had been supported after his initial 1981 election. In her own councilmatic District 1, she only received 58 percent of the vote and in the four largely Mexican American districts, she got only 57 percent of the total vote. In contrast, these same districts gave Cisneros 85 percent of the total vote when he first ran in 1981. She only received 5 percent of the total white vote. A major factor in her victory was the bitter and antagonistic campaign waged between Cockrell and Wolff, which developed over the issue of Mayor Cockrell's alleged payoff to business elites in the form of lucrative city contracts. But perhaps another more significant factor for victory was the Applewhite reservoir issue. She was the only major candidate who opposed it.

1991 Runoff Election

On the surface, Berriozabal appeared the stronger of the two by virtue of her victory on May 4. In addition, she was more experienced than Wolff in city government, having served 10 years on the city council compared to his 4. Finally, Wolff, like Cockrell, had endorsed the Applewhite project, whereas Berriozabal had not. Given the voters' rejection of that referendum, political pundits predicted a Berriozabal victory.

The two candidates shared some similarities of background. Both were 50 years of age and lifelong members of the liberal wing of the Democratic Party. Both grew up in Catholic, low-income working-class families. However, their racial and class differences projected two distinct ideological images. Nelson Wolff was a white, self-made millionaire and the owner of a successful chain of organic grocery stores. Although born and raised in the southside, originally a white working-class community that has since become predominantly Mexican American, he never maintained a working-class identity, and his anti-union posture was well known. Entrepreneurship had been his way out of poverty. As he put it, "It gave me a great sensitivity to the small guy who's struggling to build something. . . . I think when government intrudes itself too much, you kill that initiative" (Tolson 1991). Although not as experienced in city government, he had served in the Texas State Legislature during the 1970s where he had made a name as a liberal progressive on social issues, and had taken a leading role in the effort to revise the outdated and conservative state constitution.

Although not directly identified as a candidate for pro-growth developer interests, Wolff had served as chairman of Mayor Cisneros' "Target '90" committee. After the defeat of the business elite's candidate, Mayor Cockrell, that group rallied behind Wolff. Wolff's campaign was based on his message that he would be "a mayor for all the people" and that he had the necessary experience to create jobs and compete for viable economic development projects for the city. He campaigned heavily in the Mexican American districts, stressing his southside roots and receiving endorsements from key Mexican American leaders as well as the Hispanic Chamber of Commerce.

Maria Berriozabal was born in Laredo, Texas, but was raised in the Mexican American west side of San Antonio. She grew up poor, the daughter of Mexican working-class immigrants. After graduating from high school, she worked to help put her brothers and sisters through college, while she herself attended night school. Twenty years later, she graduated with a bachelor of arts in political science from the University of Texas. In 1980, she served as director of the Census Bureau in San Antonio. In 1981 she was elected to the city council. Although she moved into a more affluent middle-class section of town after she married, she maintained strong ties to her old barrio.

Berriozabal's campaign strategy was not, however, based on distinct issues confronting the Mexican American community. Many of her campaign workers were grass-roots activists and some were former members of the defunct Chicano Raza Unida Party. But her campaign manager was a conservative who had directed the local Reagan and Bush presidential campaigns. Her slogan for mayor was "For those of us who believe," and she had two basic issues. The first was to reinstate trust in local government by instituting a fairer and more open political process. And second, she stressed a "marriage between economic development and human capital investment." She believed a more diversified economy would benefit all of San Antonio, not just Mexican Americans. She did not emphasize social programs at the expense of economic development. Nevertheless, in her 10 years on the city council, she came to be perceived as an antigrowth candidate. In reality, she supported many of the Cisneros projects, including "Target '90." She was never antigrowth per se, but she fought for pro-growth and economic development policies that would also contribute to the Mexican American community.

Although Berriozabal's campaign strategists were careful not to promote her as a Mexican American candidate, she and her supporters perceived her campaign as the first Mexican American challenge to the city's white corporate power structure. In contrast to Cisneros, she was a more well-defined liberal, given her grass-roots political orientation. Moreover, as a city councilwoman, she never pursued the city's economic elite. Her support came primarily from Mexican American grass-roots community activists and liberal Democratic Party politicians.

Election Results

Nelson Wolff won the runoff with 53 percent of the vote against 47 percent for Berriozabal. Wolff received approximately 80 percent of the white vote and only 5 percent of the Mexican American vote. Berriozabal received approximately 95 percent of the Mexican American vote but only about 20 percent of the white vote. Although race and ethnicity per se never emerged as an issue during the campaign, the voting was in fact polarized along racial lines. Political scientist Robert Brischetto (1991) stated: "Maria lost the election not because she was a woman but because she was Latino in a city where voting along ethnic lines is still very much a fact of political life." Berriozabal was unable to effectively counter her antibusiness image and convince white voters that she, more than Wolff, would be a mayor for "all of the people." Berriozabal was unquestionably a victim of a "nonstated race issue," and her Mexican accent and identity went against her in the white councilmatic districts where the majority of the registered voters reside. The voters ousted a pro-growth candidate in the person of Mayor Cockrell and defeated the Applewhite referendum supported by corporate developers. But when it came to electing a white or a Mexican American candidate, they voted for the white candidate who was supported by the same Cockrell pro-growth interests and who endorsed the Applewhite referendum they defeated.

Beyond this racial polarization, several other factors were significant in Berriozabal's defeat. First among these was the black vote. Interestingly, the majority of African American voters perceived the white candidate, Wolff, as the better candidate and joined white voters in rejecting Berriozabal. One explanation for this is that Wolff had recruited many of the key religious leaders in the African American community. Other factors in Berriozabal's defeat were her failure to concretize the key issues of the campaign by providing specific proposals for bringing government closer to the people or for ways to link future economic development to the benefit of the Mexican American community, especially in terms of human capital.

In conclusion, Berriozabal's campaign strategy focused on image as opposed to substance. Her Mexican American cultural and working-class identity was indeed a challenge to local white corporate power, but it was not the type of challenge that would lessen the business elite's grip on local government.

PROSPECTS FOR FUTURE MEXICAN AMERICAN EMPOWERMENT

Berriozabal's defeat bodes ill for the future political and economic empowerment of Mexican Americans in San Antonio. The election of Cisneros in 1981 was interpreted by some as the beginning of a more inclusive and pluralistic civic political culture (Brischetto 1991). But the mayoral election of 1991 proved that racism, although less vulgar than in the past, remains alive and well. White voters made clear that only Mexican American candidates who underplay their identity can effectively persuade them that they can be a "mayor for all the people." The majority of the city population may be Mexican American, but whites will continue to dominate at the polls because they are the majority of the city's registered voters (Mexican Americans comprise only 38 percent of San Antonio's registered voters).

Berriozabal's loss also portends a pessimistic future with regard to the emergence of a Mexican and African American political coalition in San Antonio. The fact that 60 percent of the city's African American vote went to Nelson Wolff and only 40 percent to Berriozabal may mean that African Americans do not perceive a common ground with Mexican Americans. A basic mistrust exists among African Americans and Mexican Americans, which has been exploited by both liberal and conservative politicians. In general, African

Americans regard Mexican Americans as white and not as fellow people of color. Similarly, most Mexican Americans do not identify themselves as people of color, as evidenced by their growing preference for the term *Hispanic* (Muñoz 1989).

Most middle-class Mexican American politicians have historically promoted a white identity for Latinos, which has contributed to a lack of interest in building coalitions with African Americans. The prospects for such coalition building will be enhanced if Latinos and African Americans accurately perceive each other as peoples of color sharing a common political agenda and a common history of racial oppression.

Finally, the 1991 mayoral campaign emphasized the lack of Mexican American community organizations in San Antonio as resources for electoral mobilization. COPS, the only visible community organization in the city during the past decade, has declined as a political force. It has not played a role in developing or actively supporting Mexican American candidates for political office and has limited its role in the Mexican American community to voter registration activity. No other grass-roots political community organizations were in evidence during the campaign.

The Berriozabal defeat furthermore underscores the reality that Mexican Americans, as with Latinos in general, are not of one political mind. True, Berriozabal received overwhelming support from San Antonio's Mexican American voters, but the Mexican American political leadership has been and will continue to be divided, as manifested in the varying endorsements of each candidate. The four Mexican Americans who have served on the council generally divided along the lines of pro-growth versus antigrowth and/or pro-economic development and pro-Mexican American community interests. Class divisions were also a basis for political division. The Mexican American working class has not benefited much from the political representation of Mexican American middle-class politicians who are from the professional sector of the community. Perceptions exist within the Mexican American working-class community that most, if not all, Mexican American middle-class and political elites are coopted by the city white business elites.

Note

My analysis of the 1991 mayoral campaign is derived from local coverage of the campaign as reported in the *San Antonio Light* newspaper and interviews with the following people who first hand observed or directly participated in the mayoral campaign: Maria Berriozabal, Robert Brischetto, Choco Gonzalez Mesa, Rodolfo Rosales, Lalo Valdez, Henry Flores, Antonio Cabral, Richard Lewis, Rick Casey, Yolanda Vera, and Andy Hernandez. I am especially grateful for the assistance I received from Robert Brischetto, Director of Research for the Southwest Voter Education Project in San Antonio (SWVEP) and my two research assistants, Jesus Martinez and Jose Sigala.

References

Booth, John. 1983. "Political Change in San Antonio, 1970–1982: Toward Decay or Democracy?" *The Politics of San Antonio*, edited by David R. Johnson, et al. Lincoln: University of Nebraska Press.

Brischetto, Robert R. 1991. "The 1991 San Antonio Mayoral Campaign." Southwest Voter Project. Photocopy.

Brischetto, Robert R., and Rodolfo O. de la Garza. 1985. *The Mexican American Electorate: Political Opinions and Behavior across Cultures in San Antonio*. Occasional Paper 5. San Antonio, Tex.: Southwest Voter Registration Project.

Cantu, Tony. 1987. "Cisneros' Decision Not to Seek Statewide Texas Post May Be Only a Detour En Route to National Office." *Wall Street Journal*, Sept. 10.

Diehl, Kemper, and Jan Jarboe. 1985. *Cisneros: Portrait of a New American*. San Antonio, Tex.: Corona Publishing Co.

Flores, Henry. 1988. "Structural Barriers to Chicano Empowerment." In *Latino Empowerment*, edited by Roberto E. Villarreal, et al. New York: Greenwood Press.

————. N.D. *Chicanos and Economic Development*. Photocopy.

Garcia, Ignacio. 1990. *United We Win: The Rise and Fall of La Raza Unida Party*. Tucson: University of Arizona Press.

LaFranchi, Howard. 1988. "Cisneros Bows Out—For Now." *Christian Science Monitor*, Sept. 14.

Muñoz, Jr., Carlos. 1989. *Youth, Identity, Power: The Chicano Movement*. London: Verso Press.

Muñoz, Jr., Carlos, and Charles P. Henry. 1986. "Rainbow Coalition in Four Big Cities: San Antonio, Denver, Chicago, and Philadelphia." *PS*, 19 (3, Summer): 598–609.

————. 1990. "Coalition Politics in San Antonio and Denver: The Cisneros and Peña Mayoral Campaigns." In *Racial Politics in American Cities*, edited by Rufus P. Browning, Dale Rogers Marshall, and David H. Tabb. White Plains, N.Y.: Longman Publishing Group.

National Association of Latino Elected and Appointed Officials. 1991. *1990*

National Roster of Hispanic Elected Officials. Washington, D.C.: Author.

Partnership for Hope. 1991. *Pride and Poverty: A Report on San Antonio.* San Antonio, Tex.: Partnership for Hope.

Tolson, Mike. 1991. "Mayor's Race a Tale of Two Cultures." *San Antonio Light,* May 23.

Zwick, Barry. 1991. "Lots of Laughs and Plenty to Eat in the New, Improved San Antonio." *Los Angeles Times,* May 5.

Chapter Seven

CITY GOVERNMENT AND MINORITY ECONOMIC OPPORTUNITY: THE CASE OF MILWAUKEE

Peter K. Eisinger

As in many other big cities in the United States, Milwaukee's glass and granite office tower district virtually collides at its edges with the city's most decrepit and ruined neighborhoods, an architectural metaphor for the class and racial friction that drives much of urban life and politics. Here, as elsewhere, Michael Harrington's "other America" is scarcely invisible anymore, for the destitute and the poor, many of them black, stand or sleep in the public streets in plain view (Harrington 1963). If this observation is hardly novel, it scarcely diminishes the moral urgency implied by the contrast or its political intractability.

A number of analysts explain the coincidence in American cities of great poverty and a booming white-collar economy as the product of economic restructuring. Like other metropolises, Milwaukee lost jobs during the 1980s, particularly in heavy manufacturing, the city's bread and butter. But in 1990, city employment increased slightly, a boomlet that led the *Wall Street Journal* to write of the "Milwaukee Miracle" (Bailey 1990). At the same time, however, the unemployment rate among blacks in the city remained among the highest in the country. Meanwhile, suburban employment in the Milwaukee metropolitan area traced a steady upward trend over the decade, with dramatic gains in the broad service sector.

As job opportunities declined in the city, whites migrated to the surrounding suburban counties. But such mobility has not been open to black Milwaukeeans. A study conducted for the city's major newspaper concluded that only about 500 blacks had moved from the city to the suburbs between 1980 and 1987 (*Milwaukee Journal*, Dec. 27, 1987). Indeed, the metropolitan area is classified as one of the most segregated in the nation: 1990 Census figures show that 98 percent of all black residents of Milwaukee County lived in the central city, compared to only 56 percent of all whites. Many inner-city black residents cannot easily commute to suburban jobs: in 1980 39.6 percent of all black households did not own a car (compared to 20.2 percent of white households) (McNeely and Kinlow 1988: 47); public transportation in the Milwaukee metropolitan area, as in most places, is geared to the needs of inbound commuters.

The constricted opportunities for economic and residential mobility for blacks became a source of serious concern at the beginning of the 1990s for the city's public officials, business elites, and leaders in the minority community. What is striking, perhaps, is that this concern was more than talk: it has resulted in a host of social experiments, pilot programs, and policy commitments addressed to housing, education, business formation, and jobs among the disadvantaged.[1]

Yet, these local efforts ultimately raise the question of what local government can in fact do to generate significant opportunities for its minority citizens. Are the good ideas—the social technology— adequate to the task? Can local government command or leverage adequate resources? Can it galvanize and sustain the necessary political will to see its efforts through? Do the efforts of local government ultimately affect the life chances and situation of the black population? This chapter examines the degree to which local government action and policy actually generate or influence the creation of employment opportunities for minorities in both the public and private sectors. In particular, we analyze the effects of the main targeted economic development programs, the record of the local public sector in employing blacks, and city efforts to channel government contracts to minority-owned businesses.

ECONOMIC RESTRUCTURING AND RACE IN MILWAUKEE: THE BACKGROUND

It is a matter of bitter historical irony that black migration to Milwaukee did not achieve substantial proportions until after economic restructuring in the city was well under way. By the time blacks began to arrive in significant numbers, opportunities in manufacturing were already on the decline.

Blacks had been slow to come to Milwaukee. In 1950, a year in which the Allis Chalmers corporation was still employing nearly 20,000 workers in the city (Marchetti 1980: 2), Milwaukee ranked 23rd among the largest 25 cities in the proportion of its black popula-

Figure 7.1 BLACK POPULATION GROWTH AND MANUFACTURING DECLINE,
MILWAUKEE, 1960–1990

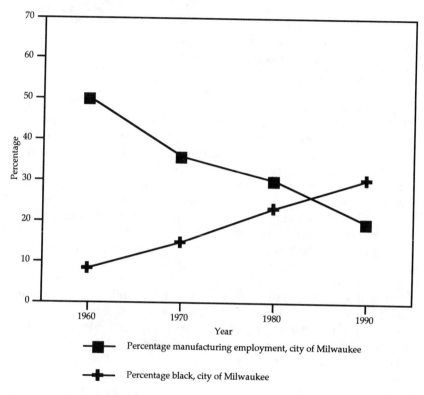

Percentage manufacturing employment, city of Milwaukee

Percentage black, city of Milwaukee

Sources: Manufacturing data are from Employment Database, Urban Research Center,
University of Wisconsin–Milwaukee, unpublished data. Population data are from U.S.
Bureau of the Census.

tion (Bernard 1990: 177). By 1960, when fully half the city's workers
were still employed in various manufacturing establishments, blacks
comprised only 8.4 percent of the population (see figure 7.1). (Contrast this figure with that of other Great Lakes industrial cities: in
1960 blacks constituted nearly 23 percent of Chicago's population,
28.6 percent of Cleveland's, and 29 percent of Detroit's.) Over the
next three decades the black community in Milwaukee grew by nearly
130,000, accounting by 1990 for 30.4 percent of the city's people; at
the same time manufacturing employment was declining steadily to
its present level, roughly one-fifth of the work force.[2]

Like many other northern cities, Milwaukee sits at the center of a

Table 7.1 EMPLOYMENT CHANGE IN MILWAUKEE AND ITS SUBURBS,
1979–87

	1979	1987	Percentage Change
Metropolitan total	650,628	657,959	1.1
City only	349,826	320,580	−8.4
Suburbs only	300,802	337,379	12.2

Source: White et al. (1989: 8).

booming metropolitan area. While the city itself was losing 30,000
jobs between 1979 and 1987, the suburbs were gaining over 37,000
(see table 7.1). The bulk of the lost jobs in the central city were in
manufacturing, but losses were recorded in wholesale trade, retail,
construction, utilities, and public administration. Suburban areas
gained in every sector except manufacturing, though the decline in
suburban manufacturing was not as severe as in the city (see table
7.2). As the 1980s came to an end, a majority of all jobs in the
metropolitan area were located outside the central city.

Declining manufacturing employment, continuing black in-migra-
tion, and constricted suburban housing opportunities have converged
to produce chronically high levels of black distress. In the mid-
1980s William O'Hare (1986) ranked Milwaukee 46th out of 48 major
metropolitan areas in terms of black well-being, using a composite
measure of nine different factors. The city routinely ranks among the
top cities in the proportion of minority households headed by women
and in the teenage pregnancy rate. Unemployment, in particular,
among blacks has been extremely high. In 1970 the black unemployment rate was estimated at 2.5 times the white rate; by 1977 the black
rate was 3.7 times the white rate; and by 1985, with 27.9 percent of
all blacks unemployed, the rate had risen to 4.7 times the white rate

Table 7.2 JOB SHIFTS IN MILWAUKEE, BY SECTOR, 1979–87

	City	Suburbs
Manufacturing	−33,334 (−33%)	−18,795 (−16%)
Construction	−1,677 (−18%)	131 (1%)
Transportation/utilities	−1,668 (−7%)	4,697 (42%)
Wholesale	−3,145 (−17%)	5,495 (32%)
Retail	−3,857 (−8%)	11,649 (23%)
Fire	2,806 (10%)	5,837 (57%)
Services	12,023 (12%)	26,697 (41%)
Public administration	−1,505 (−7%)	204 (2%)
Total	−29,246 (−8%)	36,577 (12%)

Source: White et al. (1989: 8).

(Milwaukee Metropolitan Sewerage District 1990: 36). According to the U.S. Department of Labor, the disparity between black and white unemployment in 1986 was worse in Milwaukee than in any other city in the country (ibid: 139). Recent figures (from 1990) put black unemployment around 21 percent, just over four times the white rate (from author's interview with BLS official, 2/22/91).

Chronic black unemployment is reflected in the county's welfare statistics. Although blacks comprised only about 20 percent of the county's population, they accounted in 1990 for 63.4 percent of the county's Food Stamp recipients and 64.5 percent—more than one out of every three blacks—of all people receiving Aid to Families with Dependent Children (AFDC) (data from Milwaukee County Social Services, January 1991).

Given these conditions, it was scarcely a surprise when one of the city's black aldermen, Michael McGee, organized a Black Panther Militia group in the early spring of 1990 and threatened to lead his cadre of shock troops in a series of terrorist attacks if dramatic actions were not taken by the city to deal with black poverty. Specifically, McGee threatened, among other things, to disrupt the annual summer circus parade in downtown Milwaukee, shoot commuters on the freeway entering the city, and terrorize fans at professional basketball games, if the city and state refused to finance a $100 million emergency job program for the inner city. Although most civic leaders, both black and white, denounced McGee, there was nevertheless a sense among many blacks in the city that his threats (none of which materialized) sent what a black colleague on the city council called "a very deep and concerned message" (*Milwaukee Journal*, Mar. 1, 1990).

MUNICIPAL ECONOMIC DEVELOPMENT AND THE DISADVANTAGED

Politics of Minority Opportunity in Milwaukee

Milwaukee maintains an extraordinary variety of separate economic development programs, some funded with local revenues, others with intergovernmental grants. Those that maintain at least some provision for targeting job creation or business development among minorities or the disadvantaged are listed, by year of their establishment, in table 7.3. Many of the programs have been modestly funded: for example, the city had granted less than $200,000 of its Community Development Block Grant (CDBG) monies to the Community-Based Ventures Fund, and it allocated only about $100,000 from the same source to the Storefront Improvement Grants program. Other programs have received more generous treatment: for instance, the city spent about $1 million of its own revenues to launch the Milwaukee Enterprise Center small business incubator, it allocated $3.5 million in CDBG funds to establish a revolving loan fund for disadvantaged businesses, and it loaned over $1.2 million to minority- and women-owned businesses between 1988 and 1990 through programs of the Milwaukee Economic Development Corporation.

Table 7.3 underscores the veritable explosion of minority-targeted programs after the election of John Norquist as mayor in April 1988. These initiatives represent Norquist's partial, if substantial, fulfillment of promises to facilitate minority advancement made during his mayoral campaign and subsequent first term.

Norquist's 1988 election marked a genuine sea change in Milwaukee politics, whose contours and character had been dominated for 28 years by the mercurial personality of the dean of American mayors, Henry Maier. Maier was no friend of black Milwaukee, principally, perhaps, because he did not need their votes.[3] The Maier years were filled with episodes of stormy racial conflict: a major riot in 1967, months of marches led by Father James Groppi in an unsuccessful effort to persuade the city to pass a fair housing ordinance, incidents of police misconduct that never seemed to disturb Police Chief Harold Brier or move him to action.[4] When Maier decided at last not to run again in 1988, a prominent Milwaukee black educator and administrator noted that his "legacy for black people is steeped in policies and practices that have helped to foster black political, economic, and social disenfranchisement. . . ." (*Milwaukee Journal*, Feb. 1, 1988).

In his initial mayoral campaign, Norquist promised black Milwaukeeans a new era, and in so doing, won early black support, including the enthusiastic endorsement of Michael McGee, the future firebrand. In his victory speech on the night he beat former governor Martin Schreiber, Norquist described his election as a mandate for change and a historic opportunity to break down the divisions between the races. Black leaders hailed the election as the start of a "new era of openness in City Hall" (*Milwaukee Journal*, Apr. 16, 1988; *Milwaukee Sentinel*, Apr. 20, 1988).

During the mayoral campaign there had been little explicit discussion of minority job or business creation, except for a pledge to create

Table 7.3 MILWAUKEE TARGETED ECONOMIC DEVELOPMENT PROGRAMS,
BY YEAR OF ESTABLISHMENT

Prior to 1988

Milwaukee Economic Development Corporation
Minority and Women's Business Loan Program: low-cost, subordinated loans

Micro-loan Guarantee Program: city loan guarantee

Community Based Ventures Fund: grants to community-based organizations to
create for-profit businesses

Neighborhood Commercial Revitalization Program: develops revitalization plans
and eliminates blight in Community Development Block Grant (CDBG) areas

1988

Milwaukee Enterprise Center: small business incubator

Transportation for Central City Workers: bus transport for central city residents to
Northwest Side Industrial Land Bank businesses

1989

Fair Lending Action Committee: investigates discrimination in lending

Development Zones: state-sponsored, city-supported enterprise zones

Inner City Land Bank: city acquisition of inner-city land to sell for business
development

Step Up: summer school to employment program for young people

1990

Fair Lending Project: funded effort to increase bank reinvestment in central city
homes and businesses

Socially Responsible Investment Program: city funds are invested in financial
institutions that hire minorities and make loans in the central city

Contractor Development Training Program: training seminars for potential minority
vendors seeking city contracts

Targeted CDBG funds: revolving loan fund for disadvantaged businesses

Storefront Improvement Grant: small grants for improving facades

1991

Capital Access Program: city-sponsored loan loss reserve fund to encourage high-
risk lending

Milwaukee Community Service Corps: paid work on community projects combined
with individualized education for 18- to 23-year-olds at or near poverty level

Work Place Job Training: links central city residents to job training for openings
offered by local companies

Operation Bootstrap: city job training for rent assistance recipients

First Source Employment Program: city and Private Industry Council (PIC) team
businesses that receive financial assistance from the city with unemployed city
residents, who will be offered job training by the PIC

Performance Bond Fund: guarantees letters of credit issued by a lender to a surety
company on small businesses to enable disadvantaged firms to obtain performance
bonding

a program for summer youth employment. Instead, in the months leading to the election, Norquist sought to offer more oblique reassurances about the city's role in fostering minority economic opportunity by speaking mainly about the need for a *neighborhood*, rather than a downtown, focus for economic development. The advantage of the neighborhood focus was that it not only represented a clear way to differentiate himself from Henry Maier's development efforts, but it also permitted a more inclusive interpretation of Norquist's concerns. *Neighborhoods*, a term loaded with much appealing emotional freight, are, after all, the home of white ethnic groups as well as minorities.

As table 7.3 shows, however, much of Norquist's agenda was in fact oriented toward minority development. But rather than make this explicit when announcing individual programs, Norquist often signaled his commitment to minority development early on in more subtle ways. For example, in contrast to Schreiber, his opponent in the mayoral race, Norquist refused to promise to keep Mayor Maier's director of City Development, William Drew, who had made Milwaukee a "developer's dream" (*Milwaukee Journal*, Jan. 3, 1988), and had been a key player in the development of the Rouse Company's Grand Avenue Mall and other downtown projects. When Drew finally resigned three months after Norquist's inauguration, the mayor replaced him with Ricardo Diaz, director of a Hispanic community center, and let the facts speak for themselves.

Later in his mayoralty, Norquist was more explicit in communicating his concern for minority development: among other examples, he dropped all references to neigborhood development in his state of the city speech in 1990, and spoke instead of the need to promote minority businesses and jobs (*Milwaukee Journal*, Jan. 23, 1990). In a series of well-publicized meetings, he pushed banking executives to make more loans to minority home buyers and businesses (*Milwaukee Journal*, Feb. 26, 1991), and he began to speak with increasing frequency about the necessity to ensure that black Milwaukeeans enjoyed the same economic opportunities as whites (*Milwaukee Journal*, Apr. 28, 1991).

Milwaukee is a city where discrimination in housing, schools, union halls, apprenticeship programs, and business financing has a long, deep, and continuing history (Milwaukee Metropolitan Sewerage District 1990: chap. 8). Conflict between white ethnics and black Milwaukeeans over school desegregation, fair housing, and police behavior has been endemic. Thus, Norquist's initial impulse to cloak his agenda for minority development in the more inclusive embrace of neighborhood made good political sense. Casting his development agenda initially in racial terms would have risked exacerbating existing divisions.

Yet, in hindsight, Norquist's invocation of neighborhood objectives bespoke, perhaps, an excess of political caution. For one thing, from the outset he enjoyed business support for his efforts on behalf of minority development. To complement the city's initiatives in this area the major business organ in the city, the venerable Greater Milwaukee Committee, established an Inner City Task Force late in 1990 whose mission was to "explore the needs of the inner city from a business perspective and make recommendations or propose new initiatives that will tackle problems facing our central city" (Greater Milwaukee Committee 1990). The GMC task force's subcommittee on Jobs and Minority Business Development offered a set of recommendations in March 1991, which, among other things, called for including minority contracting, employment, or training opportunities in every major development project in the city (ibid. 1991).

A second factor that enabled the mayor to speak forcefully for minority development was the absence of vocal opposition either to any particular targeted program or to the more general concept of minority-targeted economic development. The white ethnic neighborhoods of the south side have been silent on this issue, and there have been no complaints from construction contractors or union officials. Resistance to minority business development has not been so much political as the product of well-established institutional patterns: banks, for example, are still reluctant lenders to minority entrepreneurs (*Milwaukee Journal*, Mar. 15, 1991) and minority vendors still have difficulty obtaining insurance and bonding. But as a plank in the city administration's political platform, minority development, it is fair to say, has not been particularly controversial.

Emergence of Targeted Local Development in American Cities

Although the effort to induce economic activity by stimulating private-sector investment through the use of public-sector authority and resources is now a virtually universal practice in U.S. cities, Milwaukee has been especially active in this regard. Nevertheless, Milwaukee's shift from a virtually exclusive preoccupation with downtown redevelopment to one that evinces a greater awareness of neighborhood and disadvantaged economic concerns is not uncommon in U.S. cities. Before examining the job effects of several of

Milwaukee's major initiatives, it is important, therefore, to set the city's efforts in this more general context.

In most cities the engine of municipal economic development efforts was set into motion in the two decades after World War II and typically took the form of a group of business elites and local government actors, loosely organized as a "growth machine" (Logan and Molotch 1987) or a "progrowth coalition" (Mollenkopf 1983). Fueled mainly by federal urban renewal money and local matching resources, the chief objectives of these growth coalitions were to create profitable opportunities for the owners of capital (Ferman 1989) and to enhance the local property tax base. Job generation, a secondary consideration, was assumed to occur through the trickle-down process.[5] The effort to create employment for particular disadvantaged groups was almost never a goal.

Distributive issues in economic development first became important during the 1960s, a trend that originated both in response to the civil rights movement's interest in employment and the growing neighborhood resistance to the clearance strategies of urban renewal programs.[6] In response to growing grass-roots discontent, most cities by the 1980s had not only made job creation an explicit goal of their increasingly numerous and complex capital subsidy programs but had, in the case of many initiatives, identified disadvantaged target populations as the principal intended beneficiaries.

A study by Carla Robinson (1989: 283–94) found that 108 of the 139 cities she surveyed in 1986 maintained some economic development initiatives that targeted disadvantaged workers or businesses. For example, 52 percent of Robinson's sample had programs that provided training or job set-asides for low-skilled workers, while slightly higher percentages did the same for low-income workers (64 percent) and minorities (62 percent). Seventy-eight percent said that assisting community-based organizations was very important or somewhat important. Only slightly over a fifth of the cities were still committed exclusively to a "corporate center" approach to development, which seeks primarily to improve the climate for downtown capital investment.

Cities have often believed that they had to tread a fine line in targeting disadvantaged groups for special attention. This is particularly the case where economic development involves redistributing municipal public resources from well-off taxpaying firms and households to the less well-off. Consider the fate of a so-called linkage program in Hartford, Connecticut. In the early 1980s neighborhood groups in that city sought passage of an ordinance that would require payments by downtown developers to a low-income development fund as a quid pro quo for the property tax abatements the developers enjoyed. But as a Hartford political columnist pointed out, "Make the linkage tax high enough, and commercial geese will find some suburban nest in which to lay their golden taxable eggs" (Neubeck and Ratcliff 1988: 316). Despite some political and business support for the idea, the city council never enacted a linkage requirement. In Hartford, as elsewhere, taxpayer mobility typically has tended to limit the degree to which a local government is willing to use revenues generated from its own sources for redistributive development.

The disciplining effect that capital and household mobility may have on municipal taxing and spending for the disadvantaged means that many cities are loathe to make direct expenditures of their own funds for development programs targeted to the disadvantaged. One way they have avoided the problem is to fund development programs with money from other governments. The Urban Development Action Grant (UDAG) is a case in point. No longer funded by Congress, the UDAG existed from 1978 to 1988 as a categorical grant to distressed localities to leverage private investment for a variety of development projects aimed at revitalizing the community by increasing employment and the tax base. Although localities were required to estimate the job impacts of the projects for which they sought grant monies, the U.S. Department of Housing and Urban Development (HUD) did not insist that recipients reserve employment for disadvantaged or minority workers.[7] Whatever employment targeting took place, then, actually occurred as local initiatives. Data compiled by HUD, however, suggest that substantial employment benefits did in fact go to those target groups.[8]

Despite its being discontinued, the UDAG has had a lasting impact beyond the first generation of 3,000 development projects. Cities have used the repayment of UDAG loans by businesses and developers to seed revolving loan funds, permitting them to broaden their development focus beyond the hotel and downtown office tower complexes that dominated the early UDAG funding rounds to subsidization of a more eclectic set of business undertakings. Many of these latter are small and minority-owned businesses that would not have qualified for original UDAG monies. The Milwaukee Economic Development Corporation, discussed later here, provides a case in point.

With the demise of the UDAG program, the most common source of outside funding for targeted economic development became the Community Development Block Grant (CDBG) program, also used by many cities to seed various revolving loan funds for small and disadvantaged businesses and to make modest grants. Milwaukee, as noted, uses some of its annual entitlement for these purposes.

Another common development initiative, the urban enterprise zone, is heavily subsidized by foregone state revenues. At least 36 states have passed such programs since the early 1980s (Eisinger 1988: 188–99; Wolff 1990). The basic form is similar from state to state: businesses locating, forming, or expanding in designated limited geographical areas exhibiting high levels of economic distress enjoy various special tax credits and other incentives. The most common incentives the zones offer are credits against state income and sales tax liability.

To encourage job creation, about half the state zone programs offer job tax credits against state income tax liability. In a few states, including Wisconsin, credits are available when a firm hires a member of a disadvantaged targeted group, including zone residents, AFDC recipients, Supplemental Security Income (SSI) recipients, and dislocated workers. Job creation effects in enterprise zones, particularly with respect to targeted categories of workers, tend to be modest. In 1990, the first year of the Wisconsin enterprise zone program, for example, administrators of the eight zones, scattered about the state, reported that they expected to create a total of 300 new jobs. Of these, 136 were to be filled by targeted workers. Only 64 of these had actually begun work by September 1990, of whom only 6 were black (Wisconsin Department of Development 1990).

In summary, even though some cities still use their economic development resources primarily to subsidize downtown development, it is now common for them also to require job set-asides for disadvantaged groups or to administer special incentives for their employment, particularly when they are able to use intergovernmental revenues or other forms of subsidy to fund such programs. Milwaukee exemplifies this pattern. The city's economic development efforts began by clearing the downtown through the urban renewal program, subsidizing industrial sites through a pioneering municipal land bank program, and providing capital and infrastructure subsidies for big downtown projects. In the last few years, however, the city has also put into place a broad array of innovative, targeted development initiatives, funded primarily with federal grants, to implement city hall's commitment to neighborhood and minority development. I now turn to the various city programs.

Milwaukee's Development Zones

Wisconsin's version of the urban enterprise zone program was enacted by the state legislature in 1987 and implemented two years later in 1989. Development zones are designed to encourage business investment in targeted geographical areas by offering an array of state tax incentives. The most important of these is the Targeted Jobs Tax Credit, equal to 40 percent of the first $6,000 in wages for the first two years of employment of each employee drawn from any one of several eligible categories, including, as previously noted, AFDC recipients, dislocated workers, and youth participating in summer education and training programs, such as Milwaukee's Step Up (see table 7.3). To emphasize its job creation objectives, the state requires that the Targeted Jobs Tax Credit account for 65 percent of the tax incentives any business receives.

Businesses that locate in a zone may also receive a state credit for the amount of sales taxes paid on building materials and equipment, an investment credit on depreciable property, and several others. The state has allocated $4.5 million in foregone revenues to be used over a 7- to 10-year period as incentives just in the three designated Milwaukee zones.

The city has also added several incentives of its own, the main one being special low-cost financing through the Milwaukee Economic Development Corporation's (MEDC) Development Zone Loan Program, established in 1990. In that year, the MEDC loaned nearly $2.5 million to 10 different businesses at below-market interest rates. In addition, the city has promulgated certain guidelines to ensure that businesses receiving tax credits will focus on the task of generating good jobs for local residents. To win city certification for state tax credits, existing businesses must increase their employment at their zone location by at least 20 percent. City guidelines also require that 25 percent of new employees in businesses receiving any public incentives must be zone residents. Furthermore, 80 percent of new employees must be city residents or have been unemployed from full-time work for 90 days. Finally, the only jobs the city will certify as eligible for wage tax credits are those that pay $1.20 above the minimum wage.

The job impacts of the development zone program are difficult to gauge. In the city's 1990 *Development Zone Annual Report*, data on job effects are presented in the future tense. Even by the relatively unconstrained standard of "anticipated jobs," the potential impacts of the program seem small. In 1990 the city certified 15 businesses as eligible for state tax credits. Of these, 8 are located in the two zones that encompass the virtually all-black neighborhoods of the near north side (the third zone, covering the port area and the near south side, is heavily Hispanic). These 8 businesses anticipated creating 125 new jobs, of which 87 were supposed to go to members of one of the targeted categories. The businesses committed them-selves to reserving only 52 of the new jobs for residents of the development zones themselves.

The city imposes no restrictions on the sorts of businesses that might qualify for tax credits, and thus the actual range of enterprises is broad. They include small machine shops, metal fabrication, precision machining, weaving, commercial cleaning, metal electroplating, and fast food operations. In the two heavily black development zones, the largest certified employer was a Popeye fried chicken restaurant, which created 66 new jobs. No other business had created more than 25 new jobs.

Businesses that do not qualify for the state tax credits may nevertheless be eligible for the earlier-mentioned MEDC Development Zone Loans. Of the nearly $2.5 million in loans made in the first round, 79 percent went to noncertified businesses, including $360,000 to two firms in the largely black zones. These two businesses reported creating a total of six new jobs.

The development zone program is likely to grow somewhat. At the end of 1990 at least 10 more businesses were seeking certification for state tax credits. Those located in the largely black neighborhoods projected creating 139 new jobs, about half of which would go to zone residents. But it is difficult to imagine that the scale of the program will increase significantly. Perhaps the most that can be said of the development zone program is that it affords the city leverage in its effort to encourage targeted hiring in the inner-city small business sector.

Milwaukee Economic Development Corporation

Originally established in 1971 as a component of Milwaukee's Model Cities program, the MEDC has become the principal financing arm of the city's economic development effort. By 1991 the corporation, staffed by employees of the municipal Department of City Development, had accumulated total assets of $47 million, of which $35 million had been invested since 1979 in 198 different companies.

A major portion of MEDC assets came initially from Urban Development Action Grants ($15.8 million), which the corporation then loaned out for designated HUD projects. Since UDAG monies once granted became the property of the city, as we have seen, loans repaid with interest by the original project recipients could then be used by the city to establish a revolving loan fund. The MEDC's loans have earned the corporation $17.4 million in interest. Other sources of funds have been the federal Community Development Block Grant ($740,000), federal Economic Development Administration grants ($800,000), tax increment financing bonds ($9.8 million, representing the chief purely local contribution), and borrowings ($2.5 million) (Corporate Report Wisconsin 1991: 23).

The MEDC makes subordinated loans for partial financing of fixed assets for businesses of all sizes for the purpose of locating or expanding in Milwaukee. The corporation manages seven different loan programs, of which two are targeted at disadvantaged and minority businesses. One is the Development Zone Loan Program, discussed previously. The second is the Minority and Women's Business Loan Program, a particularly flexible program, in that instead of limiting MEDC participation to 25 percent of the total project cost, the normal limit, this program provides up to 40 percent of the total cost. Furthermore, MEDC will finance not only fixed assets of minority and women-owned firms but also allow the loan to be used for working capital. Of a total of 230 loans made by MEDC between 1979 and the end of 1990 (sometimes more than one loan is made to a single company), 83 (totaling $3.9 million) have gone to female- and minority-owned firms. A disproportionate share (about a third) of these loans was made since the election of John Norquist in 1988.

MEDC does not require that its borrowers fulfill any affirmative action hiring requirements, but it does ask that they make good-faith attempts to expand their recruitment pool to include minorities and women. If a firm's labor force does not reflect the racial and gender breakdown of the hiring pool, then MEDC will offer to link the business with the state Job Service office as a means of identifying qualified minority and female applicants.

Prior to receiving MEDC financing, the 198 firms had employed a total of 7,634 people (memorandum from Patrick Walsh, MEDC president, to members and directors of MEDC, July 25, 1991).[9] Through the end of 1990, these same firms had increased their employment to 15,878 people, of whom 23 percent (3,652) were minorities. Although it is highly probable that all but a small proportion of these are black, MEDC has no data on the exact breakdown by minority group.[10]

Nor is there any way of knowing how many of these minority workers were among the 8,244 employees hired after the firms received MEDC financing, and we do not know how many work in the businesses that received loans specifically through one of the two specially targeted programs. We cannot therefore confidently estimate the effects on black employment of MEDC. It is worth noting, nevertheless, that our estimate of the proportion of black workers in all MEDC-financed firms (19.2 percent) is somewhat higher than the proportion of black workers in the employed labor force in the city (15 percent).

BLACK EMPLOYMENT IN THE PUBLIC SECTOR

For one reason or another—whether the exercise of sheer political power, the neutral operation of merit principles, or the application of nondiscrimination laws and affirmative action—the local public sector has historically been accessible to job seekers from disadvantaged groups to a degree unmatched by the private sector. There is much evidence to support this proposition. Erie (1988: 60), for example, has traced dramatic gains by Irish ethnics in city employment in the decades around the turn of the century, and Eisinger (1983: 7) has documented the disproportionate presence of blacks in municipal service in the 1970s. By some measures, Milwaukee blacks are overrepresented in the local public sector, and by any calculation they have greatly improved their representation in local government employment over time.

Table 7.4 provides a detailed occupational distribution of black employment in Milwaukee city government for 1986 and 1990.[11] To establish employment goals, the city initially used a ratio of percentage black in the various municipal work-force categories to percentage black in the city population, which I have called a *representation ratio*. This is a highly imperfect measure, since it necessarily ignores labor force participation, labor force qualifications, and the age structure of the population. Nevertheless, it provides a rough gauge by which to measure progress in the occupational distribution of blacks over time. In a later effort to calculate more precisely whether minority hiring patterns reflected minority labor force capacities, the Affirmative Action Office in the city Personnel Department carried out a work-force availability study that used black occupational data in the denominator instead of the black city population. This enabled the calculation of *utilization ratios* for 1990.[12]

The first thing to note about the data in table 7.4 is that the percentage of blacks in the employ of the city increased slightly in the second half of the 1980s, from 18.2 percent to 20.3 percent. (Black gains were in fact steady across the decade: in 1980 they comprised 16.1 percent of the municipal work force.)[13] The actual number of black

Table 7.4 BLACK REPRESENTATION IN MILWAUKEE'S MUNICIPAL WORK FORCE, 1986 AND 1990

	1986			1990			
	Number	Percentage	Representation Ratio[a]	Number	Percentage	Representation Ratio[a]	Utilization Ratio[b]
Administrators	14	(6.6)	.248	61	(12.4)	.408	.880
Professionals	143	(11.9)	.447	130	(14.5)	.477	1.196
Technicians	49	(11.2)	.421	42	(11.4)	.375	.984
Paraprofessionals	25	(34.7)	1.470	22	(32.4)	1.070	1.312
Police	225	(11.4)	.428	217	(11.9)	.395	N.A.
Fire	146	(14.1)	.530	131	(12.7)	.422	N.A.
Office/clerical	158	(19.6)	.736	185	(23.8)	.782	1.059
Skilled craft	100	(16.6)	.725	95	(17.7)	.582	.864
Service/maintenance	411	(30.4)	1.140	388	(29.4)	.967	1.055
Total	1,271	(18.2)	.684	1,271	(20.3)	.674	—

Note: N.A., data not available.

a. Representation ratios for 1986 are based on a prorated percentage black for that year; see also text.

b. Utilization ratios are calculated by the city on the basis of black occupational availability; see also text.

employees held even between 1986 and 1990, despite a reduction
in the city work force of nearly 400 positions, indicating that black
workers were not subject to a pernicious "last hired, first fired"
policy. The data show that the percentage black increased in nearly
every job category, except for paraprofessionals, service workers, and
firefighters. Note the particularly striking gains in the "Administrators" category in the table. In 1980, incidentally, blacks comprised
only 2.7 percent of workers in this classification.

Table 7.4 furthermore reveals that blacks lost positions in most of
the middle- and solid-working-class occupations. Fewer blacks were
working in 1990 as city professionals, technicians, police officers,
and firefighters. Gains, however, were recorded in clerical jobs, where
pay scales, though higher than for comparable work in the private
sector, nevertheless generate relatively low incomes. The declines
in the two protective service occupations are surprising. Since 1975
the Police Department has been under a consent decree in which the
federal court ordered the department to hire two blacks for every
three whites. A similar consent decree for the Fire Department has
since been lifted.

A third finding in table 7.4 is that the total number of blacks
employed by the city is actually relatively small. Given the Bureau of
Labor Statistics estimate that 12,000 blacks are unemployed (author's
interview with BLS official, 2/22/91), then the size of the total black
labor force would be about 60,000, of whom 48,000 currently hold
jobs. Black municipal workers, therefore, comprise only about 2.1
percent of that labor force, and about 2.6 percent of those blacks
currently employed.

A final observation regarding table 7.4 is that despite black percentage gains in the municipal work force, blacks lost ground slightly
when measured against their presence in the population. The representation ratio declined from .684 in 1986 to .674 in 1990. Blacks
were underrepresented by this standard in every occupational category except in the small paraprofessional class. They were close to
parity in service and maintenance jobs and clerical work. The situation improves, however, if the measure is the city's utilization ratio,
based on a calculation of work-force availability. By this gauge, Milwaukee blacks are employed close to or above parity in every occupational category for which utilization ratios were estimated.

City government is not the only, nor even the main, source of
public-sector work for black Milwaukeeans. Milwaukee County government employs nearly twice as many blacks as does the city, as
shown in table 7.5. The 195,470 blacks who lived in the county in

Table 7.5 BLACK EMPLOYMENT IN MILWAUKEE COUNTY GOVERNMENT, 1987 AND 1991

| | 1987 | | 1991 | | Representation |
	Number	Percentage	Number	Percentage	Ratio[a]
Administrators	32	(8.7)	43	(12.6)	.621
Professionals	263	(10.5)	291	(10.9)	.567
Technical	136	(21.9)	122	(21.9)	1.107
Paraprofessional	512	(48.3)	715	(58.6)	2.887
Clerical	463	(25.7)	498	(29.3)	1.443
Skilled	20	(9.2)	20	(9.5)	.468
Service	557	(25.1)	520	(29.1)	1.433
Protective	100	(15.7)	145	(20.9)	1.030
Total	2,083	(22)	2,354	(25.6)	

a. Representation ratio is calculated as percentage of blacks in the particular occupational category divided by percentage black in the county population (20.3 percent).

1990 comprised 20.3 percent of the total population, although all but 4,000 of them lived inside the central city.

Unlike the city government, Milwaukee County government has expanded significantly in the last several years. Whereas the county employed a total of 7,806 full-time workers in 1986, the number grew to 8,966 in 1987 and then to 9,196 by March 1991. Idiosyncracies in the county's data-reporting procedures permitted an analysis of growth in black employment only from 1987 onward. The rate of increase in total county government employment (2.6 percent) is far lower than the rate of increase in black employment in the county government (13 percent).

The county has not performed any work-force availability studies; I thus had to rely on a population-based representation ratio to gauge black access to the county work force. By this measure blacks were solidly overrepresented in the total work force and in five of the eight job categories.

A third source of public employment for black Milwaukeeans is the Milwaukee Public School District. As table 7.6 shows, the district employs over 2,000 blacks, more than half of whom are teachers. Although the percentage black in the teaching corps has declined slightly since 1985, the proportion black at the administrative level has risen significantly. Overall, black employment was slightly greater in 1990 than in the mid-1980s.

In sum, more than 5,600 blacks are employed by the city, county, and school district. This amounts to about 9.4 percent of the available black labor force, and 11.8 percent of those actually employed. It is

Table 7.6 BLACK EMPLOYMENT IN MILWAUKEE PUBLIC SCHOOL SYSTEM,
1985 AND 1990

	1985		1990	
	Number	Percentage	Number	Percentage
Administrators[a]	106	(34.5%)	121	(37.3%)
Teachers	984	(18.5%)	1,041	(17.8%)
Professionals[b]	132	(16.1%)	161	(18.9%)
Other[c]	620	(27.8%)	715	(30.9%)
Total	1,842	(21.3%)	2,038	(21.8%)

a. Includes principals, assistant principals, and central administration.
b. Includes librarians, psychologists, and guidance counselors.
c. Includes clerical, service, maintenance, and teacher aides.

interesting to compare these figures to those for the Irish at the turn
of the century. Like contemporary blacks, the Irish found it easier to
penetrate the public sector than the private business world. Many
argue that municipal jobs served as a springboard for the Irish in
their rise from poverty (e.g., Clark 1975).[14] In 1900 at the beginning
of Irish political ascendancy, 5.6 percent of the Irish work force in
the 8 most heavily Irish cities were municipal workers. In another
set of 14 cities (over 50,000 people but with less than 13 percent
Irish), the municipal work force on average employed 7.5 percent of
the Irish work force (Erie 1988: 60). Erie does not include county
employment in his analysis (counties had not yet become the highly
diversified and large local government units they are today). Excluding black employees of Milwaukee County for purposes of historical
comparison, the city and the school district account for 5.5 percent
of the local black labor force, a figure nearly identical to that found
for the Irish in heavily Irish cities at the turn of the century.

CITY CONTRACTING WITH MINORITY
BUSINESS ENTERPRISES

Minority-owned firms in Wisconsin, as elsewhere, have historically
found it difficult to breach the well-guarded barriers surrounding the
lucrative world of city contracts (Bates 1993). To some degree the
problem has lain with the underdevelopment of the minority business community itself: there have simply been too few qualified
firms to compete for public business. An analysis by the Governor's
Committee on Minority Business based on 1980 Census data found

that minorities, although 6 percent of the state's population, owned only 1.3 percent of the state's businesses. They employed less than two-tenths of 1 percent of the state's workers. Fully 82 percent of these businesses had no paid employees, and their average annual sales in 1982 amounted only to around $43,000 (Governor's Committee on Minority Business 1988).

Wisconsin's situation was not unlike that of numerous other states whose public jurisdictions were reluctant either to serve as a stable customer base or to take responsibility for fostering minority business development through training, information, and mentoring efforts. In the 1970s many local governments, particularly those led by the first wave of black mayors, began to establish set-aside programs in which a certain percentage of the city's business was reserved for minority-owned enterprises (Eisinger 1984: 249–60). The assumption behind these programs, of course, was that the steady custom provided by the city would enable minority businesses to grow in strength and size, creating in turn employment opportunities for minority workers.

This practice began to spread, and by 1987, according to a survey by the National Institute of Governmental Purchasing, 52 percent of localities responding had some sort of program to assist minority businesses, and 24 percent had modified their purchasing policies and practices to ensure that minority firms received a share of city contracts (in MacManus 1990: 455–73). Bowman's (1987) study turned up corroborating evidence: of the 322 cities that responded to her 1987 survey for the National League of Cities, slightly over 24 percent targeted minority business development in some way.

In 1986 the Milwaukee city council formalized its commitment to using the procurement process for minority business development by passing a set-aside program, Chapter 360, that established voluntary goals for doing business with minority enterprises.[15] Then in 1989 the U.S. Supreme Court ruled in *City of Richmond v. Croson* (109 S. Ct. 706) that Richmond's 30 percent set-aside of municipal business for minority firms was not narrowly tailored to remedy particular discriminatory practices. The Court found that a generalized finding of societal discrimination was insufficient to justify a racial classification to constrain the procurement process. In the wake of *Croson*, Milwaukee modified its Chapter 360 program by establishing goals for *disadvantaged* business enterprises.[16] The program is designed to be race and gender neutral. At the same time Mayor Norquist, who in 1988 had moved the Equal Opportunities Enterprise Program (EOEP) into the mayor's office, reiterated the city's commitment to

Table 7.7 CITY CONTRACTING WITH DISADVANTAGED BUSINESS
ENTERPRISES, 1988–90

	1988	1989	1990
Purchasing Department	$780,339 (2.0%)	$1,092,642 (2.8%)	N.A.
Department of Public Works	$3,921,435 (13.6%)	$4,031,919 (12.3%)	$6,537,562 (17.0%)
Department of Community Development	$3,468,861 (15.8%)	$522,666 (8.0%)	N.A.

Source: Data from Equal Opportunities Enterprise Program, Office of the Mayor, Milwaukee.
Note: N.A., data not available.

enhancing the development of disadvantaged businesses. As the EOEP *1988 Annual Report* stated: "The City of Milwaukee supports the belief that nurturing disadvantaged and small businesses will benefit the economy of the City of Milwaukee and increase employment opportunities" (City of Milwaukee n.d.).[17]

Table 7.7 provides data from 1988 to 1990 on the percentage of city contract dollars that go to Disadvantaged Business Enterprises (DBEs). As cited in the table, the departments of Purchasing, Public Works, and Community Development are responsible for the overwhelming bulk of city procurement. Data that disaggregate contracts by ethnic group and gender of the owner are not available, although in 1989 the Department of Public Works did separate out female-owned businesses.[18] These latter accounted for only 9 percent of the more than $4 million in DBE contracts reported in table 7.7 in that year. Some of the female entrepreneurs are no doubt black. We also know that only one out of six of the large minority-owned firms in Milwaukee is Hispanic-owned. Thus, it is relatively safe to assume that most minority-owned DBEs have black proprietors.

Several things should be noted about table 7.7. First, spending by the Department of Community Development, particularly for housing rehabilitation and maintenance, fluctuates as a consequence of project and grant cycles. Much of the department's activity is funded by federal grants that do not provide a steady or predictable flow of monies from year to year.

Second, DBEs have clearly had a difficult time participating significantly in purchasing operations (see table 7.7). The Purchasing Department spends nearly $40 million a year in procuring goods and services for a range of city departments. A major barrier to increased participation by DBEs is that out of the 400 or so Milwaukee-area businesses certified as disadvantaged, only 120 sell commodities. Of these, 108 operate only on a retail basis. As the *1988 Annual Report* of the EOEP noted: "It is difficult for disadvantaged businesses to compete with distribution and manufacturing level companies in formal and informal bids. In addition, substantial monies— $8,000,000 to $10,000,000—was [sic] expended in 1988 on commodities for which there are no certified minority or women businesses" (City of Milwaukee n.d.).

A third point related to table 7.7 is that disadvantaged businesses participate most extensively in public works contracts. Bridge painting, snowplowing, street repairs, landscaping, and roof repairs are examples of public works projects.

Finally, the EOEP does not collect data on the employment effects of city contracting. There is no way, short of surveying the vendors themselves, of determining whether city contracts generated employment and whether the businesses hired minority workers. The city is seeking, however, to link city contracting and targeted employment through a residents' preference program. In the spring of 1991 the city council passed an ordinance that reserves 14 percent of all worker hours on city-funded public works projects for unemployed residents of the Special Impact Area Census tracts, high-poverty neighborhoods so designated by the federal Economic Development Administration. The rationale for the particular percentage was the finding that 36 percent of all workers on public works projects are currently city residents; the 14 percent set-aside in addition was designed to bring public works labor crews up to 50 percent city residents.

The city maintains a number of programs to facilitate disadvantaged business participation in city contracts. The oldest, from 1985, is a revolving loan fund for DBEs that have already won city contracts. Initially capitalized with federal Community Development Block Grant money, the fund makes fewer than half a dozen small loans (averaging $25,000) each year.

Several more-recently created programs include a Contractor Development Training Program (1990)—as a supplement to regular orientation programs for DBEs—and commitment of $500,000 in city funds to establish a Performance Bond Program (1991). Both programs were initiated in response to complaints voiced by black business owners (*Milwaukee Sentinel*, Dec. 26, 1988).

CONCLUSIONS

Let us return to the central question underlying this chapter: can local governments generate significant opportunities for their minority citizens? The answer is a qualified yes. They can do so both through the application of affirmative action principles in public employment and through public subsidies and contracts with firms that are likely to hire minority workers.

Local jurisdictions—municipal and county governments and school districts—are, of course, limited governments with respect to their revenue sources and formal powers. In addition, they are subject to the discipline of market forces that may stimulate outmigration of tax-paying firms and residents to locales that offer more favorable mixes of tax and spending policies. Thus, a local government cannot, for example, become an employer of last resort when the private sector has no jobs.

If some policies, such as full employment through public-sector work, are essentially unthinkable, so too must local government contend with forces beyond its control or influence. The city of Milwaukee can do nothing, for example, to change the fundamental restructuring process, understood as a shift in economic activity from centralized manufacturing activities to decentralized service occupations. Nor can it influence the value of the dollar against foreign currencies, thus affecting the scope of opportunities for local exporting firms.

Yet even given these constraints, local governments can both create and influence substantial employment opportunities for minorities. Take, for example, the number of public-sector jobs in the city, county, and school district, along with jobs that firms have added after they received public subsidies through the Development Zone program or the Milwaukee Economic Development Corporation. (This is not to claim that the economic development programs necessarily created minority jobs that would not have been generated otherwise, but it is fair to give the city government some credit at least for influencing firm expansion or formation through public subsidies.) The total comes to approximately 8,400.

This figure amounts to more than 17.5 percent of all employed blacks in the city of Milwaukee, a not insignificant proportion. In fact, the amount is slightly on the conservative side of our estimate of local government influence on employment opportunities, since one could add to this the blacks employed in Disadvantaged Business

Firms because those firms contract with city government, a sum not calculated by the city, as well as blacks employed in firms that do business with the county and the school district.[19] Furthermore, I made no attempt to calculate multiplier effects or indirect job creation as a function of these 8,400 jobs.

White workers are not as dependent on government employment or government subsidies. Adding the total number of whites in public employment and in firms located in Development Zones or financed by MEDC yields a figure of 31,500, approximately 11.6 percent of the employed white work force in Milwaukee.

Local governments, then, are important determinants of the structure of black employment opportunities. But are their resources sufficient to the task? And what are the prospects for the future?

Local governments operate under at least two significant constraints that undercut their ability to generate or influence substantial additional employment opportunities. One is that for a variety of reasons the private sector is an unreliable producer of minority jobs. The second is that the federal resources that have provided city economic development programs with leverage in the marketplace have dried up or diminished. Neither local governments nor the state have the resources to expand economic development efforts significantly, or even to replace those lost federal funds. Let us examine these two limitations.

One problem with the first limitation—private sector vis-à-vis minority employment opportunities—is that the sector is not growing nearly so fast as the minority population.[20] But beyond this obvious constraint, it is clear that blacks must still contend with widespread job discrimination in seeking private employment, particularly for entry-level positions (Turner, Fix, and Struyk 1991).

Where the public sector provides subsidies to private firms in the form of low-interest capital or other economic development assistance, it might be expected that it could or would exact as a quid pro quo some sort of affirmative action commitment. But in a recent report of the Milwaukee Black Community Relief Task Force, appointed by the city council, leaders of the city's black community contended that "the city of Milwaukee has not done an efficient job in actually enforcing minority employment goals by companies that utilize various City controlled federal, state and local funds for expansion purposes or other economic development purposes" (Milwaukee City Council n.d.). The charge applies specifically to large-scale projects that have operated with city assistance. As noted, the Milwaukee Economic Development Corporation simply asks firms that receive city loans to make a good-faith effort to hire minorities. According to a staff member for the Milwaukee Black Community Relief Task Force, "the perception of the Department of City Development in the black community is not very good. It's seen as a power unto itself. It's hard for minorities to influence its contracting and operations" (interview with Eisinger, March 25, 1991).[21]

Where the city targets assistance or contracts to disadvantaged firms in particular, which may be expected to hire predominantly minority workers, the problem is that most of these are small operations. Although some may use city contracts or city financing as a springboard for expansion (a few success stories are always reported in agency annual reports), many of these firms remain small and operate at the margins of profitability. Building a solid economic base for minority employment on the backs of small business is fraught with risk and instability.

One clear policy implication of the city's necessary reliance on the private sector as the major source of minority job opportunities is to exact a contractual commitment from firms to hire from targeted groups as a condition of city assistance. Local governments cannot rely mainly on good-faith efforts and modest hiring incentives.

The second major limitation on local governments' ability to generate jobs for minorities is that the flow of federal dollars has significantly diminished. Although there is no evidence to indicate that Milwaukee was better able during the peak period of fiscal federalism in the 1970s to influence the job prospects of minorities, the fact is that programs such as the Comprehensive Employment and Training Act, the Urban Development Action Grant, the Economic Development Administration's Title IX grants, and CDBG underwrote significant employment both in the public and private sectors. If such funds were still available, then it is likely, given the sympathetic administration of Mayor Norquist, that city efforts to address minority job opportunities would be that much more richly funded.[22]

Of the federal programs just cited, only the CDBG still exists. Milwaukee's CDBG entitlement, however, declined from about $20 million annually in the late 1980s to $14 million in 1991. Given the constraints that Milwaukee—and indeed any city—faces in spending own-source revenues for targeted economic development, the loss of intergovernmental revenues makes an expanding—and even continuing—commitment to minorities and neighborhoods a potentially fragile proposition. Yet Milwaukee continues to add programs for this purpose, and its mayor is increasingly outspoken on behalf of the city's minorities. This suggests that if Milwaukee's fiscal resources are not wholly adequate to the task, at least its political impulses provide a supportive context for public efforts to create minority economic opportunities.

Notes

1. The best summary of these programs and experiments is contained in the City of Milwaukee's *Report to the Community: Action for Goals 2000* (1991). In addition to the various city programs noted in the *Goals 2000* report, it is important to mention the New Hope project. This experimental program, to be funded in the amount of $15.5 million by a partnership of the private sector, state and local government, and the nonprofit sector, is designed to offer 600 unemployed, underemployed, or welfare-dependent people in targeted inner-city neighborhoods an alternative to welfare by guaranteeing them a job at a reasonable rate (using wage supplements, where necessary), child care support, health care, and personal counseling. Fund-raising is currently underway, spearheaded by the downtown business organization, the Greater Milwaukee Committee, and the Congress for a Working America.

2. Sammis White has collected annual manufacturing data based on state unemployment compensation files. His data show 19.5 percent of the population was engaged in manufacturing in 1990 (unpublished data, Urban Research Center, University of Wisconsin-Milwaukee).

3. Although a "sea change" in terms of sharp differences in approach to politics and to policy, the Maier-Norquist change was not a sea change in terms of political party or ethnic group. Both mayors were white males, both were Democrats, and both were elected primarily by white voters. For an analysis of Maier's electoral strategy see Eisinger (1976) and Maier (1993).

4. On Chief Brier and the black community, see Laura Woliver (1990).

5. The federal Urban Renewal Administration collected no data on the employment effects of the $13.2 billion it spent over the life of the program, although the impact of the program on urban tax bases and the leveraging effects on private investment are carefully recorded. See U.S. Department of Housing and Urban Development (1974, 1975).

6. For a critique of the impact of the urban renewal program on the poor, minorities, and the working class of New Haven, Connecticut, see Norman and Susan Fainstein (1983: 27–79).

7. In selecting among competing projects, HUD did consider the impact of the project on low- and moderate-income persons and minorities, including employment, housing, and training opportunities. This was one of nearly a dozen selection criteria, however.

8. Minority workers received 27.2 percent of the roughly 350,000 new permanent jobs created by UDAG projects, and minority-owned firms won 18 percent of all contracts (and 9 percent of dollars) in the program (HUD 1989: 60–61).

9. The MEDC does not disaggregate these data by size of firm, race or gender of owner, or date of the original loan. Neither does MEDC have data on the before-and-after racial composition of the borrowers' work forces.

10. Hispanics comprise 6.3 percent of Milwaukee's population, about one-fifth the size of the black population. If we assume for the sake of argument that Hispanics

are represented among minority workers in proportion to their presence in the population, then slightly over 600 of the 3,652 workers are probably Hispanic. This would indicate that 19.2 percent of all workers in MEDC-financed firms are black.

11. Data availability restricted the choice of a baseline date. My chief concern was to establish a benchmark prior to the 1988 election of the current mayor, John Norquist, regarded as much friendlier to minority interests than his predecessor, Henry Maier.

12. Specifically, work-force availability was determined by the city by examining both the racial composition of the potential "feeder" occupations within the city government from which promotions or transfers would be made as well as the racial composition of the relevant occupational groups in the city (or, for the highest-level occupational categories, in the nation). The utilization ratio, then, is the percentage of blacks employed in the city job category over the city's weighted average of the percentage of blacks available in the internal and external labor pools.

13. Figures for 1980 are from Eisinger (1983).

14. Erie (1988) opposed this view, pointing out that the number of jobs was too small and that too many jobs were low-paid. Public-sector work today, however, is different. For one thing, it tends to pay better than the private sector in the low- and moderate-skilled occupations. In addition, in contrast to turn-of-the century municipal employment, public employment offers a high degree of job security and extensive benefits, including health insurance. I would suggest that all things being equal, the mobility implications for modern blacks of public employment are greater than were those for their Irish counterparts a century ago.

15. Mayor Maier had originally vetoed a minority business set-aside ordinance in 1985, prompting the resignation of the city's minority business enterprise coordinator.

16. Milwaukee's effort to modify its policy was unusual. Most other jurisdictions, including Denver, Fort Lauderdale, South Bend, Minneapolis, Durham, and the state of Colorado voluntarily suspended their set-aside programs altogether. For a list of voluntary terminations and other adaptations, see Joshi (1990: 4).

17. Minority small businesses do tend to hire mainly minority workers (see Bates and Durham 1991).

18. Data in table 7.7 do not reflect this disaggregation.

19. The number of minority jobs supported by city contracts alone probably amounts to no more than 200. There is no rule of thumb for estimating the dollar amount of sales in a domestic small generic firm necessary to generate one additional job. My figure is based on U.S. Department of Commerce estimates that one job is created for every $40,000 in export business. If total city spending with minority firms in 1990 comes to $8 million, then using the same standard for domestic sales as for foreign yields a figure of 200 jobs. Data for DBE contracting with the school district were not available, although the county did release data. Since 1987, county purchases from DBEs have ranged from about $860,000 to $1.6 million per year, or slightly over 3 percent, on average, of county purchases. Other data were not available.

20. An analysis by the nonprofit Social Development Commission in Milwaukee indicated that the Milwaukee economy simply is not producing enough jobs for all those who want to work. Between 1988 and 1990, according to the commission, there were between 6.3 and 12.1 times the number of job seekers as there were available jobs (Social Development Commission 1991).

21. A black member of the city council expressed similar views (interview with Eisinger, March 25, 1991).

22. It is possible, of course, that the Clinton administration empowerment zone and enterprise cities programs may provide modest resources for Milwaukee, but the dimensions and location of these initiatives are, at this writing, still unknown.

References

Bailey, Jeff. 1990. "As Economy Falters, Old Industrial City of Milwaukee Shines." *Wall Street Journal*, November 29.

Bates, Timothy. 1993. *Banking on Black Enterprise*. Washington, D.C.: Joint Center for Political and Economic Studies.

Bates, Timothy, and Constance Dunham. 1991. "The Changing Nature of Business Ownership as a Route to Upward Mobility for Minorities." Paper presented at the "Conference on Urban Labor Markets and Labor Mobility," sponsored by The Urban Institute, Airlie, Va., March 7–8.

Bernard, Richard. 1990. "The Death and Life of a Midwestern Metropolis." In *Snowbelt Cities*, edited by Richard Bernard. Bloomington: Indiana University Press.

Bowman, Ann. 1987. *Tools and Targets: The Mechanics of City Economic Development*. Research report of the National League of Cities. Washington, D.C.: National League of Cities.

City of Milwaukee. n.d. *1988 Annual Report*. Equal Opportunities Enterprise Program. Milwaukee: Author.

————. 1990. *Development Zones Annual Report*. Milwaukee: Dept. of City Development.

————. 1991. *Report to the Community: Action for Goals 2000*. Milwaukee: Office of the Mayor, April 10.

Clark, Terry. 1975. "The Irish Ethic and the Spirit of Patronage." *Ethnicity* 2: 305–59.

Corporate Report Wisconsin. 1991. "Central City Milwaukee." February: 23.

Eisinger, Peter. 1976. *The Patterns of Interracial Politics*. New York: Academic Press.

————. 1983. *Black Employment in City Government, 1973–1980*. Washington, D.C.: Joint Center for Political Studies.

————. 1984. "Black Mayors and the Politics of Racial Economic Advancement." In *Readings in Urban Politics*, edited by Harlan Hahn and Charles Levine. New York: Longman.

————. 1988. *The Rise of the Enterpreneurial State*. Madison: University of Wisconsin Press.

Erie, Steven. 1988. *Rainbow's End*. Berkeley: University of California Press.

Fainstein, Susan, Norman Fainstein, Richard Child Hill, Dennis Judd, and Michael Peter Smith. 1983. *Restructuring the City*. New York: Longman.

Ferman, Barbara. 1989. "Democracy Under Fire: The Politics of Economic Restructuring in Pittsburgh and Chicago." Paper presented at the annual meeting of the American Political Science Association, Atlanta, August 31–September 3.

Governor's Committee on Minority Business. 1988. *The Wisconsin Chal-*

lenge: A Report on Minority Business Development. Madison: Author, September.

Greater Milwaukee Committee, Inner City Task Force. 1990. *Mission Statement.* Milwaukee: Author, December.

————. 1991. *Problem Statement.* Jobs and Minority Business Development Subcommittee. Milwaukee: Author, March.

Harrington, Michael. 1963. *The Other America.* Baltimore: Penguin.

Joshi, Pamela. 1990. "After *Croson*: New Directions for Minority Business Set-Asides." *Focus* 18 (October): 4.

Logan, John, and Harvey Molotch. 1987. *Urban Fortunes: The Political Economy of Place.* Berkeley: University of California Press.

MacManus, Susan. 1990. "Minority Business Contracting with Local Government." *Urban Affairs Quarterly* 25 (March): 455–73.

Maier, Henry. 1993. *The Mayor Who Made Milwaukee Famous: An Autobiography.* Lanham, Md.: Madison Books.

Marchetti, Peter. 1980. "Runaways and Takeovers: Their Effect on Milwaukee's Economy." *Urbanism Past and Present* 5 (Summer): 2.

McNeely, R. L., and M. R. Kinlow. 1988. *Milwaukee Today: A Racial Gap Study.* Milwaukee: Milwaukee Urban League.

Milwaukee City Council. n.d. "Recommendations of the Economic Development Committee of the Black Community Relief Task Force." Milwaukee: Author. Photocopy.

Milwaukee Metropolitan Sewerage District. 1990. *A Study to Identify Discriminatory Practices in the Milwaukee Construction Marketplace.* Milwaukee: Conta and Associates, February.

Mollenkopf, John H. 1983. *The Contested City.* Princeton, N.J. Princeton University Press.

Neubeck, Kenneth, and Richard Ratcliff. 1988. "Urban Democracy and the Power of Corporate Capital: Struggles over Downtown Growth and Neighborhood Stagnation in Hartford, Connecticut." In *Business Elites and Urban Development*, edited by Scott Cummings. Albany: State University of New York Press.

O'Hare, William. 1986. "The Best Metros for Blacks." *American Demographics* (July): 26–33.

Robinson, Carla Jean. 1989. "Municipal Approaches to Economic Development." *Journal of the American Planning Association* 55 (Summer): 283–94.

Social Development Commission. 1991. "Expected to Work but No Jobs: Job Availability in Milwaukee." Milwaukee: Author. Photocopy.

Turner, Margery Austin, Michael Fix, and Raymond Struyk. 1991. *Opportunities Denied, Opportunities Diminished: Racial Discrimination in Hiring.* Washington, D.C.: Urban Institute Press.

U.S. Department of Housing and Urban Development. 1974. *Urban Renewal Directory.* Washington, D.C.: U.S. Government Printing Office.

————. 1975. *Statistical Yearbook.* Washington, D.C.: U.S. Government Printing Office.

————. 1989. *Report to Congress on Community Development Programs, 1989.* Washington, D.C.; U.S. Government Printing Office.

White, Sammis, Peter Reynolds, William McMahon, and James Paetsch. 1989. "City and Suburban Impacts of the Industrial Changes in Milwaukee, 1979–87." Urban Research Center, University of Wisconsin-Milwaukee. Photocopy, July 5.

Wisconsin Department of Development. 1990. *Wisconsin Development Zone Program.* Annual Report. Madison: Author.

Wolff, Michael Allan. 1990. "Enterprise Zones: A Decade of Diversity." In *Financing Economic Development,* edited by Richard Bingham, Edward Hill, and Sammis White (123–41). Newbury Park, Calif.: Sage Publications.

Woliver, Laura. 1990. "A Measure of Justice: Police Conduct and Black Civil Rights, the Coalition for Justice for Ernest Lacy." *Western Political Quarterly* 43 (June): 415–436.

Chapter Eight

CITIZEN PARTICIPATION IN URBAN POLITICS: RISE AND ROUTINIZATION

Christopher Howard, Michael Lipsky, and Dale Rogers Marshall

"Citizen participation" has been a rallying cry in urban politics since the mid-1960s. Meaning different things to different groups in different contexts at different times, this term has nevertheless been important over the last quarter century in shaping expectations and actions. Calls for citizen participation are much less prominent, however, in the current era. This silence may be due in part to the growing awareness of the intractability of urban poverty, especially among racial minorities, and to the absence of debate concerning the plight of American cities—crises that have become perversely symbiotic.

This chapter examines that paradox by summarizing the recent history of citizen participation by disadvantaged groups in urban politics. Despite seemingly dim prospects for improvement, disadvantaged groups in urban areas do have political resources that were unavailable to them 25 years ago. We need to understand better the development of these resources to appreciate their strengths and limitations. We also need to examine avenues of political participation that may have been neglected or driven underground.

Our collective experience and reading of the literature suggest strongly that citizens have participated in urban politics over the last quarter century in ways fundamentally different from those of the preceding era. One of the most profound changes has been the emergence and incorporation of new actors—blacks, Latinos, and the poor. One could also highlight important developments in citizen participation by white middle-income communities. However, our focus here is on the incorporation of disadvantaged groups in urban politics.

The first and most general aim of this chapter, then, is to describe that process of incorporation. The civil rights movement and its legacy constitute a central theme. So, too, does the role of the national government, since it has historically been more responsive to the demands of disadvantaged groups than have state and local govern-

ments.[1] As disadvantaged groups demanded a more favorable distribution of political power and public services during the 1960s,
"urban politics" ceased to be the sole province of urban governments.
The national government became increasingly involved in urban
politics, but its involvement was frequently mediated by state and
local officials. The tremendous growth of federal programs during
the 1960s and 1970s, many of which were administered by urban
authorities, and the evolution of federal requirements for citizen
participation receive close attention here.

The history of grass-roots protest and of government programs are
by no means separate developments. Their frequent convergence is
an important part of the story. The second aim of this chapter, therefore, is to understand the effects of this history on the avenues of
political participation currently available to disadvantaged groups.

We contend that over the last quarter century, there has been a
pattern of expansion followed by routinization of citizen participation in urban politics. During the 1960s, groups of disadvantaged
citizens, aided for a brief but important moment by the national
government, enlarged avenues of participation in urban politics.
Their efforts resulted in a significant expansion of formal requirements for citizen participation in many areas of public policy. As a
result, ordinary citizens now enjoy greater access to urban policymaking than they did in the 1950s. Nonetheless, as the politics that led
to this expansion died down in the late 1960s and early 1970s, these
avenues became routinized. By "routinization" we mean, first, that
as citizen participation in urban politics became incorporated in law
and in practice, it became more commonplace, more routine. The
second dimension of routinization was that of increasing predictabil-
ity in the timing, process, and content of citizen participation—a
narrowing of its scope and impact. As participation became more
prevalent, it also became more limited.

As citizens gained new opportunities for participation in the 1960s,
principally in bureaucracies or via administrative procedures, they
were, in turn, expected by local officials to use those avenues and
not others. Disadvantaged groups experienced the limitations of routinized modes of participation more than others because they had
depended more upon disruption—and the threat of disruption—to
achieve their objectives. The difficulties of sustaining nontraditional
forms of participation and of achieving substantial political change
through routinized modes of participation contributed to the search
by disadvantaged groups for alternative forms of expression during
the 1970s and 1980s.

We furthermore argue that a second major development arose in part as a reaction to the routinization of participation. New modes of participation have been used by disadvantaged groups, as they discovered the limitations of administrative politics. We identify and discuss three modes: electoral politics, direct action by such groups as tenant organizations, and the development of alternative institutions. Whatever the initial potential of these modes to reshape urban politics, these, too, became routinized, largely as a result of changes in the urban political economy during the 1980s and early 1990s. Economic constraints, coupled with the growing diversity of disadvantaged groups, and at times their direct competition with each other, have extended the time lag between political empowerment and tangible benefits in the lives of many urban blacks, Latinos, and poor people. As a result, the promise of alternative modes of participation has yet to be realized.[2]

If our arguments about fundamental change in citizen participation are to have force, however, they need to be juxtaposed with what went before. To establish a baseline, we begin with an impressionistic portrait of citizen participation in the 1950s. Many of the characterizations of this era will be familiar, but are nonetheless important for the purposes here. We then describe the various ways in which new actors have emerged and have been incorporated over the past quarter century. We conclude by considering how these changes may shape the future course of urban politics.

CITIZEN PARTICIPATION IN THE 1950s

Political participation in the 1950s occurred primarily in two arenas: elections and voluntary organizations. In both cases, participation was skewed toward the more affluent. Most citizens limited their participation to electoral politics—principally to voting and to a lesser extent to working in campaigns—although a sizable fraction of the electorate did not vote at all. Participation rates correlated closely with levels of formal education and income. Racial and ethnic minorities and the poor were less politically active than other groups. As of 1960 there were no black or Latino mayors of cities with populations greater than 50,000. Minorities were better represented on city councils, but were often excluded from their governing coalitions (Banfield and Wilson 1963; Browning, Marshall, and Tabb 1986; Milbrath 1965; Nie, Verba, and Petrocik 1979).

After electoral politics, voluntary community service organizations were the most important avenue of participation in urban politics. At the local level, voluntary organizations replaced public office as a primary source of status for upper- and middle-income groups over the course of the 20th century. As the locus of political power shifted to the state and national levels, and as local politics became the preserve of white ethnics, more affluent citizens created new organizations that influenced urban public policy. Their politics were decidedly conservative. The United Community Defense Services (UCDS)—created jointly by the National Social Welfare Assembly and the Community Chests and Councils of America—was the single largest effort by voluntary associations during the fifties. The UCDS assisted communities disrupted by military-related projects such as the construction of new bases and weapons facilities. UCDS members saw themselves as integral to national defense and the struggle against communism. Another important type of community organization, the neighborhood improvement association, was oriented toward preserving property values and community homogeneity by excluding lower-income and minority groups. Liberal and radical groups dedicated to substantial community change, which had flourished during the Depression and World War II, confronted a conservative political climate in the 1950s that was much less receptive to protest and calls for reform in urban politics (Fisher 1984; Rossi and Rossi 1973).

Political scientists of this era sanctified these modes of citizen participation into a theory of pluralist democracy and typically turned to urban politics for the best evidence of pluralism. Following Joseph Schumpeter, pluralist theorists such as Robert Dahl and Edward Banfield made direct citizen participation in policymaking secondary to the election of representatives who made policy on behalf of ordinary citizens. Regular elections enabled all citizens to exert indirect influence over decision making. Although a small group of citizens might wield direct influence over specific policy areas, no single elite dominated all policy areas. Citizens were able to join a variety of interest groups or organizations to influence policy debates; barriers to entry were low.

Pluralist theorists insisted that the American political system was essentially fair and ultimately popular because all legitimate interests were heard. The essence of politics was the pulling and pushing among these many groups. Unlike earlier scholars of the Progressive era, pluralists considered political conflict to be a positive expression of democracy and not a pathology. Because pluralists denied the possibility of a unique, objectively determined common good, competition was essential in shaping public policy (see, e.g., Banfield 1961; Dahl 1961).[3]

Pluralists recognized that such a competitive system would produce winners and losers, but argued that the resulting inequalities were not cumulative for any one group. Two consequences of this view are noteworthy. First, pluralists paid relatively little attention to participation by groups—most notably racial minorities and the poor—who lacked political resources such as money, status, and social influence. The pluralist model did not consider fully the possibility that some citizen groups so lacked resources that they were effectively denied participation within the constellation of pluralist forces. Nor did pluralists consider decisions to participate as calculations of costs and benefits in which high costs and low perceived benefits functioned to discourage mass participation. At best, pluralists viewed minority involvement in urban politics as structured by participation by whites; more often they treated it as unimportant (for partial exceptions to this generalization, see Banfield and Wilson 1963; Wilson 1960). Yet, as E. E. Schattschneider (1960) and other scholars argued at the time, formal rights of participation meant little to those lacking in income, formal education, or free time.

Second, and closely related to the first point, pluralists never questioned the adequacy of the existing channels of participation. If only two-thirds of the electorate voted in mayoral elections, one could in theory assume that nonvoters were satisfied with the political system. Thus, pluralists, among others, did not anticipate the degree to which blacks, Latinos, and the poor would challenge the political system and transform citizen participation in the years to come.

Besides local elections, national urban policy was one political arena that potentially affected the well-being of low-income and minority communities. In number of programs and dollar amounts, federal aid to cities was relatively minor in the 1950s, with the majority of funds coming from state and local revenues. As the junior partner in many of these programs, national officials provided technical assistance and monitored the efficient use of funds, but wielded little influence in policymaking. National-urban relations thus lacked the complexity that would characterize later decades. Overall, the national government's emphasis during the 1950s was on enabling cities to realize their own objectives, rather than on requiring them to conform to some national purpose (Sundquist 1969a).

The best-known (and by many accounts most notorious) example of national involvement in urban politics in the 1950s was urban renewal, often referred to as "Negro removal" by critics. Numerous studies have chronicled the rise and fall of urban renewal (see, e.g., Anderson 1964; Dahl 1961; Domhoff 1978; Hartman 1964; Lewis 1959; Nathan et al. 1977; Rossi and Dentler 1961). Of interest here is the extent to which the controversies over citizen participation in urban renewal programs prefigured subsequent debates. Urban renewal originated in Title I of the Housing Act of 1949 which, building on the New Deal model of physical development, emphasized residential slum clearance and construction of new commercial buildings. A statutory requirement for relocation did not prevent the widespread perception that not enough attention was given to the human costs of urban renewal. Officials in many cities repeatedly failed to secure housing for those residents whose neighborhoods had been razed.

After these practices led to protests concerning the lack of citizen input, Congress passed the Housing Act of 1954, which mandated more comprehensive planning in urban renewal projects. The language of the legislation called for participation but was nonetheless vague; it required only that "the entire community" be given an "opportunity" to "participate." The legislation was not intended as an invitation to serious participation, nor was it so implemented. Who formed the entire community and what constituted an opportunity to participate was left largely to the discretion of city officials. Even in cities like New Haven, Connecticut, where the mayor consciously sought the views of a wide cross section of interest groups, the citizens most directly affected by urban renewal were still not represented after 1954. Not until the civil rights movement began to change the balance of power in urban politics would citizen participation carry significant meaning for the poor and minorities. Then, with the dramatic growth of federal programs targeted at the cities, questions surrounding federal requirements of citizen participation—who was entitled to participate and to what extent—would assume central importance in urban politics.

CITIZEN PARTICIPATION IN THE 1960s

Of course, racial minorities and the poor were politically active during the 1950s, but not in the electoral arena that pluralist theorists usually equated with political participation by mass publics. A much wider conception of political participation during this period is therefore warranted. If we understand political activity as encompassing efforts by individuals or groups to gain or preserve (1) political power, (2) a distribution of public goods and services favorable to themselves, or (3) protection against government intervention in their lives, then electoral, legal, administrative, and protest activities are all political. By this definition, the legal struggles culminating in the 1954 *Brown v. Board of Education* school desegregation decision were certainly political. So, too, was the 1955–56 Montgomery, Alabama, bus boycott, as well as lesser-known boycotts throughout the South. Where these efforts failed or fell short, they forced blacks to reconsider the openness of the political system and the likely effectiveness of a gradualist approach to full political equality. And whether these efforts succeeded or not, they served to educate a new generation of black leaders. They in effect created the political tinder of the civil rights movement.

A modest lunch-counter demonstration in Greensboro, North Carolina, in February 1960 sparked the sit-in phase of the civil rights movement. By April of that year, demonstrations had erupted in 54 cities. One historian observes, "It was as if an entire generation was ready to act, waiting for a catalyst" (Chafe 1986: 169). As the movement gained momentum, whites resisted more violently. Freedom Riders testing desegregation in interstate travel were beaten in South Carolina, then beaten again and their bus firebombed in Alabama in May 1961. Federal troops were called in the next year to protect James Meredith, a black Air Force veteran, from angry mobs trying to prevent him from registering at the University of Mississippi. Newspaper and television images of the Birmingham, Alabama, police using clubs, tear gas, fire hoses, and dogs against demonstrators, many of whom were schoolchildren, outraged the nation in May of 1963. One month later, civil rights leader Medgar Evers was murdered in Mississippi. These incidents and accounts of daily intimidation increasingly mobilized public opinion in support of blacks who demanded to be treated as equal citizens. By the time 250,000 black and white protesters gathered for the March on Washington that August, the civil rights movement had moved the issue of racial inequality to the top of the national agenda (Chafe 1986).

Linear (and highly truncated) summaries, such as this one, of the early civil rights movement run the risk of obscuring its loosely coordinated, spontaneous, trial-and-error nature. It is tempting to view Martin Luther King, Jr., as the leader of a single, coordinated movement comprising the Southern Christian Leadership Conference (SCLC), the Student Nonviolent Coordinating Committee (SNCC), the Congress of Racial Equality (CORE), and the National Association for the Advancement of Colored People (NAACP). In fact, however, black students, ministers, and lawyers in many communities pursued desegregation from very different angles, and they frequently clashed over strategy (Branch 1988). Even in cities where black leaders were united and successfully mobilized a protest community, they could call for demonstrations but never completely control their size or direction (which sometimes facilitated their bargaining with local white leaders). The most skillful civil rights leaders knew how to combine careful planning and an understanding of local circumstances with real-time improvisation. They tried a wide range of nonviolent political strategies—from petitions, rallies, boycotts, picket lines, and marches to sit-in demonstrations and other direct confrontations intended to overload local governments or provoke violent resistance—whose use and success varied by community and over time.

The sum total of these efforts, which may be referred to collectively as forms of political protest, helped to make visible a dimension to citizen participation in urban politics that had long lain dormant. Protests seemed increasingly the best means of influencing public policy, particularly for those who saw little difference between candidates in periodic elections, who lacked the resources of time and money to organize around a specific issue, or who simply were frustrated by the pace of change. Protests greatly increased the capacity of ordinary citizens to determine the timing, target, and substance of participation. They allowed the disadvantaged to reorder the priorities of the political system in fundamental ways that elections and voluntary organizations could not. The early civil rights movement created a model of how people without access to formal institutions but enjoying some latent sympathy from more powerful groups could generate political resources (Lipsky 1968).

Although the civil rights movement had not yet shifted its focus from social to economic issues by 1963, the movement had influenced the administration of John F. Kennedy to gather statistics on the "Negro question." Data collected by the Council of Economic Advisers (CEA) provided clear evidence of economic inequality. Still, Kennedy did not encourage CEA Chairman Walter Heller to draft antipoverty legislation until the fall of that year. Two days after Kennedy was assassinated, Lyndon Johnson was briefed on the project and adopted it as his own. "That's my kind of program," he indicated, "move full speed ahead" (quoted in Sundquist 1968: 137).

The next few months proved decisive in charting the future course of the War on Poverty, which strongly influenced the development of citizen participation. Invoking the legacy of Kennedy, President Johnson appealed directly to the American people and declared an "unconditional" War on Poverty in his first State of the Union address, in January 1964. Johnson's "war" (at home) would be fought at all levels of government and would rely considerably on community participation.

Jeffrey Tulis has described one set of problems President Johnson created by rushing the implementation of his program.

> Before Congress could act and the people enlist, the president had to draft the legislation. For a month and a half after the State of the Union message, the Budget Bureau, CEA, and White House staffs attempted to fashion a program of community action; but they faced the problem that, though there was private program experience with the strategy through several community action programs in Manhattan, New Haven, and elsewhere, the idea had only been seized upon by the president's men in late December under the pressure of a deadline for an "idea" for the State of the Union message. (1987: 165)

Architects of the War on Poverty consequently had little time to evaluate and choose among three available models of community action, each of which had distinct implications for federal-urban relations and contained profoundly different ideas about the proper role of citizen participation in urban politics. In the first model, the federal government could work through municipal officials and agencies to effect change, the approach used in the Ford Foundation's Grey Areas Program for decaying neighborhoods. In the second model, the government could rely on technical expertise and comprehensive planning to ensure the maximum efficiency of existing urban programs. This had been the emphasis of President Kennedy's Committee on Juvenile Delinquency and Youth Crime. Neither of these models, however, had a history of promoting citizen participation.[4] In the third model, the federal government could bypass existing municipal organizations and organize the disadvantaged directly. Richard Cloward and Lloyd Ohlin of Columbia University's School of Social Work had developed this approach in their Mobilization for Youth program in New York City.[5] These three models would come to define the parameters of national-urban relations from the early 1960s to the present. The choice of model could promote, contain, or reverse the expansion of citizen participation initiated by the civil rights movement.[6] The War on Poverty initially incorporated elements of all three models.[7]

Different models were championed by different actors in the policymaking process. To sell the antipoverty programs to the Bureau of the Budget (predecessor of the Office of Management and Budget), federal officials emphasized the increased efficiency of service delivery. The proposed Community Action Program, they argued, would help to coordinate the piecemeal antipoverty efforts of federal and state agencies at the local level. Better coordination of existing programs and relatively small additions to the budget seemed more attractive options politically and fiscally than a major income redistribution program. The value of citizen participation was subordinated to administrative efficiency, much as it had been in Kennedy's Committee on Juvenile Delinquency and Youth Crime.

This approach downplayed a key and ultimately controversial provision of the 1964 Economic Opportunity Act mandating "maximum feasible participation of residents of the areas and members of the groups" to be served. Although calls for "maximum feasible participation" were entirely consistent with the rhetoric of war, the implications for actual program implementation were unclear. According to Daniel Patrick Moynihan, one of the architects of the act, this clause "was intended to do no more than ensure that persons excluded from the political process in the South and elsewhere would nonetheless participate in the *benefits* of the community action programs of the new legislation" (Moynihan 1969: 87). In his view, everyone took for granted that the actual design and administration of these programs would fall to local government authorities (as in the Ford Foundation Grey Area Program model).

Many planners within the Office of Economic Opportunity (OEO), however, viewed "maximum feasible participation" differently. They hoped to mobilize the urban poor directly (the Mobilization for Youth model) and empower them to gain a greater voice in city government, not just in antipoverty programs but in all areas of public policy. Many OEO officials believed, as Ford Foundation officials had earlier, that cities had had opportunities to alleviate poverty in the past but had declined to do so. They doubted the willingness of southern officials to establish a program that would benefit blacks. They also doubted the ability, if not the inclination, of northern urban machines to fulfill the objectives of any antipoverty program. The OEO's solution was to work around city hall. This decision was reinforced by OEO planners' commitment to grass-roots democracy and desire to create a constituency distinct from those of other federal and state agencies.

Although the models that informed the development of OEO can be spelled out in some detail, in practice the consequences of choosing a particular model, or of combining models, were never fully articulated. Widespread disagreement over the correct approach to antipoverty policy characterized the program from the beginning. Should program functions be centralized or decentralized? Should the national government work through local governments, or should it attempt directly to empower the disadvantaged? These questions persisted largely because different powerful actors held different points of view, and no one with authority was able or willing to impose a single view on the antipoverty agency.

Critical issues involving the locus of control of antipoverty policies were more important in some places than others, largely because of the manner in which the Johnson administration developed political support for the War on Poverty. By appealing directly to the American public, President Johnson went over the heads not only of Congress but also of state and local officials. He excluded congressional Republicans entirely from the process of drafting the Economic Opportunity Act of 1964 and did not share credit for its passage with his own party. Administration officials failed to consult with state and local officials or to include them in the design of the programs. Only the unusual convergence of the civil rights movement, Kennedy's assassination, and President Johnson's own persuasive powers and use of the media enabled him to ignore traditional political channels in securing passage of the act.

But Johnson had to gain the cooperation of elected officials to guarantee the act's successful implementation. Both the rhetoric of war and the need for a wide base of political support prevented the Johnson administration from starting small. All communities would be able to apply for federal funds, as would nonprofit organizations within those communities. Within a few years the OEO had funded over 1,000 Community Action Agencies (CAAs), urban and rural, to serve as the local outposts of the War on Poverty.

The emphasis on speed meant that the OEO did not have the time to specify the meaning of citizen participation requirements, even if it had been able to impose a single view. In practice, the OEO approved projects lacking established mechanisms for participation so long as those projects were consistent with participation once they were later implemented. For the next two years, the OEO resisted attempts to formalize citizen participation requirements, hoping to foster the independence and creativity of local CAAs. The closest the OEO came to standardization was its decision to study 12 of the most "interesting" local participation plans in 1966 and somehow incorporate the main lessons learned in fiscal year 1968.

Local actors consequently determined the nature and scope of citizen participation in the War on Poverty. Typically, city officials and local social service agencies established Community Action Agencies with little to no input from disadvantaged groups. In a sample of 20 cities with populations between 50,000 and 1 million, Stephen Rose (1972: 128) found that "in *none* of the twenty cities were any poor people, any representatives of the neighborhoods, or members of the groups to be served involved" in the initial design of the agency. Early involvement by these established local agencies translated into control over the administration of most community action programs. The newly created CAAs subcontracted most of the work back to established local agencies. Only 20 percent of all community action programs in Rose's study were directly adminis- tered by the CAAs themselves. A similar study by Kenneth Clark and Jeannette Hopkins (1969), covering 51 cities and for one year rather than three, supported these findings.

Thus, from the beginning, the influence of members of disadvan- taged groups in the Community Action Program was circumscribed. They could participate as administrators of a minority of community action programs or as directors on the CAA advisory board. Participa- tion in CAA advisory boards was hotly contested in many cities. Some mayors (e.g., Samuel Yorty of Los Angeles and Richard Daley of Chicago) refused to include the disadvantaged on their CAA boards, and then handpicked a few representatives when the OEO withheld funds. Even where participation by disadvantaged groups was accepted in principle, many (white) political and civic leaders felt that these groups required guidance in assessing their communi- ties' needs and in spending considerable sums of public monies. Representatives of impoverished communities argued otherwise and pointed out that those same city leaders had long ignored their demands. Persisting in its view, the OEO recommended as a general rule that at least one-third of CAA board members be representatives of the groups to be served by the program. Congress formalized this requirement in 1966.

Actual control over CAA boards varied. A coalition of political, business, and civic leaders usually formed a majority. In cities where disadvantaged groups were politically active or allied with sympa- thetic groups from other parts of the city, they sometimes controlled the CAA board. Yet, when one considers that few cities provided technical staff support to their CAA boards, which would have helped the poor transform their demands into concrete programs; that disad- vantaged groups never controlled the majority of CAA boards nation-

ally; and that established political and civic leaders directly administered the majority of the Community Action Programs, then one
realizes how limited "maximum" and "feasible" participation by
disadvantaged groups was.

Not every community action effort followed the model of elite
dominance. In a second pattern, less common but far more publicized, disadvantaged groups used the local CAAs in an effort to gain
more political power. Where disadvantaged groups controlled the
local CAA board, or where they had successfully applied for direct
funding from the national government, they had leverage with which
to challenge local officials. The proportion of programs designed to
redistribute political power was probably no more than 5 percent
nationally; the vast majority of community action programs were
designed to provide better social services to disadvantaged groups.
Federal funds in a few cities like Syracuse (New York), Oakland
(California), and Newark (New Jersey) helped local groups with a
history of activism challenge city hall. Syracuse University, for example, applied directly to the OEO for funds to support a community
action training center, whose mission was to teach organizing and
protest techniques to prospective community activists.

Urban officials seized on these few examples in accusing the
national government of undermining their authority. Some accused
the OEO of "fostering class struggle" (Selover 1969: 181). The U.S.
Conference of Mayors protested the use of federal funds to undermine
local authority and pressured the OEO and the Johnson administration for changes late in 1965. The mayors were particularly concerned
about the ability of community groups to apply directly to Washington, D.C., for funds. The two sides reached an informal compromise
early the following year, whereby city officials gained veto power
over any part of a CAA proposal in exchange for a minimum of one-
third representation by the poor on local CAA boards. Since the OEO
already provided for a one-third representation by the poor, they and
the disadvantaged groups they represented gained no substantive
advantage in the bargain. This agreement effectively terminated federal efforts to bypass city government and mobilize disadvantaged
groups directly.

Congress soon formalized the mayors' agreement and applied it
nationwide. Frustrated with the OEO's unwillingness or inability to
clarify what it meant by citizen participation, Congress offered a
more precise and more restrictive definition in 1967 when it extended
the Economic Opportunity Act. The Green Amendment, known as
the "bosses and boll weevil amendment" because it appeased south-

ern and urban Democrats, required that all local CAAs be designated by the state or local government. The federal government would thereafter work through established public authorities to achieve its objectives. To many in Congress, which had become more conservative since the 1966 elections, unchecked citizen participation was the cause of urban unrest. In the wake of the 1967 riots, Congress wanted to channel mass participation as narrowly as possible. The Green Amendment only confirmed what urban mayors and federal officials had agreed upon in early 1966—citizen participation had to be reined in. Any claim that poor people and racial minorities controlled the Community Action Program must therefore be limited to a few cities, for a few months.

During this same period, federal officials were also shifting the emphasis of the War on Poverty from local initiatives to national programs. The reasons are not hard to identify. President Johnson had created unreasonably high expectations of success within Congress and the American public. The wide distribution of funds limited the potential impact in any one community. Where community groups had been encouraged to address major problems, they had only enough funds to undertake conventional projects such as building playgrounds or installing street lights. The initial priority on local solutions to local problems, without federal guidance, meant delays as many communities took time to plan their programs. These factors made it structurally impossible to demonstrate early success.

At the OEO's suggestion, Congress began to appropriate a larger percentage of funds to national programs like Head Start, programs that were prepackaged, politically safe, and had quantifiable benefits. This transition encountered less opposition than might have been expected, because many communities found it easier to participate in national programs than to develop their own. By 1967, funding for national programs had surpassed that for local programs. Head Start alone received more funds than all local programs combined that year. In sum, by the time President Johnson left office, responsibility for the War on Poverty had moved steadily upward, from citizen groups to city officials to the federal government. The War on Poverty may have started by employing three distinct strategies, but by 1968 it was clear that the federal government intended to address inequality by working through established local governments.

What tangible benefits did the War on Poverty produce for disadvantaged groups? In retrospect, it is remarkable that it accomplished much of anything. The process by which it was enacted alienated congressional Republicans, as well as state and local officials of both parties. Moreover, any federal social program enacted in 1964 would have been opposed strenuously in the South. Ambiguous objectives, conflicting strategies, and the broad distribution of funds made success elusive. Federal officials responded to the turmoil created by the program by executing a "strategic retreat on objectives," to use Aaron Wildavsky's phrase (1979), and dropped the most controversial of the features they had advocated.

By creating a new bureaucracy, the Johnson administration had generated friction with the U.S. Department of Health, Education & Welfare and local social service agencies. CAA employees often went into poor neighborhoods, sought out those who were eligible for public assistance but were not receiving it, and encouraged them to demand their rights, thereby adding to welfare costs as well as the regular social workers' caseloads. Whenever the OEO or the local CAAs made their inevitable mistakes, the traditional agencies publicized them and accused the CAAs of being disorganized and unprofessional. The idea that the OEO, through the CAAs, might coordinate local antipoverty programs quickly fell victim to bureaucratic infighting.

Despite these obstacles, the War on Poverty provided needed social services to the urban (and rural) poor. Antipoverty law offices funded by the Legal Services Corporation helped resolve landlord-tenant disputes and acted as a buffer between the urban poor and police and juvenile authorities. However poorly funded relative to the need, the poverty program established the principle of providing legal assistance in civil cases to people too poor to afford a lawyer. The Job Corps offered much-needed vocational training and basic education to urban youths between the ages of 14 and 21. Head Start, perhaps the most successful of the Great Society programs, provided compensatory preschool education to thousands of poor four- and five-year-old children. Even the creation of a simplified guide to public welfare was of real benefit to the poor.

Community Action Agencies provided an important medium for empowering disadvantaged groups. Indeed, political activity was often the prerequisite of better access to social services. In a survey of 100 CAAs in cities with population greater than 50,000, James Vanecko found that a political mobilization approach produced greater institutional change and a better distribution of material benefits to the poor than did attempts to improve the coordination and delivery of existing services (cited in Peterson and Greenstone 1977: 246). Although the services approach would come to dominate subsequent governmental programs, the process of empowerment had significant implications for the future of urban politics. In many cities the CAA provided the only forum where disadvantaged groups could present their demands and expect a sympathetic audience. Unlike social services, empowerment could not be restricted to specific programs or problems. "As the poor were organized to discuss and make known their problems and their needs, and as they developed confidence, they inevitably extended their concern beyond the planning and operation of the local community action program" to issues such as Model Cities, busing, and rezoning (Sundquist 1969a: 63).

Equally important, many CAA employees became the core of an urban leadership class. Between 25 percent and 35 percent of CAA field representatives were blacks and Latinos. According to one OEO official, "It was probably the ablest and largest group of minority-group professionals ever assembled in one government program" (Wofford 1969: 90; see also Eisinger 1979; Piven and Cloward 1971). These leaders played a key role in urban politics over the next 25 years. Their continued influence attested to the power of the national government—even with too little time and money—to assist in the transformation of urban politics.[8]

As it became clear that the War on Poverty could not possibly live up to its advance billing, the Johnson administration adopted a second strategy that marked a further retreat from a mobilization strategy. President Johnson announced a new, more comprehensive approach to urban problems in his 1967 State of the Union message, one that would soon be referred to as the Model Cities program (see, e.g., Friedan and Kaplan 1975; Marris and Rein 1982; Millett 1977; Nathan 1975; Strange 1972; and Sundquist 1969a). Its designers were concerned about criticisms of urban renewal and wanted to find a means of rebuilding the cities' physical environments without destroying the social environments.

Without explicitly saying so, Johnson intended Model Cities to replace the Community Action Program as the primary federal program for addressing urban problems. The newly created Department of Housing and Urban Development (HUD) would administer Model Cities, thus diminishing the status of the more confrontational OEO. There would be fewer Model Cities than Community Action Agencies in order to maximize their potential impact. An early version called for 36 Model Cities, but congressional leaders recommended that the number be at least 50 so that each senator could feel that his state might receive one. HUD initially approved 63 programs in November 1967; the total eventually reached around 150. The architects of Model Cities did not specify the content of local programs except to provide for a general emphasis on comprehensive solutions and physical rehabilitation, particularly in the construction of low-income housing. In contrast to social programs, which were designed to change behavior, the success or failure of physical development projects was relatively easy to determine. Model Cities thus constituted a transition in antipoverty policy from the categorical social welfare programs of the War on Poverty to the revenue sharing and block grants under President Richard Nixon. It also incorporated responses to prevalent criticisms of the urban renewal program.

The design and implementation of Model Cities continued the trend toward limiting citizen participation by disadvantaged groups. HUD worked closely with local officials from the beginning and made them the central actors, returning to the earlier Ford Foundation model. Mayors had to approve all local applications for federal funding and designate which organization would administer the local Community Development Agency (CDA), just as they had with the Community Action Program after 1967. According to Millet (1977: 40), "this character of administrative conservatism was widespread and insured not only City Hall's dominance in the program but also in the intervention process: maximizing *existing* resources, rehabilitating *existing* structures, preserving *existing* neighborhoods, and, of course, using *existing* political institutions to deal with the problems of poverty."

Semantic changes in the requirements for citizen participation signaled a further retreat from the early Community Action Program's stress on mobilization. The legislation establishing the Model Cities program required cities to promote "widespread" rather than "maximum feasible" participation. HUD interpreted this to mean that planning "should be carried out *with* as well as for the people living in the affected area." The city should create mechanisms for "communication and meaningful dialogue" between the CDA and local citizens that guaranteed them a "meaningful role" and "active involvement" (HUD guidelines quoted in Sundquist 1969a: 85–86).

HUD left interpretation of these guidelines up to city officials in order to give them maximum flexibility in defining their specific needs and potential solutions. Unlike the requirement for CAAs, disadvantaged groups were not assured of any representation on the CDA advisory boards, much less one-third. HUD believed that Model Cities had to respond more to the needs of the entire community instead of singling out one group for special consideration. On the other hand, more widespread representation on CDA boards helped to build a broader base of support for Model Cities. Whereas many citizens viewed the Community Action Program as a program for poor people, Model Cities promised to provide benefits to all. Instead of community action, which carried the potential for a redistribution of political power and public services, Model Cities promised community development. Instead of maximum feasible participation of all groups to be served, Model Cities assured maximum flexibility for city officials.

Even more so than in the Community Action Program, local actors and circumstances determined the precise meaning of citizen participation in the Model Cities program. In an analysis performed for HUD, Marshall Kaplan (cited in Marris and Rein 1982) concluded that the nature of citizen participation depended on the level or amount of conflict already occurring in the city and the organizational strength of local citizens' groups.[9] When both factors were low, city officials controlled the program. If either factor was high, city officials, local business interests, and citizens' groups shared responsibility for administering the CDA. And if both factors were high, citizens groups representing the poor and minorities exercised considerable influence. Previous federal programs certainly made a difference. According to James Sundquist (1969a), the existence of an active Community Action Agency usually translated into a larger role for minorities and the poor in the new CDA. Cities without a tradition of organized protest or activism, however, tended to stay that way. Overall, the Model Cities program helped to institutionalize the patterns of citizen participation in urban politics established by the Community Action Program.

Outside of these federal grant programs and the civil rights movement, other developments were also important in shaping citizen participation in the 1960s. Rent strikes, protests against urban renewal and highway projects, demonstrations by public employees, student opposition to the Vietnam War, and marches in support of the women's movement all became familiar events. In addition, city politics and agendas began to change in ways that would develop more fully in the 1970s. School desegregation was accompanied by controversies over busing and by white flight, police brutality was linked to demands for civilian review boards, and blacks began to win electoral offices.

Perhaps the most important development was the escalation of protest. The civil rights movement had represented an intense form of what Ralf Dahrendorf (1959) called "regulated conflict": black protestors generally constituted an organized interest group whose leadership and demands were easily identified; and although all parties did not always agree on the justice of each others' claims, each side couched its arguments in a common language of democratic rights and upheld democracy as its political ideal. Thus, a certain measure of agreement concerning the "rules of the game" facilitated the political incorporation of disadvantaged groups, albeit in ways that simultaneously opened and closed avenues of participation to them.

In contrast, the extraordinary urban riots of the 1960s constituted "unregulated conflict." Starting with the Watts (Los Angeles) riot in 1965, and building to involve dozens of large and small cities in the "long hot summer" of 1967 and the spring of 1968 (after the assassination of Martin Luther King, Jr.), these unpredictable outbreaks violated traditional norms of political participation. Rioters were essentially leaderless and unorganized; their demands seemed at once limitless and (to white elites, at least) unintelligible.

Indeed, questions were even raised at the time as to whether the ghetto riots should even be considered "political." Some analysts equated them with sprees and other politically inconsequential events. However, systematic research conducted by the Kerner Commission, which was charged by President Johnson with studying the events of the summer of 1967, demonstrated that there was reason to think riots at least in part were engaged in by people acting purposefully to protest their circumstances. In particular, rioters tended to have a greater stake in the community and to have been community residents longer than nonrioters, when a "riff-raff" theory of riot participants would predict the opposite. And in many cities, stores operated by whites were targeted by arsonists and vandals, while shops operated by black proprietors were passed over.

Ultimately, whether the riots were political depends on whether they were endowed by participants—and the larger society that was their putative target—with political content. It is here that the role of the riot commissions seems most central. After every major race-related riot in the United States this century, riot commissions have been established. Their role seems to be twofold. On the one hand, because they comprise high-status citizens and, in the modern period, representatives of important constituencies, they provide assurance that causes will be identified and just grievances redressed. On the other hand, because they are advisory to the executive who appoints them, their recommendations are nonbinding and may be ignored. They may be ignored, too, because their report is delivered significantly after the riot events, when tempers have cooled and executives' actions and nonactions will be received in a more stable environment.

The executive of the jurisdiction is critical in determining the political content of riots because he or she is in a position to respond positively, thereby acting as though a (political) message has been received. By the same token, he or she is in a position to ignore the riots and the recommendations of the riot commissions, thereby communicating that, in a sense, no important message was sent (Lipsky and Olson 1977).

Thus, the ghetto riots of the 1960s did send a political message but the message was not received. President Johnson responded to the alarm of whites and most blacks over the unrestrained violence the riots seemed to represent when he appointed the Kerner Commission. But he diluted the political content of the message by ignoring the commission's recommendations. Preoccupied with the Vietnam War, the president was unwilling to undertake the reconstruction of society called for by the commission. When the tangible results of the commission are assessed, only modest insurance relief for ghetto merchants can be said to have emerged.

For concrete responses to the riots, one has to look beyond the immediate results of the Kerner Commission. James Button (1978) has suggested that between 1963 and 1966, relatively infrequent yet severe riots prompted the national government to direct more funds for antipoverty programs in the cities affected (e.g., Rochester and Los Angeles). The Model Cities program was in part a response to the Watts riot of 1965. More vigorous national antidiscrimination legislation in housing, passed in 1968, may be attributed in part to the atmosphere of support for improving the conditions of blacks after the riots following the death of Dr. King.

Urban riots continued through the late 1960s and 1970s, though they received far less coverage in the mass media. Law and order became the dominant response to this phase of urban riots. Between 1969 and 1972, national, state, and local law enforcement authorities increasingly added new equipment and created specialized units capable of controlling riots. In the long run, urban riots led to greater police in the cities, not increased benefits for the communities from which the riots emerged (Button 1978; Feagin and Hahn 1973).

CITIZEN PARTICIPATION AFTER THE 1960s

For our purposes the most noteworthy development in citizen participation in urban politics after the 1960s was what we term its routinization. As stated earlier, one dimension of routinization was that new laws and practices made citizen participation more commonplace, more routine. Ordinary citizens no longer had to fight over the right to participate in the direction and evaluation of public programs.

The creation of Community Action Agencies and Community Development Agencies, which had to answer in some meaningful way to citizen advisory boards, created greater expectations of accountability in other areas of public policy. This was particularly evident in the emerging areas of environmental and energy policy; for example, Congress in 1969 required environmental impact statements and public hearings for every activity that significantly affected the quality of the environment. Altogether, almost one-third of all federal grants to state and local governments required some form of citizen participation by 1978 (DeSario and Langton 1987; Gormley 1986; U.S. Advisory Commission on Intergovernmental Relations [henceforth, ACIR] 1979).

Either by state law or local initiative, cities also established citizen advisory committees or commissions to oversee everything from economic development to police and fire protection. The U.S. Advisory Commission on Intergovernmental Relations (ACIR), in conjunction with the International City Management Association, conducted a survey of 1,464 cities in 1977 that revealed the magnitude of these developments. Only 5 percent of the sample had no citizen advisory committees; over 30 percent had 10 or more committees; a total of 100 or more citizens participated in almost one-quarter of the cities surveyed; and in 17 cities over 500 citizens served on committees (ACIR 1979: 274–75).

In light of the decomposition of political parties, routinization brought an important measure of stability to urban politics. Without these mechanisms, Ira Katznelson's warning in 1976 would carry more force:

> Over the period of the past four decades, the locus of urban political power has shifted from the party organization to independent, autonomous, but not apolitical bureaucracies. The shift has weakened the social-control position of authorities, for unlike the machines, bureaucratic control mechanisms deal only with the output side of politics. They have taken over the machines' function of distributing services and benefits without assuming the vital control function of the organization of participation in politics. As a result, bureaucratic, as opposed to party, control, leaves authorities potentially more vulnerable to challenge from below. (1976: 225)

The advent of citizen advisory committees, mandatory public hearings, and other routine forms of participation furnished bureaucracies with important mechanisms of political input, which became
the bureaucratic equivalent of periodic elections. Even if the value
of these mechanisms was primarily symbolic, they in fact functioned
to organize political participation.

However, effective use of these new avenues of participation
required certain political resources that disadvantaged groups lacked
relative to other urban groups. Based on a survey of school organizations in Atlanta, Boston, and Los Angeles in the 1970s, for example,
Marilyn Gittell found that only members of middle- and upper-
income groups could sustain genuine advocacy efforts. They had
greater access to information and decision makers, were more knowl-
edgeable about the educational bureaucracy, and were better able
to attend frequent meetings than members of lower-income groups
(Gittell 1980).[10] Her findings are supported by Katznelson's (1981:
chap. 7) case study of the Washington Heights-Inwood section of
Manhattan, New York, and by the ACIR's broader survey of citizen
participation. The latter concluded that "the impact of different kinds
of federal citizen participation requirements varies, but overall it is
modest. The major participants in the process are the middle class,
and even special efforts targeted to certain low income groups often
do not produce significant participation by them" (ACIR 1979: 4).
Recent evidence indicates that even in cities committed to greater
citizen involvement, important disparities remain between the haves
and have-nots (Berry, Portney, and Thomson 1993).

Moreover, even as citizens gained new channels of political participation, these channels had distinct contours and boundaries. A second dimension of routinization was that as participation became
more widespread, it became more limited—more predictable in timing, content, and process. As Lipsky has observed in another context:

> These developments were tacit forms of exchange. People implicitly
> agreed to express themselves on policy matters through the media of
> citizen participation; public officials implicitly agreed to take some
> notice of their activities, to respect if not act upon their expressed
> sentiments, and to regard their message as legitimate. However minimal
> implicit exchanges are, they present government with obligations to
> heed and maintain the legitimate channels of citizen expression in a
> policy world that calls for at least the registration of citizen views.
> Citizens may have other avenues of influence open to them [e.g.,
> protest], but they will be pressured to use these mechanisms if conflict
> over policy emerges. (1984: 14)

The evolution of federal grants to local governments after the 1960s clearly illustrated the more restrictive dimension of routinization. This is demonstrated by examining the changing requirement for citizen participation. Initially, terms such as "maximum feasible participation" mobilized disadvantaged groups, particularly when reinforced by support from Washington, D.C., or an indigenous protest community. During the Nixon, Ford, and Carter administrations, New Federalism translated into remarkable increases in income transfers, a relative decline in the importance of categorical grants for the urban poor, and the rise of block grants such as the Community Development Block Grant (CDBG), the latter of which gave priority to physical development rather than social service projects. Instead of "maximum feasible" or even "widespread" participation, each CDBG applicant merely had to guarantee that it had provided the public with "adequate" information about the program and an "opportunity to participate" in the application process (see, e.g., Auger 1987; Dommel et al. 1980; Lovell 1983; Nathan 1975; and Nathan et al. 1977).

This shift in statutory language revealed the declining importance of citizen participation in federal programs. The operational meaning of such vague and elastic terms depended heavily on the degree of involvement by federal agencies. As federal officials allowed urban officials to exercise more discretion in administering programs, cities expanded their definitions of the groups to be served and involved in decision making. Many new groups who had not previously been eligible for assistance could now claim that their development project had a "particular urgency," a key requirement for block grants. Whatever gains disadvantaged groups registered during the 1960s were effectively diluted by the entry of other community groups. In addition, exclusive reliance on urban officials to administer national funds eliminated the ability of local groups to work directly with the federal government and thus reduced their independence from city hall.

The cumulative effect of several shifts—from city-specific to national programs, from categorical to block grants, and from social welfare to infrastructure programs—limited the ways in which disadvantaged groups could exercise political power. First, local participation in national programs lessened the ability of disadvantaged groups to target specific needs and influence program content. Second, block grants meant greater competition among organized groups for a smaller federal pie. CDBG funds were spread thinly, thereby diluting the claims of disadvantaged groups and preventing a major, concentrated attack on poverty (or on any other policy problem). And third, the growing emphasis on infrastructure programs such as housing and highway projects diluted the influence of disadvantaged groups, either because the projects were seen as affecting the entire community or because effective participation required a certain level of technical expertise.

To say that citizen participation did not regain importance in the administration of Ronald Reagan is an understatement. Reagan's domestic policies, emphasizing retrenchment and devolution, represented a major shift away from redistribution and toward the promotion of economic growth, a reduction in federal domestic expenditures, and an increase in the responsibilities of state governments. The much-ballyhooed "empowerment" of the poor was little more than wishful thinking; the administration gave top priority to policies designed to promote privatization and consumerism. As a result, the state and local political economy became more important in shaping urban affairs and citizen participation (Kirlin and Marshall 1988; Marshall and Kirlin 1985; Nathan, Doolittle, and Associates 1987; Palmer and Sawhill 1982, 1984; Peterson et al. 1986). These trends persisted under the presidency of George Bush as part of a larger Republican attack on traditional Democratic programs and constituencies (Ginsberg and Shefter 1990).

Routinization took place apart from federal programs as well. The employment of disadvantaged groups in public and nonprofit social service agencies contributed to both dimensions of routinization. Many civil rights activists redirected their energies to the public or nonprofit agencies administering antipoverty programs. Public employment was in fact a primary benefit of the Great Society and helped to create an urban middle class of minorities (Brown and Erie 1981). Public employment of community leaders may increase their participation in politics, but it channels their energies in regularized ways as well.

Nonprofit agencies, which also absorbed the efforts of some civil rights activists, led a precarious life, lacking in funds and relying frequently upon volunteers. Federal funding kept these organizations alive and provided employment to some staff. As with advisory committees, federal support of these agencies carried expectations of and demands for reciprocity. In exchange, many groups accommodated their mission to the shifting demands of national agencies, refrained from challenging city officials—who administered the programs— and in some cases ultimately defined their objectives solely in terms of federal programs. Organizations that once actively confronted public officials and encouraged disadvantaged groups to do likewise often became adjuncts of the social welfare bureaucracy (Gittell 1980; Lipsky 1984).[11]

From one vantage point these developments appear cruelly ironic. Disadvantaged groups invested tremendous amounts of time and energy, often risking bodily injury, to gain greater influence in urban politics, and yet the principal beneficiaries of their efforts seem to have been the more-affluent groups. Such a conclusion underestimates the positive-sum possibilities of political protest. Middle- and upper-income citizens certainly did gain a larger direct role in policymaking during the 1960s and 1970s, largely because of grass-roots protest. Still, Norman and Susan Fainstein are right to claim that the proliferation of community planning boards, housing councils, and health boards also provided disadvantaged groups with important points of access to the political system. "Decentralization and the creation of new linkage structures enlarge the number of groups participating in the policymaking process and increase the legitimacy and bargaining power of the relatively deprived" (Fainstein and Fainstein 1976: 922). All citizens registered absolute gains in their ability to participate in urban politics. By the same token, these developments did not improve the relative position of disadvantaged groups. The consequences of maintaining the relative balance of power became evident as urban politics became more of a zero-sum contest for public goods and services during the latter 1970s and 1980s.

Routinization, whose twin meanings remained in constant tension, constituted the most important development in citizen participation in urban politics after the 1960s. The second development of note arose in part as a reaction to routinization. Beginning in the early 1970s, there was a flowering of different modes of participation as many groups discovered the limitations of routine participation in administrative politics.

We identify three primary modes in which urban citizens sought to realize the full potential of the civil rights movement and the War on Poverty. These modes are distinguished not by their novelty but by the changing opportunities they presented to disadvantaged groups. The most prominent path—facilitated no doubt by passage of the Voting Rights Act of 1965—led to electoral politics, the rise of black and Latino mayors, and the resulting redistribution of formal political power. A second path led to the continued use of direct action to pressure existing institutions. Tenant organizations and citizen action groups sought both a redistribution of political power and a more equitable distribution of public goods and services. A third path bypassed existing organizations and led to alternative institutions, newly created or built upon the foundation of existing churches, neighborhood groups, and ethnic associations. Neighborhood crime watches, nonprofit rape crisis centers, and community development corporations are examples of this approach. For a time, following the Los Angeles riots of 1992, it appeared that urban riots might also reappear as a form of political participation.

These three major modes of citizen participation continue to shape urban politics and are discussed in the remainder of this chapter. After considering the rise of minority elected officials, we treat the second and third modes of participation as a unit. They have traditionally been referred to as complementary thrusts of the "citizen movement" or "neighborhood movement," and we have chosen to work within a modified version of this framework. Much as race has served as the organizing principle of electoral politics, class and income have animated these latter modes of political participation. Each mode has, however, encountered significant obstacles in recent years—the most important of which relate to changes in the urban political economy. We conclude by speculating on the potential of these modes of participation, singly or in combination, to produce significant changes in the lives of disadvantaged citizens.

Electoral Politics

The rise of minority mayors has often been cited as the best evidence that disadvantaged groups have made gains in urban politics over the last 30 years. The change has indeed been dramatic. Whereas there were no black or Latino mayors of cities with populations greater than 50,000 in 1960, there were 27 black and three Latino mayors of cities this size by 1985. By 1991, there were 33 black mayors in cities this size (Joint Center for Political and Economic Studies 1992). They became the elected leaders of some of America's largest cities—New York, Chicago, Los Angeles, Detroit, Atlanta, San Antonio, Newark, and Denver, among others. Some, like Newark's Kenneth Gibson and Atlanta's Andrew Young, were veterans of the civil rights movement and the War on Poverty.

The total number of black elected officials, who far outnumber Latino officials nationally, grew 138 percent between 1970 and 1975, 40 percent from 1975 to 1980, and 23 percent between 1980 and 1985. Part of the explanation for the declining rate of growth lies in demographics. The 1970–75 surge came primarily in cities with large black populations. Comparable data for Latino officials are unavailable. What is clear is that between the early 1970s and 1990, the total number of elected officials grew at a faster rate than the rate of growth of Latino populations in Arizona, California, Florida, New Mexico, New York, and Texas (Pachon and DeSipio 1992).

By the 1980s, there were few cities left with large minority populations that had not elected a black or Latino official. As rapid as these changes have been, continued growth in the number of minority elected officials is likely to be less rapid. Minorities are currently declining as a percentage of population in many urban areas as white professionals return to the central cities. Faster growth can be expected for Latino officials than black officials, principally because of faster growth in the (naturalized) Latino population. Of course, minority population size does not fix a ceiling on the potential number of minority elected officials, but the clear (not perfect) split of recent urban elections along racial or ethnic lines indicates that this factor is important (Browning, Marshall, and Tabb 1990; Pachon and DeSipio 1992; Williams 1987).[12]

As one might expect with such a large increase, no one model of political organization predominated. Based on an investigation of 10 northern California cities over 20 years, Browning, Marshall, and Tabb (1984) produced a study that identified four general patterns of minority mobilization and incorporation in urban electoral politics. In descending order of minority influence, these patterns are biracial electoral alliance, cooptation, protest and exclusion, and weak mobilization. The key to higher levels of responsiveness—the degree to which minority demands are translated into public policy— is not simply representation but incorporation into the governing coalition. Election to city council, for instance, is less meaningful if the council member represents the minority party or is excluded from the dominant faction of the majority party. A tradition of protest and activism helped to accelerate the process of incorporation, but was not in itself sufficient to produce tangible benefits to the minority community. Blacks and Latinos achieved the highest levels of incorporation in those cities in which they formed alliances with liberal whites.

Incorporation brought tangible shifts in public policy. Cities where it occurred not only experienced a sharper increase in city minority employment and in the percentage of city contracts awarded to minority businesses but appointed more minorities to city boards and commissions, established many more minority programs, created police review boards, and were in general more responsive in delivering services than cities in which minority representation was either negligible or was coopted (Browning et al. 1984, 1990; Button 1989; Eisinger 1982).[13]

A number of scholars have questioned the significance of these findings because the sample communities came from a relatively prosperous region of the country with a reputation for liberal views and included only two major cities, San Francisco and Oakland. Subsequent testing of the thesis that "protest is not enough" has borne out the primary finding, with several important qualifications. First, inclusion in a dominant coalition does assure a much stronger minority position than does just representation, but the value of political incorporation will be tempered by the larger context of the urban political economy. In a context of fiscal crisis, the need for economic development constrains the kinds of redistributive policies that blacks and Latinos might have been expected to favor. Second, entrenched party machines have created barriers to incorporation in cities such as New York and Chicago. Third, as New York City and Miami demonstrate, blacks and Latinos cannot be assumed to be natural political allies; they have at times worked at cross-purposes. Mollenkopf (1986) warns of a possible rollback of minority gains in New York City. Thus, even incorporation may not be enough to provide minorities with meaningful control over urban public policy (see essays in Browning et al. 1990).[14]

These qualifications bring into question the impact that minority electoral participation has had on the black and Latino communities. Students of urban politics have divided sharply in their assessments of how effectively minority officials have worked within these constraints. Most would agree that incorporation seems to have incre, sed levels of political participation and trust in government among minorities (Bobo and Gilliam 1990). Their disagreements relate to the size and distribution of material benefits. Among the optimists, Bette Woody has argued that

> black mayors . . . blended a sophisticated mix of managerial reform principles, good government and grass roots participation, designed to compete in regional and national arenas for a larger slice of the social and economic pie. . . . The black mayors thus proved some of the more successful practitioners of an amalgamation of populist and socially responsive goals on the one hand and on the other, leaders of the fight for management reform and sound government operation. (1982: 3)

Less-sanguine observers have emphasized the degree to which benefits have accrued disproportionately to more-upwardly mobile blacks and Latinos, leaving behind a significant underclass. In their view, the election of minority officials and federal initiatives like the War on Poverty have helped to create a black middle class of government employees but failed to alleviate poverty. William Nelson, Jr., offered a typical judgment of this group:

> The upsurge in the election of "new breed" black politicians to public office has been most effective in the promotion of the social and economic interest of upwardly mobile, elite sectors of the black community.
>
> Elected on reform platforms that promised profound changes in the policy-making process, black mayors have almost uniformly embraced corporate-centered strategies that have virtually precluded the redistribution of major benefits to broad segments of the black community. (1987: 172, 174)

A third perspective—and in our view the most persuasive—has emphasized the numerous obstacles to reform common to black, Latino, and white officials. Decentralized and overlapping authority, the product of "good government" reforms, has lowered the potential for any one city official, including the mayor, to affect public policy. Weak political organizations and candidate-centered elections have depressed voter turnout and produced officials who owe sustained allegiance to no group. Where urban machines have dominated, competing views have been ignored and new actors discouraged from participating. Perhaps most important, city officials, regardless of race or ethnic background, have come under increasing pressure to make economic development their overriding policy objective. The combination of slower rates of economic growth, the exodus of more-affluent residents to the suburbs (and, hence, declining tax bases of many cities), public resistance to tax increases, and the increasing mobility of capital has limited cities' ability to engage in redistribution (Reed 1988; Stone 1989). Meanwhile, the national government, a prime sponsor of programs for disadvantaged groups in the 1960s and 1970s, has reduced aid to the cities—a policy some have termed "fend-for-yourself federalism" (Altshuler and Howard 1991; Kirschten 1989).

As a result, many mayors who campaigned on a progressive or populist platform have actively pursued corporate investment once in office. Coleman Young of Detroit and Tom Bradley of Los Angeles are the most-commonly cited recent examples; Andrew Young of Atlanta, Federico Peña of Denver, and Lionel Wilson of Oakland also fit this pattern (Judd 1986). These same pressures have changed the types of candidates likely to run for office, the tenor of their campaigns, and the substance of their message. Referring to the second generation of minority mayors (e.g., Wilson Goode of Philadelphia, Kurt Schmoke of Baltimore), one observer has written: "More pragmatists than pioneers, professionals than preachers, coalition builders than confrontationists, they came to power during a period of drastic cutbacks in federal money for cities, and they are hawking economic progress and managerial expertise" (Moore 1988: 373).

Moreover, minority officials have faced an additional set of constraints. Their core constituency has become a smaller portion of the electorate as affluent whites and other racial and ethnic immigrants have moved to the cities. As the black middle class has grown, its participation in civic matters has declined or dispersed over a larger metropolitan area. Traditional black organizations like the NAACP have lost membership and support. In this third view, then, black and Latino officials on the whole have been as constrained, or as ineffective, in addressing the poverty-related problems of their constituents as their white counterparts. Ironically, the process of generating real benefits for the black middle class may have undercut political support for minority officials and reoriented urban politics more along income and class divisions than along racial lines (Nelson 1987; Rich 1987; Williams 1987).

Looking back over the last quarter century of minority participation in electoral politics, we foresee three issues becoming more important in the near future. The first is that of growing income disparities and class divisions within the minority community. Although these disparities are most obvious within the black electorate, Miami and Los Angeles provide comparable evidence for Latinos. These schisms are most evident in Atlanta, Chicago (since Harold Washington's death in 1987), Cleveland, and Philadelphia. According to Carolyn Adams, "it is increasingly difficult for a single black candidate to appeal to the disparate socioeconomic groups within the black community" (chap. 2, this volume; see also Stone 1990).

A second and related issue is that of generational succession. The mature generation of minority officials, which grew up with the civil rights movement and various federal antipoverty programs in the 1960s, succeeded in replacing more conservative businessmen, politicians, and civil rights leaders because they better represented the views of a population coming of age. There is some evidence, still mostly anecdotal, that this process is repeating. In New York City, for instance, black leaders divided sharply over their responses to racial incidents such as the Howard Beach murders and Washington

Heights riots. A younger generation of ministers and lawyers has gained visibility in characterizing these incidents as the most obvious signs of a profoundly racist society and has challenged city leaders, regardless of color, to be more open and aggressive in confronting racism. These leaders regularly question the wisdom of working through the Democratic party to achieve their goals, and sometimes advance independent candidates and policy platforms. Alternatively, pragmatic mayors like Goode and Schnoke may represent the future generation. James Jennings (1993) suggests that neither set of leaders will alone speak for the black community. They will instead share power, and ideally will discover ways to combine their respective resources to effect meaningful policy change (see also Morris 1992).

The extent to which the next generation adopts the politics of confrontation will have a profound effect on the third issue in minority electoral politics, the growing importance of multiethnic electoral coalitions. Demographic changes will continue to force minority officials, even in cities where minorities now outnumber whites, to develop closer alliances with white constituencies. The increasing racial and ethnic diversity of cities will create the potential for many different types of coalitions. Obviously it will be difficult to forge such alliances if the parties view each other more as the problem than as the solution. At such a moment of political flux, the side that expands its constituency by mobilizing disadvantaged citizens who currently refrain from participation may well tip the balance of power in its favor.

Urban Populism

Most scholars use the term "neighborhood movement" or "citizen movement" to capture the diversity of grass-roots organizing and protest that emerged during the 1970s and 1980s. One 1978 survey identified over 1,000 community and neighborhood groups organized around 40 different issues. Gary Delgado (1986) estimated the number of these groups at over 8,000 by the mid-1980s. Neither of the terms for these activities, however, is adequate. Although neighborhoods did reemerge as important actors in urban politics, considerable activity took place elsewhere. Statewide organizations like Massachusetts Fair Share and national organizations such as the Associated Communities Organized for Reform Now (ACORN) were central actors. Nor is it clear whether "neighborhood" refers to a geographic entity, type of organization, or a particular set of values. "Citizen movement" is a catchall phrase whose vagueness seems designed to capture as many developments as possible under one heading. Those who use this term tend to highlight the more progressive organizations and ignore the more conservative and even reactionary elements. Further, the inclusion of "movement" in both terms overstates the unity of these organizations.

A different conceptual framework is needed. The richness and ambiguity of these efforts may be better understood through the concept of "urban populism": urban because the majority of these organizations operate in cities; populism because, like the agrarian populists of the late 19th century, they are openly suspicious of concentrated power, whether in the form of big business or big government. Urban populists stress local solutions to local problems and build upon the strength of community churches, ethnic associations, and similar organizations. They work through and around existing institutions, much as their 19th-century counterparts did. Their membership also cuts across traditional political divisions of left and right, liberal and conservative.[15] This term also captures a central tension. Whereas many urban populists affirm the highest democratic ideals, others demand local control to preserve their communities racially and culturally—a reminder of the racism that tainted populism a century ago.

The analogy to agrarian populism should not be taken too far, however: urban populism of the 1980s and 1990s has been geographically fragmented and oriented toward short-term goals; urban populists have devoted little attention to fundamental critiques of capitalist democracy and have created nothing like the Farmers Alliance or the People's party. Still, the similarities appear close enough to make the analogy useful.

The roots of urban populism are as numerous as its branches. All of the protest movements of the 1960s appear to have influenced it (Boyte 1980; Delgado 1986; Fisher 1984; Perlman 1976; Piven and Cloward 1979; Rosenbloom 1979). The combination of Nixon's reelection, the end of the Vietnam War, and the winding down of civil rights/black power compelled many activists to rethink their approaches to social change. Some began to focus on tangible issues in their local communities.[16] A 1976 poll of leaders in 32 grassroots organizations found that 12 traced their roots to the civil rights movement, 6 to the National Welfare Rights Organization (NWRO), 6 to Saul Alinsky's Industrial Areas Foundation (IAF), and 6 to the Students for a Democratic Society (SDS) or to the antiwar movement (Perlman 1976).

Because the predecessor movements had different goals and used different strategies, the community organizations that emerged were remarkably diverse. Some of the activists who came through the civil rights movement and SDS favored the creation of alternative institutions such as food co-ops and credit unions. Welfare rights advocates argued for mass protests leading to systemic breakdown. Organizations like ACORN, a descendant of NWRO, emphasized grass-roots organizing around local issues. Some SDS veterans preferred to use the media to mobilize the population around long-term goals. And many organizations have employed any number of combinations of these strategies.[17]

Admittedly, some elements of urban populism did not spring from the protest movements. Many white, working-class neighborhood groups originated as a response to major development projects (e.g., highways and stadiums). These projects either displaced working-class whites directly or displaced blacks who moved into white working-class neighborhoods. These groups were essentially conservative; they wanted to shield their neighborhoods from outsiders. They were less interested in organizing for more political power or a better distribution of goods and services than in being left alone to determine the character and composition of their neighborhoods. Some of the best-known groups, such as Restore Our Alienated Rights (ROAR) in South Boston and BUSTOP in Los Angeles, developed in opposition to court-ordered school busing. Although these organizations used the same rhetoric of community control as other urban populists, their motive was racism and their politics were the politics of exclusion (Ackerman 1977; Davis 1978; Fisher 1984; Perlman 1976; Thomas 1986). Whereas some of these organizations are truly inclusive and progressive, a "parochial and reactive 'Not in My Backyard' stance" appears to have become more prevalent over time (Boyte 1991: 60).[18]

Perhaps the least well-understood element of urban populism has been the growth of alternative organizations providing goods and services. Examples of typical organizations that spread rapidly in the 1970s and 1980s include community development corporations (CDCs), which promoted economic development, affordable housing, and job training in particular neighborhoods; rape crisis centers; battered women's shelters; food co-ops; and housing co-ops. Despite their diversity, all of these groups originated out of a desire to meet basic human needs in a decentralized, democratic, face-to-face setting. Their brand of urban populism may have been less confrontational than the practice of ACORN and ROAR, but distrust of big government and big business runs through all of them. Such an attitude would seem to create conflicts between many of the new nonprofit social service agencies and the government whose funds support them. The relationship persists because of mutual need: alternative organizations need to survive and governments need to develop flexible mechanisms to deliver public services in the wake of new service demands, fiscal constraints, and widespread public dissatisfaction with the results of established agencies and approaches (Smith and Lipsky 1993).

Pressure to create these kinds of alternative organizations has increased in recent years. Spurred by the decrease in national funding for cities and the increasing mobility of capital, many neighborhood groups have created local development organizations to fill in the gaps left by state and market.

> "It's been a remarkable transformation," says Norman Krumholz, professor of urban planning at Cleveland State University and former city planning director under three Cleveland mayors. "What began in the early '70s as a group of grass-roots activist organizations, very strident in style and confrontational in expression, has been transformed into a set of enormously competent community development corporations that are now doing economic development, housing, and commercial development." (quoted in Katz 1990: 49)

Many of these goods and services are desperately needed, and the involvement by community organizations signals an expansion of their influence in urban politics. On the other hand, participation has forced these same organizations to stress collaboration over confrontation. Their housing and development projects often require a coalition of public and quasi-public agencies, churches, foundations, and private banks, none of which is legally required to cooperate. Put simply, "the era of 'baiting the establishment' is ending" (Katz 1990: 48).[19] "While LDCs [local development corporations] offer a route to community preservation and autonomy, their search for funding restricts their usefulness as independent neighborhood advocates and produces inherently co-optative tendencies" (Fainstein 1987: 330). Thus, urban populism provides further evidence of the rise and routinization of citizen participation.

Not surprisingly, the strengths of urban populism are also its basic weaknesses. First, alternative organizations that develop and remain outside existing structures of economic and political power can provide citizens with new avenues of political participation; such organizations are also by definition incapable of affecting the larger questions of public policy. To date, many of these organizations have eschewed electoral politics. Those representing less-affluent citizens fear cooptation by local governments and middle-income groups. They also believe that no matter how populist the rhetoric, elected officials will ultimately emphasize economic development without sufficient attention to redistribution. Many of those concerned with consumer and environmental issues claim that nonpartisanship is a key to their credibility. Other organizations steer clear of partisan politics to preserve their tax-exempt status (Paget 1990). Unless these organizations find some means of influencing traditional arenas of politics, they will be forced to continue reacting to decisions made elsewhere. And to the extent that they are financially dependent on government, they may be reluctant to advocate significant change.

Second, although the range of strategies and tactics has given urban populism tremendous flexibility in achieving local objectives, this same diversity has hindered its ability to transcend local issues and become a unified, national movement. Urban populists have succeeded to the extent they have previously because of their emphasis on short-term goals. There is no inherent reason why tenant groups in New York City cannot forge alliances with environmental activists in Seattle. But so long as the democratic ideal of urban populism gives priority to values of community over values of justice and equality, the conservative and clannish tendencies of urban populism will persist.

Finally, urban populism has yet to succeed in incorporating the urban poor. With few exceptions, the majority of populist organizations operate in working-class and middle-class neighborhoods. So far, the principal unifying force of urban populism has been the Reverend Jesse Jackson, whose broad democratic vision recognizes the value of community and places it within a larger framework of justice and equality. Whether Reverend Jackson (or anyone) can accommodate urban populism's conservative tendencies, and mobilize those who consider electoral politics pointless, remains to be seen.

CONCLUSION AND DISCUSSION

In trying to understand the larger meaning of citizen participation in urban politics over the last quarter century, it may be helpful to draw a few analogies to the Progressive era. Scholars have frequently commented upon the paradox of Progressivism—the simultaneous expansion and contraction of mass democracy (for a recent statement, see McDonagh 1993). The introduction of the referendum, recall, and initiative enabled ordinary citizens to have more influence over the timing and content of public debate, as well as more control over elected officials. Women gained the right to vote toward the end of the era. In theory the Seventh Amendment requiring direct election of U.S. senators opened the political process, as did direct primaries. On the other hand, personal registration requirements placed the burden on voters to make themselves eligible to participate in elections. Council-manager forms of city government permitted some measure of popular representation while shifting daily operation of the city to appointed professionals. Most important, the shift from ward to at-large representation diluted the influence of ethnic and working-class voters who had recently emerged as important actors in urban politics.

Recent changes in citizen participation have similarly moved in opposing directions. It seems clear that the political system is more open than it was in the 1950s. This expansion would not have happened without the civil rights movement. Blacks developed multiple modes of political protest as a substitute for traditional electoral activity, which had been ineffectual in producing equal rights for blacks. The national government, at least for a time, provided direct support to disadvantaged groups attempting to gain a better distribution of public goods and services and sometimes even political power. These relatively modest efforts helped to institutionalize some of the gains made by political protest. For example, bureaucracies that once were closed to political input now routinely mandate and seek citizen involvement. Members of minority groups have been elected mayors of many of America's largest cities. Thousands of community groups have sprung up around the country and engaged in debates over every imaginable area of urban policy.

Yet each of these gains has been accompanied by corresponding constraints on citizen participation. The national government no longer tries to mobilize disadvantaged groups; local circumstances are allowed to determine the appropriate level of citizen participation.[20] Citizens may have been incorporated into the decision-making process of public agencies, but primarily in ways that produce small, incremental changes in public policy. In a cruel twist of fate, minorities have reached city hall "precisely at the moment when the real power to deliver jobs, money, education, and basic services is migrating to higher levels of government and the private sector" (Williams 1987: 129). And many community groups have eschewed the larger questions of urban policy and failed to address the needs of the poorest neighborhoods.

One way to resolve this paradox, for both the Progressive era and the recent past, is to examine exactly who has benefited from these changes. Progressive-era reforms were explicitly designed to regain control of municipal government from ethnic immigrants by limiting the power of urban machines and "ward heelers." The cumulative effect of these reforms increased the political power of the middle class, especially professionals, at the expense of ethnic immigrants. Although it is impossible to explain the most recent reorganization of citizen participation with reference to explicit strategies of disfranchisement, the effect has been distressingly familiar. Middle- and upper-income groups have more of the political resources needed to be effective in routine modes of participation. While routinization has limited the potential for significant changes in urban policy, such changes are at the same time almost totally closed off to disadvantaged groups. Routine modes of political participation exhibit the same skew toward better-educated and higher-income groups as electoral politics. While absolute gains have been made since the 1950s, disadvantaged groups remain relatively powerless in urban politics. It does not seem too severe to conclude that racial minorities and the poor have once again lagged behind all other groups in reaping the benefits of change in urban politics.

If there is one lesson to be drawn from the last quarter century of urban politics, it is that political mobilization is a precondition to any meaningful approach to the problems of the urban poor. The most politically active groups of the last few decades have consistently done better, in terms of political power and distribution of public goods and services, than groups who were simply the targets of government programs. Disadvantaged groups have found ways to compensate partially for their lack of traditional political resources via political mobilization. Spontaneous protest has produced immediate results for disadvantaged groups, but not on issues of the magnitude of chronic poverty; those require political organization and the capability to participate effectively in electoral, administrative, and protest politics. Participation by disadvantaged groups in these different political arenas has become far more legitimate and open than it was in the 1950s. This is perhaps the most positive development in urban politics over the last few decades. Nevertheless, major changes in citizen participation have not been matched by fundamental shifts in public policy.

The difficulties of developing political coalitions that give priority to the challenge of poverty and the plight of American cities must not be underestimated. It seems unlikely but not impossible that the current generation of elected officials will genuinely attempt to address these problems. If so, these officials will undoubtedly make disadvantaged groups the targets of government action rather than providing them with the political resources needed to bargain as political equals. A more promising but less likely scenario would involve an alliance between the next generation of minority elected officials or urban populist groups and the disadvantaged. Together they could constitute a governing coalition in some cities and form a crucial swing bloc in state and national politics.

There is an additional reason for emphasizing the need for greater political participation by the urban poor, besides material benefits. Politics is more than an instrumental activity, more than a working out of who gets what and when, though this is a crucial dimension. Politics is also a process of becoming, a means for individuals to establish themselves in their own eyes and those of their neighbors as equal citizens. Equal citizenship is a precondition of self-respect for individuals in any society (Bowles and Gintis 1987; Gutmann 1988). Lacking the resources needed to participate as equals, low-income urban citizens are much less likely to be engaged politically than more-affluent citizens. Although signs of hope can be found (Berry, Portney, and Thomson 1993), considerable evidence indicates that the urban poor have become alienated (Cohen and Dawson 1993). After decades of neglect, it has increasingly become rational for the urban poor to sever their ties to the body politic. To make the American polity whole, this calculus must be changed.

To those who are unmoved by our vision of democracy, we appeal to self-interest. Urban poverty, drugs, and crime will not yield even to enlightened policy intervention unless the urban poor are able to mobilize to change destructive community patterns. For this reason, the entire society may be said to have a stake in increasing the scope and substance of citizen participation in American cities. Otherwise, we can fully expect disadvantaged citizens to again practice the politics of disruption, perhaps even on the scale of 1967 and 1992.

Notes

1. Some have argued that national government is inherently better equipped to address redistributive issues than are state and local governments, which must devote the

bulk of their resources to public safety, infrastructure, and economic development (Peterson 1981). We recognize the merits of this argument and do not mean to imply that municipal officials have always had the ability to alleviate urban poverty and have simply chosen to ignore the problem. We do reject, however, the assumption that the objectives of economic development and equality are mutually exclusive.

2. Readers familiar with the literature on urban politics and minority politics will recognize that our perspective is somewhat broader than that of other scholars who have stressed the transition from protest to electoral politics (see, e.g., Smith 1981).

3. See Shefter (1984) for a useful and perceptive summary of how political scientists have characterized urban politics.

4. "In none of the 18 projects created by the two programs did the organizational structure give the persons served a significant voice in formulation of policy, hiring of staff, or control of funds" (Hallman 1970: 4).

5. This framework is outlined by Peter Marris in Sundquist (1969b: 23–24).

6. Admittedly, these models are ideal types, and none of the examples of programs corresponds precisely to any one model.

7. In describing the War on Poverty, it may help to start by specifying what it was not. It was not intended to be a job creation program; federal officials assumed that substantial tax cuts in 1964 would spur economic recovery, generate jobs, and cut poverty in half. It was not an economic development program, which was usually considered a regional responsibility. And it most definitely was not a "war." Funding was limited and not directly tied to enhancement of individual incomes. In the broadest sense, federal officials envisioned the War on Poverty "as an opportunity program to assist the poor to begin to pull themselves up by their own bootstraps" (Wofford 1969: 74). The Economic Opportunity Act of 1964, the foundation of the War on Poverty, contained several different programs aimed at this objective, including the Job Corps and Head Start. This chapter's account of the War on Poverty draws on Cloward and Piven 1971; Friedman 1977; Haveman 1977; Lemann 1988, 1989; Levine 1970; Levitan 1969a, b; Marris and Rein 1982; Moynihan 1969; Peterson and Greenstone 1977; Rose 1972; Selover 1969; Strange 1972; Sundquist 1968, 1969a, b; Tulis 1987; Wofford 1969; and Yarmolinsky 1969.

8. Clearly, the civil rights movement was an important training ground for minority leaders. Still, even for those individuals already politically active, the War on Poverty provided an important source of material support and legitimacy (Browning, Tabb, and Marshall 1984).

9. The Kaplan study included 11 large- and medium-sized cities: Atlanta; Cambridge, Mass.; Dayton; Denver; Detroit; Gary, Ind.; Pittsburgh and Reading, Pa.; Richmond, Va.; Rochester, N.Y.; and San Antonio (cited in Marris and Rein 1982).

10. Interestingly, this pattern holds in the courts as well. When a local group sued the local school board over desegregation plans, the judge frequently mandated that the local group become an integral part of the desegregation order.

11. Nor surprisingly, the ability of disadvantaged groups to secure employment depended on the tradition of protest and the strength of municipal bureaucracies and mayors. One study in the early 1970s found that even though ghetto residents were supposed to receive hiring preference in Model Cities, they held less than one-half of the jobs and earned less than nonresidents in comparable positions (Harrison 1974).

12. Clearly, blacks have won elections in majority-white cities such as Seattle, New Haven, Gainesville (Fla.), and Rockford (Ill.). Our point is not that blacks cannot win where they are a minority, but that previous rates of growth are not sustainable.

13. For similar findings concerning the political incorporation of women in urban politics, see Saltzstein (1986).

14. An earlier version of articles included in Browning et al. 1990 appeared in *Political Science* 19 (3, Summer 1986).

Mladenka (1989) has argued that the impact of minority elected officials also depends on region (South versus non-South), the form of city government (reformed or unreformed), and the method of electoral representation (ward versus at-large).

15. One of the more fascinating features of urban populism is that support comes from both ends of the political spectrum. On the right, Peter Berger and Richard John Neuhaus (1977) have called for greater reliance on "mediating structures"—such as family, church, neighborhood, and voluntary association—to compensate for the alienating and unreliable aspects of the public and private sectors. In their view, any future growth in the welfare state should be channeled through these structures. From the left, Harry Boyte (1980) has pointed to citizen activism as a means of wresting control from big business and big government. In his view, the national government still plays an important role so long as key decisions are made by those most closely affected.

Both perspectives regard citizen participation not just as an instrumental good but a good in itself. The health of the community depends directly on the extent and vitality of political participation. The urban populist vision is clearly more normative than descriptive, and its implications for concrete practices and institutions have yet to be worked out in full detail. Nevertheless, it represents a challenge to the pluralist model of political behavior that has predominated since the 1950s.

16. In the words of Bill Thompson, who had been a Black Power activist and later joined Massachusetts Fair Share, "No line, no Ho Chi Minh, Kim Il Sung, Che. We tried to get back to real, everyday things, to a calm style. We switched issues from Vietnam and Cambodia and just moved in with the community" (quoted in Boyte 1980: 34).

17. If there has been one dominant strategy, it probably derives from Saul Alinsky and the Industrial Areas Foundation in Chicago. Since the late 1950s, Alinsky had been practicing a pragmatic, experimental approach to community organizing that emphasized tangible, short-term goals. He believed that achieving a series of small victories was more likely to create a sense of empowerment than championing abstract, often unwinnable causes. There was no preferred mode of organizing; whatever tactics worked were to be used. Alinsky further believed that the community's cultural resources should be used, not discarded or ignored, and that local institutions should be strengthened in democratic ways. Preexisting, authentic community institutions like local churches and ethnic associations became the foundations for grass-roots organizing. Class lines were more important than race. He offered his services to urban working-class communities, sometimes black or Latino but just as often ethnic white. Instead of racism or imperialism, the dominant issues were bank redlining, property tax rates, electric rates, and community right-to-know laws.

18. The conservative tendencies of urban populism have been downplayed by authors who have wished to emphasize the progressive potential of active working-class participation in politics (but see Boyte 1991). Yet like agrarian populism, the most recent incarnation is fundamentally ambiguous in its political orientation. The role of the Catholic church captures this ambiguity nicely. Over the course of the 1970s the Catholic church became a crucial source of funding for working-class (and other community) groups. The church-sponsored Campaign for Human Development donated over $50 million to more than 1,000 community groups during the decade. Church support helped to free many local groups from dependence on government funding, which enabled them to make broader demands of local and federal officials. Their support was crucial to the success of innumerable groups fighting for neighborhood improvements, lower utility rates, and similar tangible goods and services. On the other hand, the Catholic church's strong anticommunism has inhibited working-class groups from forging alliances with political groups on the left (e.g., Ackerman 1977).

19. Katz also cites the experience of the South Austin Coalition Community Council in Chicago. According to its executive director, the council regularly relied on protest to achieve its objectives in the 1970s. Now, "'we've gotten sucked into social services,'" he said. As governments have reduced their services, residents "'just bring their problems to us'" (quoted in Katz 1990: 51).

20. National and state governments have even encouraged, then discouraged, disadvantaged citizens from participating as consumers of public goods and services by establishing and then cutting spending on antipoverty programs, loosening and then tightening eligibility requirements, and decreasing and then increasing the bureaucratic hurdles for recipients of public assistance.

References

ACIR. *See* U.S. Advisory Commission on Intergovernmental Relations.

Ackerman, Frank. 1977. "The Melting Snowball: Limits of the 'New Populism' in Practice." *Socialist Revolution* 7 (5, September–October): 113–24.

Almond, Gabriel, and Sidney Verba. 1963. *The Civic Culture*. Princeton, N.J.: Princeton University Press.

Altshuler, Alan, and Christopher Howard. 1991. "Local Government and Economic Development in the United States." Paper presented at the Organization for Economic and Comparative Development–Kennedy School conference on "Local Development in Multi-Party Democracies," July 8–10, Paris.

Anderson, Martin. 1964. *The Federal Bulldozer: A Critical Analysis of Urban Renewal, 1949–1962*. Cambridge, Mass.: M.I.T. Press.

Auger, Deborah Ann. 1987. "Bureaucratic Policymaking through Administrative Regulation: Congressional, Clientele, Agency Interactions, and the Implementation of the Community Development Block Grants. Ph.D. diss., Massachusetts Institute of Technology, Cambridge.

Banfield, Edward C. 1961. *Political Influence*. Glencoe, Ill.: Free Press.

Banfield, Edward C., and James Q. Wilson. 1963. *City Politics*. Cambridge, Mass.: Harvard University Press and M.I.T. Press.

Berger, Peter, and Richard John Neuhaus. 1977. *To Empower People: The Role of Mediating Structures in Public Policy*. Washington, D.C.: American Enterprise Institute.

Berry, Jeffrey M., Kent E. Portney, and Ken Thomson. 1993. *The Rebirth of Urban Democracy*. Washington, D.C.: Brookings Institution.

Bobo, Lawrence, and Franklin D. Gilliam, Jr. 1990. "Race, Sociopolitical Participation, and Black Empowerment." *American Political Science Review* 84 (2, June): 377–93.

Bowles, Samuel, and Herbert Gintis. 1987. *Democracy and Capitalism*. New York: Basic Books.

Boyte, Harry C. 1980. *The Backyard Revolution*. Philadelphia: Temple University Press.

————. 1991. "Democratic Engagement: Bringing Populism and Liberalism Together." *The American Prospect* 6 (Summer): 55–63.

Branch, Taylor. 1988. *Parting the Waters: America in the King Years, 1954–1963*. New York: Simon & Schuster.

Brown, Michael K., and Steven P. Erie. 1981. "Blacks and the Legacy of the Great Society: The Economic and Political Impact of Federal Social Policy." *Public Policy* 29(3, Summer): 299–330.

Browning, Rufus P., Dale Rogers Marshall, and David H. Tabb. 1984. *Protest Is Not Enough: The Struggle of Blacks and Hispanics for Equality in Urban Politics*. Berkeley: University of California Press.

————. 1986. "Protest Is Not Enough: A Theory of Political Incorporation." *PS* 19 (3, Summer): 576–81.

————, eds. 1990. *Racial Politics in Amerian Cities*. White Plains, N.Y.: Longman Publishing Group.

Button, James W. 1978. *Black Violence*. Princeton, N.J.: Princeton University Press.

————. 1989. *Blacks and Social Change*. Princeton, N.J.: Princeton University Press.

Chafe, William H. 1986. *The Unfinished Journey: America Since World War II*. New York: Oxford University Press.

Clark, Kenneth B., and Jeannette Hopkins. 1969. *A Relevant War against Poverty*. New York: Harper & Row.

Cloward, Richard, and Frances Fox Piven. 1971. *Regulating the Poor*. New York: Vintage Books.

Cohen, Cathy J., and Michael C. Dawson. 1993. "Neighborhood Poverty and African-American Politics." *American Political Science Review* 87(2, June): 286–302.

Dahl, Robert. 1961. *Who Governs?*. New Haven, Conn.: Yale University Press.

Dahrendorf, Ralf. 1959. *Class and Conflict in Industrial Society*. Stanford, Calif.: Stanford University Press.

Davis, Mike. 1978. "Socialist Renaissance or Populist Mirage? A Reply to Harry Boyte." *Socialist Review* 8 (4–5, July–October): 53–63.

Delgado, Gary. 1986. *Organizing the Movement: The Roots and Growth of ACORN*. Philadelphia: Temple University Press.

DeSario, Jack, and Stuart Langton, eds. 1987. *Citizen Participation in Public Decision Making*. New York: Greenwood Press.

Domhoff, G. William. 1978. *Who Really Rules?*. New Brunswick, N.J.: Transaction Books.

Dommel, Paul R., et al. 1980. *Targeting Community Development*. Washington, D.C.: Brookings Institution.

Eisinger, Peter K. 1979. "The Community Action Program and the Development of Black Political Leadership." In *Urban Policy Making*, edited by Dale Rogers Marshall (127–44). Beverly Hills, Calif.: Sage Publications.

————. 1982. "Black Employment and Municipal Jobs: The Impact of Black Political Power. *American Political Science Review* 76: 380–92.

Fainstein, Norman I., and Susan S. Fainstein. 1976. "The Future of Community Control." *American Political Science Review* 70(3, September): 905–23.

Fainstein, Susan S. 1987. "Local Mobilization and Economic Discontent." In *The Capitalist City: Global Restructuring and Community Politics*, edited by Michael Peter Smith and Joe Feagin (323–42). Oxford: Basil Blackwell.

Feagin, Joe R., and Harlan Hahn. 1973. *Ghetto Revolts*. New York: Macmillan Co.

Fisher, Robert. 1984. *Let the People Decide: Neighborhood Organizing in America*. Boston: Twayne Publishers.

Friedan, Bernard J., and Marshall Kaplan. 1975. *The Politics of Neglect: Urban Aid from Model Cities to Revenue Sharing*. Cambridge, Mass.: MIT Press.

Friedman, Lawrence M. 1977. "The Social and Political Context of the War on Poverty: An Overview." In *A Decade of Federal Antipoverty Programs*, edited by Robert H. Haveman. New York: Academic Press.

Ginsberg, Benjamin, and Martin Shefter. 1990. *Politics by Other Means*. New York: Basic Books.

Gittell, Marilyn. 1980. *Limits to Citizen Participation: The Decline of Community Organizations*. Beverly Hills, Calif.: Sage Publications.

Gormley, William T., Jr. 1986. "The Representation Revolution: Reforming State Regulation through Public Representation." *Administration & Society* 18 (2, August): 179–96.

Gutmann, Amy, ed. 1988. *Democracy and the Welfare State*. Princeton, N.J.: Princeton University Press.

Hallman, Howard W. 1970. *Neighborhood Control of Public Programs*. New York: Praeger Publishers.

Harrison, Bennett. 1974. "Ghetto Employment and the Model Cities Program." *Journal of Political Economy* 82 (2, March/April): 363–70.

Hartman, Chester. 1964. "The Housing of Relocated Families." *Journal of the American Institute of Planners* 30 (4, November): 266–86.

Haveman, Robert H., ed. 1977. *A Decade of Federal Antipoverty Programs*. New York: Academic Press.

Jennings, James. 1993. *The Politics of Black Empowerment*. Detroit: Wayne State University Press.

Joint Center for Political and Economic Studies. 1992. *Black Elected Officials: A National Roster, 1991*. Washington, D.C.: Joint Center for Political and Economic Studies Press.

Judd, Dennis R. 1986. "Electoral Coalitions, Minority Mayors, and the Contradictions in the Municipal Policy Agenda." In *Cities in Stress*, edited by M. Gottdiener (145–70). Beverly Hills, Calif.: Sage Publications.

Katz, Jeffrey L. 1990. "Neighborhood Politics: A Changing World." *Governing* 4 (2, November): 48–54.

Katznelson, Ira. 1976. "The Crisis of the Capitalist City: Urban Politics and Social Control." In *Theoretical Perspectives on Urban Politics*, edited by Willis D. Hawley (214–29). Englewood Cliffs, N.J.: Prentice-Hall.

————.1981. *City Trenches*. New York: Pantheon Books.

Kirlin, John J., and Dale Rogers Marshall. 1988. "Urban Governance: The New Politics of Entrepreneurship." In *Urban Change and Poverty*, edited by Michael G. H. McGeary and Laurence E. Lynn, Jr. (348–73). Washington, D.C.: National Academy Press.

Kirschten, Dick. 1989. "More Problems, Less Clout." *National Journal* (August 12): 2026–30.

Lemann, Nicholas. 1988. "The Unfinished War" (Pt. 1). *Atlantic Monthly* 262 (6, December): 37–56.

————. 1989. "The Unfinished War" (Pt. 2). *Atlantic Monthly* 263 (1, January): 53–68.

Levine, Robert A. 1970. *The Poor Ye Need Not Have with You: Lessons from the War on Poverty*. Cambridge, Mass.: MIT Press.

Levitan, Sar A. 1969a. "The Community Action Program: A Strategy to Fight Poverty." *Annals* of the American Academy of Political and Social Science 385 (September): 63–75.

————. 1969b. *The Great Society's Poor Law*. Baltimore, Md.: Johns Hopkins University Press.

Lewis, Gerda. 1959. "Citizen Participation in Urban Renewal Surveyed." *Journal of Housing* 16 (March): 80–87.

Lipsky, Michael. 1968. "Protest as a Political Resource." *American Political Science Review* 62 (4, December): 1144–58.

————. 1984. "Bureaucratic Disentitlement in Social Welfare Programs." *Social Service Review* 58 (1, March): 3–27.

Lipsky, Michael, and David J. Olson. 1976. "The Processing of Racial Crisis in America." *Politics & Society* 6: 79–103.

Lovell, Catherine. 1983. "Community Development Block Grant: The Role of Federal Requirements." *Publius* 13 (Summer): 85–95.

Marris, Peter, and Martin Rein. 1982. *Dilemmas of Social Reform*, 2d ed. Chicago: University of Chicago Press.

Marshall, Dale Rogers, and John J. Kirlin. 1985. "The Distributive Politics of the New Federal System: Who Wins? Who Loses?" In *Urban Policy in a Changing Federal System*, edited by Charles R. Warren (127–62). Washington, D.C.: National Academy Press.

McDonagh, Eileen L. 1993. "The 'Welfare Rights State' and the 'Civil Rights State': Policy Paradox and State Building in the Progressive Era." *Studies in American Political Development* 7 (2, Fall): 225–74.

Milbrath, Lester. 1965. *Political Participation*. Chicago: Rand McNally.

Millett, Ricardo A. 1977. *Examination of "Widespread Citizen Participation" in the Model Cities Program and the Demands of Ethnic Minorities for a Greater Decision Making Role in American Cities.* San Francisco: R & E Research Associates.

Mladenka, Kenneth R. 1989. "Blacks and Hispanics in Urban Politics." *American Political Science Review* 83, (1, March): 165–91.

Moore, W. John. 1988. "From Dreamers to Doers." *National Journal* 20 (7, February 13): 372–77.

Mollenkopf, John. 1986. "New York: The Great Anomaly." *PS* 19 (3, Summer): 591–97.

Morris, Aldon. 1992. "The Future of Black Politics: Substance versus Process and Formality." *National Political Science Review* 3: 168–74.

Moynihan, Daniel P. 1969. *Maximum Feasible Misunderstanding.* New York: Free Press.

Nathan, Richard P. 1975. *The Plot That Failed: Nixon and the Administrative Presidency.* New York: John Wiley & Sons.

Nathan, Richard P., Fred Doolittle, and Associates. 1987. *Reagan and the States.* Princeton, N.J.: Princeton University Press.

Nathan, Richard P., et al. 1977. *Block Grants for Community Development.* Washington, D.C.: Brookings Institution.

Nelson, William E., Jr. 1987. "Cleveland: The Evolution of Black Political Power." In *The New Black Politics* 2d ed., edited by Michael B. Preston, Lenneal J. Henderson, Jr., and Paul L. Puryear (172–99). New York: Longman.

Nie, Norman H., Sidney Verba, and John Petrocik. 1979. *The Changing American Voter.* Cambridge, Mass.: Harvard University Press.

Pachon, Harry, and Louis DeSipio. 1992. "Latino Elected Officials in the 1990s." *PS* 25 (2, June): 212–17.

Paget, Karen. 1990. "Citizen Organizing: Many Movements, No Majority." *The American Prospect* 2 (Summer): 115–28.

Palmer, John L., and Isabel V. Sawhill, eds. 1982. *The Reagan Experiment: An Examination of Economic and Social Policies under the Reagan Administration.* Washington, D.C.: Urban Institute Press.

————. 1984. *The Reagan Record: An Assessment of America's Changing Domestic Priorities.* Cambridge, Mass.: Ballinger.

Perlman, Janice. 1976. "Grassrooting the System." *Social Policy* 7 (2, September/October): 4–20.

Peterson, George E., et al. 1986. *The Reagan Block Grants: What Have We Learned?* Washington, D.C.: Urban Institute Press.

Peterson, Paul E. 1981. *City Limits.* Chicago: University of Chicago Press.

Peterson, Paul E., and J. David Greenstone. 1977. "Racial Change and Citizen Participation: The Mobilization of Low-Income Communities through Community Action." In *A Decade of Federal Antipoverty Programs,* edited by Robert H. Haveman (241–78). New York: Academic Press.

Piven, Frances Fox, and Richard Cloward. 1971. *Regulating the Poor.* New York: Pantheon.

————. 1977. *Poor People's Movements.* New York: Patheon.

Preston, Michael B., Lenneal J. Henderson, Jr., and Paul L. Puryear, eds. 1987. *The New Black Politics*, 2d ed. New York: Longman.

Reed, Adolph, Jr. 1988. "The Black Urban Regime: Structural Origins and Constraints." In *Power, Community, and the City*, vol. 1, edited by Michael Peter Smith. New Brunswick, N.J.: Transaction Books.

Rich, Wilbur C. 1987. "Coleman Young and Detroit Politics: 1973–1986." In *The New Black Politics*, 2d ed., edited by Michael B. Preston, Lenneal J. Henderson, Jr., and Paul L. Puryear (200–21). New York: Longman.

Rose, Stephen M. 1972. *The Betrayal of the Poor: The Transformation of Community Action.* Cambridge, Mass.: Schenkman.

Rosenbloom, Robert A. 1979. "The Politics of the Neighborhood Movement." *South Atlantic Urban Studies* 4: 103–20.

Rossi, Peter H., and Robert A. Dentler. 1961. *The Politics of Urban Renewal: The Chicago Findings.* New York: Free Press of Glencoe.

Rossi, Peter H., and Alice S. Rossi. 1973. "A Historical Perspective on the Functions of Local Politics." In *Social Change and Urban Politics: Readings,* edited by Daniel H. Gordon (49–60). Englewood Cliffs, N.J.: Prentice-Hall.

Saltzstein, Grace Hall. 1986. "Female Mayors and Women in Municipal Jobs." *American Journal of Political Science* 30 (1, February): 140–64.

Schattschneider, E. E. 1960. *The Semisovereign People.* New York: Holt, Rinehart & Winston.

Selover, William C. 1969. "The View from Capitol Hill: Harrassment and Survival." In *On Fighting Poverty,* edited by James Sundquist. New York: Basic Books.

Shefter, Martin. 1984. "Images of the City in Political Science: Communities, Administrative Entities, Competitive Markets, and Seats of Chaos." *Cities of the Mind,* edited by Lloyd Rodwin and Robert M. Hollister (55–82). New York: Plenum Publishing Corp.

Smith, Robert C. 1981. "Black Power and the Transformation from Protest to Politics." *Political Science Quarterly* 96 (3): 431–43.

Smith, Steven Rathgeb, and Michael Lipsky. 1993. *Nonprofits for Hire: The Welfare State in the Age of Contracting.* Cambridge, Mass.: Harvard University Press.

Stone, Clarence N. 1989. *Regime Politics.* Lawrence: University Press of Kansas.

————. 1990. "Race and Regime in Atlanta." In *Racial Politics in American Cities,* edited by Rufus P. Browning, Dale Rogers Marshall, and David H. Tabb (125–39). White Plains, N.Y.: Longman.

Strange, John H. 1972. "Citizen Participation in Community Action and Model Cities Programs." *Public Administration Review* 32 (Special Issue, October): 655–69.

Sundquist, James. 1968. *Politics and Policy.* Washington, D.C.: Brookings Institution.

————. 1969a. *Making Federalism Work.* Washington, D.C.: Brookings Institution.

Sundquist, James, ed. 1969b. *On Fighting Poverty.* New York: Basic Books.

Thomas, John Clayton. 1986. *Between Citizen and City.* Lawrence: University Press of Kansas.

Tulis, Jeffrey K. 1987. *The Rhetorical Presidency.* Princeton, N.J.: Princeton University Press.

U.S. Advisory Commission on Intergovernmental Relations. 1979. *Citizen Participation in the American Federal System.* Washington, D.C.: U.S. Government Printing Office.

Wildavsky, Aaron. 1979. *Speaking Truth to Power.* Boston, Mass.: Little, Brown.

Williams, Linda. 1987. "Black Political Progress in the 1980s: The Electoral Arena." In *The New Black Politics,* 2d ed., edited by Michael B. Preston, Lenneal J. Henderson, and Paul L. Puryear (197–135). New York: Longman.

Wilson, James Q. 1960. *Negro Politics.* Gelncoe, Ill.: Free Press.

Wofford, John. 1969. "The Politics of Local Responsibility: Administration of the Community Action Program, 1964–1966." In *On Fighting Poverty,* edited by James Sundquist (70–102). New York: Basic Books.

Woody, Bette. 1982. *Managing Crisis Cities: The New Black Leadership and the Politics of Resource Allocation.* Westport, Conn.: Greenwood Press.

Yarmolinsky, Adam. 1969. "The Beginnings of OEO." In *On Fighting Poverty,* edited by James Sundquist (52–69). New York: Basic Books.

Chapter Nine

BIG-CITY FINANCES

Helen F. Ladd

Despite a severe economic recession in 1981 and 1982, and large cutbacks in federal aid under the administration of Ronald Reagan, some observers in the early 1980s concluded that U.S. cities were weathering the pressures extremely well and were in surprisingly strong fiscal condition. Perhaps the recession and cutbacks in federal aid were just what the doctor ordered to force big cities to manage themselves more efficiently and effectively than they had during the 1970s. Moreover, the continued expansion of the national economy throughout the decade brought expectations of even better things to come. But the 1980s brought false hope to many big cities. At the end of the decade, many big cities were significantly less well equipped to deliver adequate services to their residents at reasonable tax burdens than they had been two decades before.

One manifestation of this poor fiscal condition has been the budgetary problems of many large cities, including, most notably, Philadelphia, Detroit, New York, and Washington, D.C. Although the immediate causes of these budget crises are complex and include political and managerial deficiencies as well as the stresses of the national economic recession, they also reflect more basic or structural fiscal problems that have made it increasingly difficult for many large cities to deliver adequate public services to their residents at reasonable tax rates. This deterioration in the ability of cities to provide services exacerbates the political problem of balancing the budget by making all the options unpleasant: budget balance in a city with poor fiscal health can only be achieved by severe service cuts or large tax hikes.

Although the economic expansion of the 1980s provided some fiscal relief, it did not nullify the adverse effects of other long-term economic and social trends affecting cities, such as the increasing concentrations of poverty in cities and the movement of upper- and middle-income households to the suburbs; the growing pressures on city spending associated with the newer urban problems of homelessness, AIDS, and crack cocaine; and the dismantling of federal aid programs to cities. Although the situation varies greatly across cities, there can be little doubt that, through no fault of their own, some cities began the 1990s in weak fiscal health.

To put the fiscal condition of big cities during the 1980s into perspective, this chapter begins with a description of the adverse fiscal pressures cities have faced since the early 1960s. These pressures come from two directions: from the spending side as cities are pressured to spend more money to offset rising costs or provide additional services, and from the revenue side as cities confront the difficulty of obtaining revenue. Pressures from both directions have been operating throughout the last three decades, with spending pressures clearly dominating in the 1960s and early 1970s.

Following an overview of this period of rapid spending growth and then of fiscal changes that occurred in the late 1970s and 1980s, the heart of the chapter then addresses the basic analytical issue: What has been happening to the fiscal condition of big cities over time? The analysis includes a close look at changes in cities' financial or budgetary condition, in their underlying fiscal health, and in their fiscal performance during the 1980s. Based on the conclusion that social and economic trends outside the control of city officials have led to a significant deterioration in the fiscal health of many big cities, the final section argues that these cities need additional intergovernmental assistance from both state and federal governments.

SPENDING GROWTH, 1960–75

The hallmark of the fiscal picture in America's largest cities during the 1960s was the rapid growth in their spending. In particular, spending by the 28 largest cities (including that of their overlying school districts) nearly tripled between 1962 and 1972 and grew about 20 percent faster than that of the state and local sectors combined, which together increased their share of gross national product (GNP) from 10.3 percent to 14.2 percent (G. Peterson 1976: 41). Thus, as shown in table 9.1, public spending in U.S. cities represented a growth component of a growing sector of the U.S. economy.[1]

The rapid rise in spending by the largest cities increased the gap between the per capita spending of large cities and that of smaller cities. Between 1965 and 1973, for example, the per capita spending of cities with populations over 1 million increased at more than

Table 9.1 GROWTH IN BIG-CITY SPENDING RELATIVE TO STATE AND LOCAL
SECTORS, 1962–72

| Governmental Units | Spending Per Capita ($) | | Growth Rate, |
	1962	1972	1962–72 (%)
All state and local governments	250.36	659.02	163
All local governments	176.97	428.89	142
28 big cities[a]	191.68[b]	570.49[b]	198[b]

Sources: Reproduced from G. Peterson (1976: table 2). Original sources (published by
U.S. Bureau of the Census, Washington, D.C.) are: *Census of Governments*, 1962 and
1972; *Finances of School Districts*, vol. 4, no. 1; *Finances of Municipalities and
Township Governments*, vol. 4, no. 4; *Compendium of Government Finances*, vol. 4,
no. 5.
a. The big cities are Baltimore, Boston, Buffalo, Chicago, Cincinnati, Cleveland,
Columbus, Dallas, Denver, Detroit, Honolulu, Houston, Indianapolis, Jacksonville,
Kansas City, Los Angeles, Memphis, Milwaukee, New Orleans, New York, Philadelphia, Phoenix, Pittsburgh, Saint Louis, San Antonio, San Diego, San Francisco, and
Seattle.
b. City government expenditures plus expenditures of independent school districts,
population weighted.

double the rate of smaller cities (G. Peterson 1976: 43), so that by
1973 the largest cities spent three times as much per capita as cities
with 50,000 to 100,000 people. In many metropolitan areas, especially the older areas in the Northeast and Midwest, the rapid spending growth in the largest cities also widened the gap between the per
capita spending burdens in central cities and their suburbs (for city-
suburban comparisons, see Schultze et al. 1972: 294).

Because most of the differentially high spending in the central
cities relative to the suburbs probably did not translate into higher
services, yet was associated with higher tax burdens, such differen-
tials reinforced a variety of other economic pressures for middle-
and high-income households to move out of central cities. In some
cities there was concern that these incentives would lead to a vicious
cycle of economic and fiscal decline: the loss of middle- and upper-
income households leads to lower services and higher taxes for
remaining residents, which in turn encourages more outmigration
and further deterioration of public services (see Bradbury, Downs,
and Small 1982).

Explanations for Growth in Spending

Three major factors accounted for the spending growth in big cities:
rapid growth in public-sector labor costs, population decline and the

changing mix of city populations, and federal grants that promoted the proliferation of public services provided to city residents.[2]

RISING LABOR COSTS

Inflation, particularly inflation in labor costs, accounted for a large portion of the growth in state and local spending.[3] Because of rapid increases in the compensation of government employees between 1960 and 1971, the price index for goods purchased by state and local governments rose almost twice as fast as the consumer price index. Wages for municipal employees increased at about the same rate as manufacturing wages until 1965, but after that rose substantially faster. Throughout the period, the increasing generosity of fringe benefits for public-sector workers also pushed up labor costs in the public relative to the private sector. These fringe benefits, which included liberalized pension benefits and health plans, plus significant changes in working conditions such as longer sick leaves, lunch breaks, and vacations as well as shorter working days, significantly raised municipal labor costs.[4]

Coincident with the rapid rise in public-sector labor costs was the growth and expanding power of public-sector unions. Although one must be careful not to conclude that public-sector unions were the primary cause of the rise in labor costs, they undoubtedly played a role in assuring that the pressures of the tight labor market at that time were translated into higher compensation packages for state and local employees. Prior to this period, cities, counties, and school districts unilaterally set wage rates for public employees, who were largely unorganized. With the growth of public-sector unions came collective bargaining rights for workers and an increased willingness to strike. The number of person-days lost in the local public sector as a result of "job actions" or strikes tripled in 1966 and more than doubled each of the next two years. This 1966 acceleration in public employee strikes coincided closely with the sharp upsurge in relative wages of municipal employees in that year (Schultze et al. 1972: 298).

Studies of the effect of public-sector unions on wages suggest that unions are able to raise the wages of their workers by about 10–15 percent over those of nonunionized workers (see summary in G. Peterson 1976: 111). Though not insignificant, this differential hardly makes unions the primary cause of the growth in state and local spending. Nonetheless, the effect of crippling strikes and rising wages in the late 1960s brought city workers and taxpayers into open conflict and led many cities to adopt measures to strengthen the power of voters relative to that of public employees. For example, San Francisco voters forbade the city to tie the city's public wage rates automatically to the highest levels paid elsewhere in the state, Texas required voter authorization before cities could bargain collectively with police and firefighters, and some cities, such as New Orleans and Los Angeles, required city workers to live in the city so that they would view themselves as taxpayers as well as workers (ibid.: 111).[5]

These actions plus the recession of 1974–75 altered the trend in public-sector compensation. Between 1973 and 1975, state and local public-sector employees experienced declines in average real wages both absolutely and relative to private-sector workers (Bahl et al. 1979: 10). At this same time, however, fringe benefits continued to increase at a rate greater than inflation, partly in response to a continuing rapid rise in health insurance costs and the ratchet effect of inflation on pension liabilities. In addition, public officials may have traded restraint in current wages for less visible, and perhaps less immediate, increases in fringe benefits.

POPULATION DECLINE AND CHANGING MIX OF POPULATION

Also contributing to the rise in the per capita spending of large cities during this period was the fact that many of them were losing population at an accelerating rate. Between 1960 and 1970, 345,000 people left the central cities of U.S. metropolitan areas; between 1970 and 1975, another 1,404,000 people moved out. Because this outmigration exceeded the natural increase in population associated with an excess of births over deaths, the population in many large cities declined. Of the cities with population greater than 200,000 in 1960, 45 percent declined in size between 1960 and 1970 and 73 percent between 1970 and 1973 (G. Peterson 1976: 43–44).

This population decline increased the per capita spending of city governments because cities were unable or unwilling to reduce spending in line with the loss of residents. Many cities found that once road systems, sewers, and water networks had been built to accommodate the needs of a larger population, it was difficult to downsize them to accommodate the current, smaller population. Hence, spending for maintenance and repair of large and, in many cases, antiquated systems could not be reduced and had to be spread over fewer residents. Similarly, as cities lost residents, they found it difficult to reduce spending on police and fire services; as residents and firms left the city, they left behind vacant and abandoned buildings that required increased government spending simply to maintain prior levels of public safety.

In addition, because city pension plans typically were not fully funded, the growth in such plans during the 1960s created a debt to be paid by future city taxpayers; the generous pension benefits for current retirees who provided public services to past residents then had to be paid by a smaller number of current taxpayers. Although the full burden of the generous pension plans negotiated during the 1960s had not been felt by 1975, a few cities experienced dramatic increases in pension costs during the 1960–75 period. For example, Detroit's spending for retirement benefits increased by over 100 percent between 1969 and 1972 and amounted to over 21 percent of the city's budget in 1972–73 (G. Peterson 1976: 46).

Cities that were losing population also found it politically difficult to cut back public employment because many had come to be the sole source of new jobs in a stagnant or declining economy (G. Peterson 1976: 112). Adding to the political difficulty of cutting public-sector jobs was the fact that many major cities had become increasingly important employers of minority workers. By 1974, for example, the share of public-sector jobs going to blacks in cities such as Detroit, Newark, New York, and Philadelphia exceeded their share in the general population (ibid.: 113–14). And the Baltimore city school system at that time employed as many black professionals (2,400) as were employed in the entire private sector of the metropolitan area, which had eight times as many professional jobs as the city school system (ibid.: 114). In many cities, the necessity of laying off workers pitted unions (who supported the seniority system under which newly hired minority workers would be the first to go) against civil rights groups (who favored minority hiring goals).

Because middle- and upper-income people are more mobile than other groups, cities that lose population often end up with a poorer, more nonwhite, less-well-educated, and more elderly population than they once had. Because many of these population characteristics are associated with higher dependence on local government services (for example, the elderly's dependence on health and human services or the poor's need for social services) or with higher costs of producing a given quality of service (for example, the need to spend more to educate a child from a disadvantaged household or to provide fire protection for the densely packed older housing often inhabited by poor people), the increasing concentration of these groups boosts spending for public services.[6]

Proliferation of Services and Federal Assistance

A third factor contributing to the growth of big city spending was the expansion of services, much of which was financed by federal assistance. Under the rubric of the "Great Society" and the War on Poverty, the federal government sought to provide many new public services to poor and minority households. Ranging from early childhood education to neighborhood health care, to manpower training, and to legal aid, many of these new programs provided special benefits to the older cities both because many of the intended recipients resided there and because city officials aggressively sought federal funding.[7] With limited amounts of local revenue, city officials were able to provide expensive new programs for their impoverished residents. At the same time, however, many of these federal programs probably also led to increased local spending from the cities' own resources.

New federal assistance for cities and other subnational governments was also provided in the form of general revenue-sharing grants. This type of assistance reflected a different philosophy, namely the belief that the superior revenue-raising capacity of the federal government should be harnessed to provide no-strings-attached aid to state and local governments to use as they pleased. Under the 1972 General Revenue Sharing program, assistance was distributed to state governments and all general-purpose local governments. Large central cities benefited from some elements of the distribution formula (e.g., the tax effort component), but in some cases were hurt by limitations on the amount a particular jurisdiction could receive relative to statewide and county averages.[8] The categorical programs together with revenue sharing resulted in a dramatic upsurge in federal assistance to all cities.

Several factors accounted for this federal largess toward cities. Federal policymakers recognized that there were unmet fiscal needs in urban areas, such as inadequate housing and transportation, deteriorating neighborhoods, high crime, failing schools, and limited job opportunities, especially for minorities, and believed that the cities had neither the financial nor the political capacity to deal with these needs. Direct federal assistance to cities, it was believed, would provide the necessary financial resources and could be used to change the existing local power structure. Because states were viewed as uninterested in the problems of the underprivileged, assistance to states was seen as an ineffective way to help the cities; instead, direct federal aid to urban areas was required. Moreover, program-specific federal assistance gave political benefits to congressmen "in the form of health clinics to open, new city buses to deliver, and ribbons to cut at economic development projects" (Reischauer 1990: 229).

City Fiscal Health

Higher spending is often associated with higher-quality public services. As noted, however, much of the spending increase of big cities during the 1960s and early 1970s reflected increased costs of inputs (for example, wage costs) or increased costs related to factors outside the control of local officials (for example, population loss and change). The quality of public services provided by large cities probably did not improve much, except possibly in some of the functional areas supported by federal programs. The fact that streets were becoming dirtier and more dangerous, the schools poorer, and city services less dependable than in the past—at the same time that the number of municipal employees was expanding—often gave the impression that the problem was one of stagnant or declining productivity of city workers. Although there may be some truth to this impression, the more important reality was one of a changing population mix and an aging infrastructure that increased the costs of providing public services. The rising costs of providing a given quality of public services weakened the fiscal health of many cities—that is, they diminished the cities' ability to provide adequate services at reasonable tax rates.[9] Especially hard hit were the declining cities in the Northeast and Midwest. Added to the cost pressures in these cities was the erosion of their tax bases and their growing dependence on intergovernmental assistance.

Erosion of Tax Base

The burden of these rising costs was exacerbated in the older cities by the erosion of their tax bases. Historically, central cities had relatively large taxable capacity. Relative to their suburbs, for example, cities typically had higher per capita property values, higher retail sales, and higher resident incomes. With the movement of middle- and upper-middle-income households to the suburbs, the suburbanization of industry, and the movement of industry from the Frostbelt to the Sunbelt, the relative advantage of the cities deteriorated. Between 1950 and 1970, per capita property values typically grew much more slowly in central cities than in the suburbs and actually declined in some areas (Schultze et al. 1972: 202). Although the decline in commercial and industrial property accounts for some of the change, the more important factor in many cities was the decline in the demand for housing. For example, population losses of the order of 20 percent or greater in cities such as Buffalo, Cleveland, Pittsburgh, and Saint Louis between 1960 and 1973 significantly reduced the demand for and, consequently, the prices of city housing (G. Peterson 1976: 54). Associated with the loss of residents was also the loss of retail sales and the revenues they would have generated. Although only a few cities taxed resident income, the reduction of that tax base in cities such as New York and Philadelphia added to the revenue problems in those cities.

Whereas the sensitivity of local tax bases to population change hurt the declining cities, it helped the growing cities in the South and Southwest. New investment in growing cities combined with rising prices of housing and land generated by a vigorous demand for housing boosted their taxable property values and their overall revenue-raising capacity. These changes led to rising tax burdens in declining cities and falling tax burdens in growing cities. Between 1967 and 1972, average effective property tax rates increased by about 25 percent in declining cities and declined by about 28 percent in growing cities (G. Peterson 1976: 56).

GROWING DEPENDENCE ON INTERGOVERNMENTAL ASSISTANCE

The gap between cities' rising expenditures and their eroding revenue-raising capacity was largely filled by intergovernmental aid. Indeed, the massive increases in federal aid to cities, both directly and indirectly through the states, largely fueled the expenditure increase, especially in the older declining cities. As shown for selected cities in table 9.2, almost two-thirds of all additional revenue received by declining cities in this period came from state and local governments or was borrowed. Only 35 cents of each dollar came from local revenue sources. This division represented a major change from earlier periods when cities had relied much more on their own revenues.

Although this increasing federal largess greatly benefited cities and their residents, it made them vulnerable to cutbacks in aid or to changes in the mechanisms through which aid was delivered. Cities such as Cleveland and Detroit, for example, that relied on federal assistance for more than 17 percent of their general revenue in 1974, were hurt by the slowdown in the growth rate of federal aid to cities in 1974 and 1975. Moreover, cities that had been particularly successful in securing federal programmatic aid suffered significant

Table 9.2 SOURCES OF CITIES' REVENUE GROWTH, 1965–73

(MILLIONS OF DOLLARS OF GROWTH AND PERCENTAGE OF TOTAL REVENUE GROWTH)

| | Revenue Source[a] | | |
	Local Revenue	State and Federal Aid	Net Annual Borrowing
Declining Cities			
Baltimore	165	390	16
	(29%)	(68%)	(3%)
Boston	170	217	32
	(40%)	(52%)	(8%)
Buffalo	41	87	13
	(29%)	(62%)	(9%)
Detroit	260	279	45
	(44%)	(48%)	(8%)
Newark	41	125	9
	(23%)	(71%)	(6%)
Philadelphia	371	349	60
	(47%)	(45%)	(8%)
Growing Cities			
Atlanta	132	43	61
	(56%)	(18%)	(26%)
Houston	142	67	34
	(58%)	(28%)	(14%)
Memphis[b]	42	47	−1
	(48%)	(53%)	(−1%)
Portland	51	40	3
	(54%)	(43%)	(3%)
San Diego[b]	75	54	3
	(57%)	(41%)	(2%)
New York	2,386	3,619	508
	(37%)	(55%)	(8%)

Sources: Reproduced from G. Peterson (1976: table 10). Original sources (published by U.S. Bureau of the Census, Washington, D.C.) are: *City Government Finances,* 1964–65 and 1972–73; and, for Memphis and San Diego school district revenues, *Census of Governments,* 1967, and *Finances of School Districts,* 1972. All other school district revenues are from local budgets.
a. City government and school district.
b. 1967–72.

losses in federal aid with the shift to the formula-driven revenue-sharing program. For example, Boston, which was known for its skillful grantsmanship during the late 1960s, lost 20 percent of its federal aid between 1971 and 1975, while growing cities such as Houston, which had not aggressively sought federal aid, experienced large increases in aid (G. Peterson 1976: 62). New York City's failure to adjust to the slowdown in aid helped precipitate its financial crisis, as discussed in the next section.

New York City's Fiscal Crisis

The fiscal problems of U.S. cities hit the national headlines in 1975 when New York City effectively defaulted on its short-term debt. Although New York's fiscal health in the early 1970s was no worse than that of many other older cities, its financial crisis demonstrated what can happen when cities fail to adjust to their changing economic situations. Like many other older cities, New York suffered from the failure of its tax base to grow in line with the revenue needs of an increasingly dependent population and from the negative budgetary effects of inflation and recession. Also like many other older cities, its heavy reliance on intergovernmental assistance made it vulnerable to reductions in external aid. Poor fiscal health turned to financial crisis when the city failed to raise tax rates or to reduce expenditures in response to the 1974–75 recession and the slowdown in intergovernmental assistance.

New York City had historically provided a wider range of public services than other cities. In addition to the standard municipal services such as public safety and sanitation, the city also had partial financial responsibility for schools, it had to pay for part of a generous welfare program (financed fully by the state government in many other states), and it subsidized a variety of services—such as a major transit system, a city university system, public housing, and hospitals—that redistributed resources from middle- and upper-income taxpayers to low-income households (see Gramlich 1976). Although economic factors such as the demand for more space and lower production costs undoubtedly were the primary force motivating middle- and upper-income households' and firms' choice to relocate to the suburbs or out of the Northeast, the city's provision of these redistributive services gave firms and households an added incentive to leave; by moving elsewhere, mobile firms and households might find more favorable fiscal packages.

With the outflow of middle- and upper-middle-income households, the natural aging of the population, and immigration from the South, the city's residents became increasingly poor, uneducated, elderly, and non-English-speaking and, consequently, increasingly dependent on city services. Between 1950 and 1970, for example, the fraction of city residents over 65 increased from 8.0 percent to

Table 9.3 NEW YORK CITY'S SOURCES OF REVENUE GROWTH
(ANNUAL AVERAGE INCREASES IN REVENUE, IN MILLIONS OF DOLLARS, AND
PERCENTAGE OF TOTAL REVENUE INCREASE FROM EACH SOURCE)

Period	Local Revenue ($)	State and Federal Aid ($)	Net Annual Borrowing ($)	Unfunded Budget Gap ($)
1965–73	341 (37%)	517 (55%)	73 (8%)	—
1973–75	354 (22%)	125 (8%)	1,130 (70%)	—
Preliminary budget, 1976	206 (25%)	−7 (−1%)	—	641 (76%)

Source: Reproduced from G. Peterson (1976: table 12).

12.1 percent, and the proportion of the city's families with income less than the national median rose from 36 percent to 39 percent (U.S. Congressional Budget Office 1977: 289). But the city's tax base failed to keep pace with the increasing demand for city services. The number of private-sector jobs in the city grew only slightly between 1960 and 1970, but then declined by 12 percent between 1970 and 1975 (ibid.: 290, table 4).

The secular problems of the city were exacerbated by the short-term effects of the 1974–75 recession and high inflation rates. Because the city obtained a significant share of its tax revenue from cyclically sensitive income and sales taxes, New York's revenues were more sensitive to economic downturns than those of other cities that relied more heavily on property taxes. For example, the recession limited the growth of taxable sales to 1.5 percent in 1975 at a time when consumer prices were increasing by 9.3 percent (U.S. Congressional Budget Office 1977: 286). The recession also raised the demand for city services by increasing the number of welfare recipients and the number of households dependent on subsidized city services such as hospitals. Rising prices added to budgetary pressure by boosting expenditures more than revenues, especially those generated from the property tax, and raising interest rates on city bonds.

Like many other large cities, New York had become increasingly dependent on external sources of revenue. As shown in table 9.3, between 1965 and 1973, 55 percent of its new revenue came from state and federal aid. When the growth in aid leveled off in 1973, however, the city failed to raise tax rates or to reduce spending enough to offset the decline. Instead, as shown in the table, the city accelerated its net borrowing between 1973 and 1975. The city circumvented the legal requirement of a balanced budget by using a variety of gimmicks, such as borrowing on a short-term basis against overdue taxes that would never be collected, by reclassifying certain current account expenditures as capital expenses eligible for debt financing, and borrowing from the city's pension funds. During this period, the city's outstanding general-purpose debt escalated from about $9 billion to $12.4 billion (G. Peterson 1976: 65), and the city had about $3 billion in short-term tax and revenue anticipation notes outstanding and another $3.5 billion in housing project bond anticipation notes outstanding. This debt placed the city in the precarious position of being dependent on the willingness of investors to continue lending money to the city at a time when the investment community was nervous because of the January 1974 default of the New York Urban Development Corporation.

The financial crisis was triggered when investors lost confidence in the city's ability to repay its loans and the New York banks stopped lending to the city, thereby making it impossible for the city to redeem its short-term notes when they became due. Only with the intervention of New York State and eventually of the federal government was the crisis averted. The state used its own credit to borrow on the city's behalf; the banks and other investors were persuaded to accept a moratorium on debt repayment; the federal government, after much debate, in December 1975 made $2.3 billion of emergency loans to the city; and the city had to increase taxes, lay off 40,000 workers, and turn the management of its financial affairs over to the state.

New York's financial crisis spilled over to other large cities primarily through the municipal bond market. During 1975, borrowing costs for cities with low credit ratings increased substantially more than those for cities with higher ratings as investors became more cautious and began to distinguish more carefully among the quality of different borrowers. As a result, the average spread between the yields on high-grade municipals (those rated "Aaa" by Moody's Investors Service) and those of medium investment grade (those rated "Baa") almost doubled, from .64 percentage points in 1974 to 1.2 percentage points in 1975 (Browne and Syron 1977: 6). Even as the financial markets began to settle down in 1976, the gap continued to widen. Investors seemed to be especially concerned about the bonds of cities that had characteristics similar to those of New York. For example, between 1975 and 1976, Buffalo's interest costs shot up from 92 percent to 144 percent of the Moody's average long-term bond index. Investors were probably concerned both about Buffalo's own fiscal problems and about the ability of New York State to help its other cities. Other cities that had to pay higher interest costs—either as a result of the more intense scrutiny by investors or simply because, in the absence of good information about true credit worthiness, investors suspected they might be managed as badly as New York by virtue of their being old industrial cities—included Philadelphia, Boston, Newark, Detroit, and Cleveland (ibid.: 7).

But despite higher interest costs and continuing fiscal problems, none of these cities (with the exception of Cleveland, where a political conflict between the city's banks and the mayor briefly led the city to the brink of a financial crisis) experienced as severe a financial crisis as that faced by New York City, and by the late 1980s, no other city had had to turn to the federal government for an emergency bailout. Instead, other cities seem to have muddled through. As a result of the New York crisis, however, they began to face closer scrutiny from potential investors and new pressures to improve their financial management.

CHANGES IN FISCAL ENVIRONMENT, 1977–89

For the first few years after the New York City fiscal crisis, big cities benefited from the expansion of the national economy and the injection of new countercyclical aid. In 1978, however, federal aid to state and local governments began to decline, and two years later the economy slid into recession. After a brief economic recovery, the economy deteriorated again in 1981 as the country entered its worst recession since the Great Depression. Simultaneously, cities faced significant additional cutbacks in federal aid at the hands of the Reagan administration and, in many states, a revolt against local and state taxes. By the end of 1982, the economy began to recover, but federal assistance to cities continued to fall. The recession, high interest rates, and loss of federal aid in the early 1980s presented major new fiscal challenges for city governments and caused many observers to worry about how the cities would cope.

The long national economic expansion that continued throughout the 1980s provided some relief. To the extent that big cities shared in this economic growth, it may have helped them cope with the fiscal challenges they faced during the decade. As argued in subsequent sections, however, the expansion may have diverted attention from the underlying fiscal problems of many large cities.

Table 9.4 GROWTH IN BIG-CITY SPENDING RELATIVE TO STATE AND LOCAL
SECTORS, 1977–89
(CONSTANT DOLLARS)

	General Spending Per Capita (1989 dollars)			Growth Rate (%)	
	1977	1984	1989	1977–84	1984–89
All state and local governments	2,569	2,611	3,064	1.6	17.3
All local governments	1,633	1,566	1,851	−4.1	18.2
32 big cities	1,106	1,073	1,232	−3.0	14.9
New York City	3,413	3,165	3,850	−7.3	21.6

Sources: From U.S. Bureau of the Census, Washington, D.C.: *Census of Governments*,
1977; *Finances of Municipalities and Township Governments*, vol. 4, no. 4 (table 19:
38); *Governmental Finances in 1983–84*, table 13; *Government Finances in 1988–89*,
table 2; *City Government Finances*, 1976–77, 1983–84, and 1988–89.
Note: Data are weighted by population. New York City is reported separately because
of its large size. See note 10 in text for list of 33 big cities.

Slowdown and Resurgence in City Spending

George Peterson began his 1976 comprehensive study of big city
finances with the statement that 1975 would be remembered "for its
rediscovery of the budget constraint" (p. 35). That year, he argued,
marked a turning point in the rate at which the spending of big cities
would grow. No longer would cities be viewed as a growth sector of
the economy. As shown in table 9.4, Peterson's prediction was correct
for the late 1970s and early 1980s.

Table 9.4 provides data for 33 big cities and state and local governments on per capita spending for the years 1977, 1984, and 1989,
and growth rates for the periods 1977–84 and 1984–89.[10] The years
1977 and 1984 were chosen because they bear a similar relationship
to the national economic cycle; both follow the end of a national
recession (the 1974–75 and the 1981–82 recessions) by two years.
Consequently, spending changes during the 1977–84 period can be
interpreted primarily as secular, rather than cyclical, changes. The
period 1984–89 is one of economic expansion. The 33 big cities
represent the set of cities used for purposes of analysis throughout
the rest of this chapter. New York City is treated separately in table 9.4
because its large size would give it a disproportionate impact in the
calculation of weighted city averages.

Between 1977 and 1984, inflation-adjusted per capita spending
declined by 3 percent in the 32 big cities and by 7.3 percent in New
York (see table 9.4). Not only was city spending falling absolutely,
it was also falling relative to that of all state and local governments

at the same time that spending by the state and local sectors was declining as a share of GNP, from its 1975 peak of 14.7 percent to a low of 12.6 percent in 1984. Thus, Peterson's earlier characterization of big-city spending as a growth sector of the economy does not apply to the early 1980s; the growth in big-city spending lagged behind that of total spending in a sector that was declining relative to the rest of the economy.

The situation changed somewhat during the 1984–89 period of economic growth when spending by state and local governments grew by over 17 percent in real terms and increased as a share of GNP from 12.6 percent to 14.7 percent. During this same period, inflation-adjusted spending by the 32 big cities also rebounded and increased by almost 15 percent in real terms, with New York City increasing its inflation-adjusted spending by 21.6 percent. Although large, the 15 percent increase for the 32 big cities still falls short of that for all state and local governments (see table 9.4).

Between 1977 and 1984, real spending by big cities declined the most in the areas of education and libraries, welfare and social services, and police and fire protection. It increased most rapidly in the areas of corrections, environment and housing (particularly the subcategory of housing and urban development), transportation, administration, and interest outlays (see table 9.5, which excludes New York City). These rates of growth and decline are generally similar to those for all state and local governments. The most notable differences are the relatively larger increases in city spending on the environment and housing and on transportation. During the subsequent period of economic expansion, real spending both in the big cities and for all state and local governments increased in all categories, but most notably in corrections and interest outlays.

None of the rates of growth of spending in table 9.5 should be interpreted as changes in service levels. Over time, shifts in the division of responsibilities among levels of government and increases in the city-specific costs of providing public services can alter the relationship between city spending and the services received by city residents. For example, the 20 percent decline in inflation-adjusted city spending on welfare and social services in the first column of table 9.5 would overstate the decline in services available for city residents to the extent that it is attributable to the shifting of responsibility for these services to state governments. Alternatively, it would understate the decline in the quality of services if, all else constant, the needs for welfare and social services in big cities had increased. (See upcoming discussion of public-sector costs and service levels.)

Table 9.5 GROWTH IN SPENDING OF BIG CITIES AND ALL STATE AND LOCAL
GOVERNMENTS, BY CATEGORY, 1977–89
(GROWTH RATES IN PERCENTAGES, CONSTANT DOLLARS)

	1977–1984		1984–1989	
Category	32 Cities[a] (%)	State and Local Governments (%)	32 Cities[a] (%)	State and Local Governments (%)
Total general	− 3.0	1.2	14.9	17.4
Education and libraries	− 28.3	− 5.8	14.2	16.2
Local schools	− 23.8[b]	− 7.0	15.3[b]	18.7
Welfare and social services	− 20.2	6.2	11.0	14.9
Public safety	− 3.0	20.6	11.0	22.4
Police	− 5.3	1.9	7.9	11.7
Fire	− 4.2	4.9	12.3	12.8
Corrections	19.4	40.0	26.1	48.2
Environment/housing	12.0	7.1	17.4	21.2
Transportation	20.8	− 3.5	16.7	15.5
Government Administration	4.9	10.4	13.7	20.3
Interest	41.1	26.3	42.9	25.7

Sources: Tabulated from U.S. Bureau of the Census, Washington, D.C.: *Governmental Finances in 1976–1977*, tables 8 and 10; *Governmental Finances in 1983–84*, table 13; *Government Finances in 1988–89*, table 8; *City Government Finances*, 1977, 1984, and 1989 (table 7).
Note: Data are deflated by implicit price deflator for state and local government purchases.
a. Weighted by population. For list of cities, see note 10 in text. Sample excludes New York City.
b. Based on spending of only five cities—Boston, Baltimore, Washington, D.C., Memphis, and Buffalo—since they are the only large cities (other than New York—excluded from table) that have responsibility for schools. See text note 12 for further discussion.

Spending on schools is noteworthy because of its decrease in the 1977–84 period. Between 1975 and 1984, the number of public school pupils in the country declined from 45.1 to 40.5 million. This decline helps account for the reduction in inflation-adjusted total state and local spending on local schools and represents a significant change from the 1960s and early 1970s when the children of the baby boom generation swelled the ranks of public school pupils from 36.7 million to 45.1 million and increased pressure on state and local governments to spend more on local schools. The declining numbers of students plus additional state aid for schools in many states helped relieve the fiscal pressures of school spending on local budgets relative to the previous decade.[11] Working in the other direction for large cities, however, is the changing mix of their school populations;

higher proportions of children from disadvantaged households or with needs for bilingual education can significantly raise the costs of providing a given quality of education services. Hence, unless per-pupil spending is increased to offset the rising costs of educating city pupils, the quality of education provided in cities will decline. Overall, as shown in table 9.5, inflation-adjusted spending by big cities on local schools decreased by 28.3 percent between 1977 and 1984.[12] Having bottomed out in 1984, the number of pupils rose slightly in each subsequent year. This workload increase plus well-publicized concerns throughout the country about the quality of elementary and secondary education helped to account for the increase in inflation-adjusted spending on education in the 1984–89 period.

The spending changes documented in tables 9.4 and 9.5 reflect in various complex ways significant changes in the revenue sources available to big cities and in the fiscal environment in which they operate. The first change was the demise of the federal-local partnership and the precipitous fall in direct federal aid to cities. Second, partly as a result of the reduction in federal aid, cities became increasingly dependent on revenue from their own sources at a time when taxpayers across the country were rebelling against state and local taxes. Third, cities were buffeted by double-digit interest rates and confronted by taxpayers who were reluctant to pass bond issues.

End of Federal-Local Partnership

As early as 1974, federal assistance to cities had begun to level off. But the underlying trend in federal assistance was not fully perceived because of a temporary surge in federal jobs programs and counter-cyclical assistance provided through the Comprehensive Employment and Training Act (CETA), Anti-Recession Fiscal Assistance (ARFA), and Emergency Local Public Works. CETA funds were origi-nally intended to pay for training programs for people in areas of high unemployment, but the 1974–75 recession changed the emphasis of the program to the provision of public-sector jobs. By 1975, changes in the program guidelines enabled cities to use CETA funds to hire public employees for jobs that otherwise would have been financed by local taxpayers. Thus, the CETA program in effect provided sig-nificant general budgetary support for cities, especially older and poorer cities with high unemployment rates. During 1975, for exam-ple, 12–13 percent of the public employees in Cleveland and Wash-ington, D.C., were financed by CETA funds (G. Peterson 1976: 90).

In 1975, concern that restrictive budgetary decisions by state and local governments could threaten economic recovery stimulated congressional interest in an automatic countercyclical revenue-sharing program to help state and local governments counter the fiscal effects of recession. However, legislative debate throughout 1975 delayed the passage of the bill until 1976. In addition, Congress removed the automatic trigger and limited the program to five quarters starting in April 1976. Like CETA, this program targeted funds to areas with high unemployment and thereby boosted the revenues of many of the older and poorer cities.

Federal aid to cities, and also to all state and local governments, peaked in 1978. The elimination of the countercyclical programs and the leveling off of other programs halted the 12-year growth in federal aid to cities even before the election of President Reagan in 1980. Committed to reducing the size of government and decreasing federal involvement in state and local affairs, President Reagan proposed major cutbacks in aid to state and local governments in his first and subsequent budgets. Congress resisted some of the cutbacks but, nonetheless, federal grants bore a disproportionate share of the spending cutbacks. In the 1981 Omnibus Budget Act, for example, grant programs absorbed 29 percent of all reductions in budget authority despite representing less than 10 percent of spending on all programs that were cut.[13]

Moreover, grant programs directed toward cities tended to be harder hit than those to states. This outcome occurred in part because many narrowly defined categorical programs were consolidated into block grants. By designating state governments as the recipients of the new block grants, the administration expressed its philosophy that state governments are often in a better position than the federal government to deal with the fiscal problems of cities and other local governments. Of the 77 grants that were consolidated into block grants in 1981, 47 had formerly delivered federal funds directly to localities (Ladd 1984: 190). Although Congress mitigated to some extent the short-run effects of this reorientation by pass-through requirements and the earmarking of funds to previous recipients, the effect was generally to redistribute aid away from larger cities to rural areas and smaller communities.

In addition, three program areas of special importance to urban governments—Urban Development Action Grants (UDAGs), housing subsidies, and training and employment programs—suffered cuts of over 45 percent between 1980 and 1988 while other programs such as wastewater treatment construction, mass transit grants, and Com-

Table 9.6 PROGRAMS OF IMPORTANCE TO URBAN LOCAL GOVERNMENTS
(BUDGET AUTHORITY)

Programs	1980 (in millions)	1988 (in millions)	Percentage Change, 1980–88
Wastewater treatment construction	3,400	2,304	− 32.2
Urban mass transportation	2,430	1,736	− 28.6
Urban and secondary roads	932	948	1.7
Community Development Block Grants	3,752	2,880	− 23.2
Urban Development Action Grants	675	216	− 68.0
Housing subsidy programs	18,141	7,060	− 61.1
Training and employment services	5,532	3,023	− 45.4
Compensatory education for the disadvantaged	3,570	4,321	21.0
General revenue sharing	6,855	0	− 100.0
Grant programs of special importance to urban governments	45,287	22,488	− 50.3
All other grants	59,700	94,688	58.6
All other grants except public assistance and Medicaid	37,591	52,795	40.4

Sources: Budget authority figures are from Office of Management and Budget, 1982 and 1990, "Special Analysis H," *Special Analysis—Budget of the United States Government* FY 1982 and FY 1990, table H-11, (Washington, D.C.: U.S. Government Printing Office). Obligations figures are from Office of Management and Budget, 1982 and 1990, *Budget of the U.S. Government*, FY 1982 and FY 1990, Appendix Part I (Washington, D.C.: U.S. Government Printing Office). The spending programs are those presented by Cuciti (1990: 243, table 13.3).
Note: All figures are budget authority except in the case of urban and secondary roads, where, in recognition of the trust fund mechanism, obligations are reported.

munity Development Block Grants (CDBGs) were cut by more than 20 percent. Finally, general revenue sharing, which by this time provided aid only to local governments, was eliminated in 1986. The fall from grace of the cities during the Reagan years is documented in table 9.6; the 50 percent decline in aid programs for urban areas between 1980 and 1988 contrasts sharply with the 59 percent growth in all other grant programs.

The magnitude of these changes is portrayed in figure 9.1. By 1984 federal aid to cities (all cities, not just the largest 33) had declined to 14.3 percent of own-source revenue, its level in the early 1970s, and by 1989 it had declined further to 7.1 percent.[14] During the 1990–91 recession, federal aid declined even further, to 6.7 percent of own-source revenue in 1990 and to 6.5 percent in 1991. Moreover, the huge federal budget deficits combined with the Budget Enforce-

Figure 9.1 DIRECT FEDERAL AID TO CITIES, 1965–91

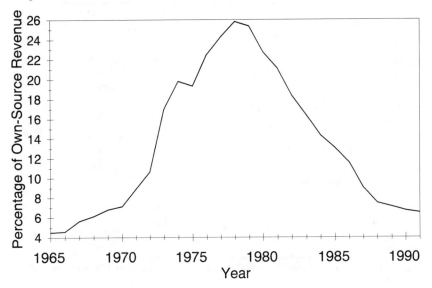

ment Act of 1990, which aimed to reduce them, portend, if not a continuation of the downward trend, certainly no turnaround absent a change in federal policymakers' attitude toward a federal tax increase. Thus, the decade of the 1980s witnessed a major change in federal-city relations. During this period, the federal government made it clear that it would no longer serve as the funding source for increased city spending or alleviate the fiscal stress of cities during recessions. Instead, the cities were left to fend for themselves or to rely on assistance from their states.

Tax Revolt

But the late 1970s and early 1980s was not a good time for cities to rely more heavily on their own revenue or that of their states. California gained national attention in 1978 as its citizens voted for Proposition 13, which rolled back property tax rates and limited the growth of assessed values. Inspired by this success at the polls and by the subsequent success of a similarly stringent measure in Massachusetts in 1980, taxpayer-voters across the country joined the tax revolt bandwagon and voiced their complaints about the burden of state and local taxes. Although voters in other states were not able to

Table 9.7 MIX OF REVENUES IN 33 BIG CITIES: 1977, 1984, AND 1989

	1977	1984	1989
Percentage of General Revenues from:			
Federal government	20.2	12.9	7.1
State government	16.6	15.9	16.4
Other local governments	2.3	2.3	3.5
Own sources	60.8	68.9	73.0
Percentage of Own-Source Revenues from:			
Taxes	68.4	60.9	60.9
Charges	20.2	21.4	22.2
Miscellaneous (not interest)	5.5	8.3	5.5
Interest	5.4	9.3	11.4
Percentage of Taxes from:			
Property	55.2	47.1	48.6
General sales	11.8	14.1	12.3
Selected sales	11.5	14.4	14.0
Income	13.8	15.7	16.4
Other	7.7	8.7	8.7

Source: U.S. Bureau of the Census, *City Government Finances* (Washington, D.C.: Author).
Note: Entries are simple unweighted averages for 33 big cities (for list of cities, see note 10 in text).

roll back property taxes as in California and Massachusetts, they succeeded in passing referenda to limit state or local taxes or both in many states and in making elected officials more reluctant to vote for tax increases. The effect of this national tax revolt was to lower total state and local taxes from 11.5 percent of personal income in 1977 to 10.3 percent in 1984.

Because state governments were feeling pressures by the cutbacks in federal aid and the tax revolt, they were not in a good position to help their big cities. Consequently, the average big city adjusted to the decline in federal aid on the revenue side almost entirely by increasing the share of revenues from its own sources. As shown in the first section of table 9.7, the percentage of general city revenues from the federal government in the average big city declined from 20.2 percent in 1977 to 12.9 percent in 1984 and to 7.1 percent in 1989. This decline was offset almost entirely by the increase from 60.8 percent to 73 percent over the same time period in the share of city revenues from the cities' own sources. In the meantime, the share from state revenues declined between 1977 and 1984 and then rebounded somewhat, but by 1989 still had not reached its 1977 level.

Between 1977 and 1984, almost every big city increased the percentage of its revenues from its own revenue sources. Boston, which was required under the Massachusetts tax limitation measure to reduce its property tax revenues by 15 percent per year for three years (to lower its effective tax rate to 2.5 percent), was one of the few exceptions. Unlike many other big cities, Boston had access to no other broad-based revenue source. Consequently, without new state aid, the double whammy of cutbacks in federal aid and local property taxes would have devastated city services. After much debate, the state government responded to the crisis in Boston and other Massachusetts cities by appropriating a substantial increase in state aid to local governments and providing Boston with only minor new revenue sources. Consequently, state aid to Boston doubled, from 21 percent to 42 percent of the city's revenue between 1977 and 1984, while Boston's reliance on its own sources decreased from 65 percent to 48 percent.[15] But Boston is an exception, not the rule.

Only in eight other big cities did the share of revenues from the state government increase during this period, and in most of them the increase was insufficient to offset the decline in federal aid.[16] Even in California, where Proposition 13 forced cities to reduce their property tax rates and where the state initially provided additional aid to cushion the loss of property taxes, the big cities still increased the share of their revenues from local sources between 1977 and 1984.[17] Compared to Boston, the California cities had much more flexibility to expand other local revenue sources. Thus, California cities maintained expenditures on basic services in the face of declines in intergovernmental aid and property taxes by increasing utility users' taxes, transient lodging taxes, franchise fees, and user charges. The shift to user-charge financing may have provided incentives for more efficient spending decisions, but the general pattern of moving away from broad-based taxes to narrow-based taxes and fees probably increased the distortions of the tax system and certainly raised questions of tax fairness.

At the same time that cities throughout the country were forced to rely more intensively on their own revenue sources, voter resistance to tax increases led them, as in California, to turn in many cases to nontax sources of revenue. As already noted, many California cities increased their reliance on user fees. For example, between 1977 and 1984 San Francisco increased the share of its own-source revenues from user charges from 18 percent to 29 percent, and Los Angeles increased its share from 18 percent to 23 percent. However, the shift in the average city was much smaller. As shown in the second section of table 9.7, the average big city increased the share of its general own-source revenues from user charges during the seven-year period only from 20.2 percent to 21.4 percent and to 22.2 percent by 1989.[18] Overall, 24 of the 33 big cities increased their reliance on user charges during the full 12-year period, while the other 9 decreased their relative reliance on fees, perhaps because the fee schedules they had at the beginning of the period were not raised to keep up with increases in the price level.[19]

The more significant source of new nontax funds for cities was interest earnings. The fiscal pressures created by the loss of intergovernmental revenue plus the opportunities provided by high interest rates encouraged cities to manage their financial assets more aggressively to increase their interest income. As a result, interest income increased from about 5.4 percent to 11.4 percent of own-source revenues in the average city during the period. Other miscellaneous revenues such as special assessments and the sale of property increased between 1977 and 1984 but then returned to their 1977 level (see table 9.7). To the extent that these miscellaneous funds derive from sales of property, they are not revenue in the standard sense; instead, they represent sales of assets and hence a diminution in the wealth of the government.

Historically, cities have relied more heavily on property taxes than on any other local tax (but cities typically derive a smaller percentage of their revenue from the property tax than do other forms of local governments such as counties or schools). In 1977, the average big city obtained 55.2 percent of its tax revenue from property taxes. Thanks in part to the tax revolt, however, property taxes declined to 47.1 percent of city tax collections in 1984, but then rose slightly to 48.6 percent in 1989. As shown in the bottom section of table 9.7, cities turned to no specific alternative tax to take up the slack. Instead, on average, big cities increased their reliance slightly on each of the other sources—general sales, selective sales, income, and other— with the largest increases in selective sales and income taxes.

Turbulence in Municipal Bond Market

Cities have historically raised about 50 percent of their funds for capital projects by issuing bonds in the municipal—or tax-exempt— bond market. During the 1970s, this proportion dropped with the increased availability of intergovernmental aid, primarily from the federal government, for capital projects. With the subsequent decline in federal aid, cities were expected to increase their reliance on the municipal bond market.

However, the early 1980s witnessed turbulence in the municipal

Table 9.8 PERCENTAGE MIX OF GENERAL-PURPOSE LONG-TERM DEBT
ISSUED IN 33 BIG CITIES: 1977, 1984, AND 1989

| | Percentage Mix of Long-term Debt | | |
	1977	1984	1989
Full faith	68.7	43.7	48.8
Nonguaranteed	31.3	56.3	53.8

Source: U.S. Bureau of the Census, 1976–77, 1983–84, and 1988–89, *City Government Finances* (Washington, D.C.: Author).
Note: Entries are simple unweighted averages for 33 big cities (for list of cities, see note 10 in text). The averages for 1977 exclude San Diego and Miami, and for 1989 exclude Columbus, because these cities issued no long-term debt in the specified year.

bond market as interest rates on tax-exempt bonds escalated, both absolutely and relative to comparable taxable bonds. For example, interest rates on high grade municipal bonds in 1982 rose to a peak of 11.57 percent, only 11 percent below the rate of return on U.S. Treasury securities. Tax-exempt municipal rates rose relative to taxable rates in part because commercial banks, one of the three major groups of lenders to the tax-exempt market (along with casualty insurance companies and households), were pulling out of the market. Between 1972 and 1983, banks responded to more profitable alternative investments and reduced their share of the outstanding municipal bonds from over 50 percent to under 35 percent. In 1982, the commercial banks absorbed only 3.5 percent of the new debt and actually reduced their net holdings in 1983 after the proportion of interest that banks were allowed to deduct on funds borrowed to buy municipal bonds was restricted to 85 percent (Poterba 1986: table 2.2 and p. 29). The reduced supply of funds by banks increased interest rates and made the market more dependent on individuals' willingness to lend. The 1981 tax act, however, reduced the marginal tax rates of individuals and increased the availability of other taxable investments, both of which reduced the attractiveness to personal investors of municipal bonds. Finally, the increased use of special purpose bonds to finance activities such as pollution control, industrial development, and mortgages increased the demand for funds, thereby contributing to the increase in tax-exempt rates.

The combined effects of record-high interest rates on long-term bonds and the tax revolt made it increasingly difficult for city officials to garner support for general obligation bonds to finance capital projects. Instead, they turned increasingly to various forms of creative financing, including sale leasebacks, revenue bonds—because they do not require a public vote—and special authorites that could issue revenue bonds financed by user charges. As shown in table 9.8, the typical big city decreased the share of its general purpose debt backed by the full faith and credit of the city from 69 percent of all new general purpose debt in 1977 to 44 percent in 1984 and then increased it slightly to 48.8 in 1989. Only by shifting to nonguaranteed bonds were cities able to raise much money through the municipal bond market.

FINANCIAL CONDITION OF CITIES

Despite the fiscal challenges of the early 1980s and the continuing cutbacks in federal aid, some observers have concluded that big cities were in stronger fiscal condition in the mid-1980s than in the late 1970s. Moreover, continuing economic expansion into the late 1980s should have boded well for big cities. But what was really going on in city finances during the 1980s and what was the condition of city finances during the 1990–91 recession?

One approach to these questions is to examine changes in the short-run budgetary or financial condition of big cities. A city is in weak financial condition if its current expenditures continually exceed its current revenues, if it relies excessively on short-term debt, or if it has difficulty meeting its cash needs. This *budgetary or financial* perspective, which is the focus of this section, is important because it is the context within which most local government spending and financing decisions are made in the short run.

However, budgetary or financial measures tell little about a city's underlying *fiscal health*—that is, the city's ability to meet the service demands of its residents at reasonable tax rates. Although budgetary condition and fiscal health are related, they need not be closely linked.[20] In some cases, fiscal mismanagement may produce a budget deficit despite a city's large capacity to raise revenue relative to the service needs of its residents. Regardless of its underlying fiscal health, any city can have a budget deficit in any year because of unanticipated changes in revenues or expenditures or because of reckless fiscal practices. In other situations, a conservative political and managerial environment may require the city to maintain a budget surplus despite the provision of inadequate services or the imposition of excessive tax burdens.[27] Hence, fiscal health and financial condition are best viewed as two distinct dimensions of city government finances that deserve separate attention. Moreover, one should be careful not to interpret an improvement in a city's budgetary condition as an improvement in the city's fiscal health, that is, in the underlying trade-off the city faces between lower taxes and more publicly provided goods and services.

Dearborn Data

Several studies during the mid-1980s concluded that the financial condition of big cities was remarkably strong at that time despite their fiscal challenges. However, this conclusion was overly sanguine. Most big cities appear to have only marginally improved their financial condition during the 1980s, and by 1990–91 many faced significant budget pressure.

The most detailed data on city financial conditions for the past two decades have been compiled by Philip Dearborn from cities' public annual reports (see Dearborn, Peterson and Kirk 1992 and references therein to earlier studies).[22] Other analysts have used the Dearborn data to argue that there was a striking secular improvement in the finances of large cities that continued, and perhaps even accelerated, through the first two years of the Reagan administration. One of these experts, George Peterson (1986), concluded that "at the end of fiscal 1982—in the trough of the national recession and after the year of steepest federal aid reduction—finances of large cities were in better shape than during any year of the 1970s" (p. 27).

Peterson supported his conclusion by comparing the 1982 performance of large cities in terms of operating deficits, accumulated deficits, and liquidity with their performance in 1971 and 1976. But 1971 and 1976 were both exceptionally bad years compared to the years immediately before or after, while 1982 was more normal. This observation emerges clearly from table 9.9 (Dearborn et al. 1992), where it can be seen that the expenditure-revenue imbalance follows a cyclical pattern throughout the entire period, with the largest city deficits tending to occur not during recession years but immediately thereafter.[23] By 1991, major cities appeared to be in as vulnerable a financial position as they had been at any time in the previous two decades.

Trends Based on Census and Other Data

Tables 9.10, 9.11, and 9.12 provide additional information about the trends in cities' financial condition based on data from the U.S. Bureau of the Census and other sources. Various measures are

Table 9.9 TOTAL GENERAL FUND REVENUES COMPARED TO EXPENDITURES
IN 28 SELECTED MAJOR CITIES

Fiscal Year	Number of Cities in which Expenditures Exceeded Revenues	Total of All Cities' Excess (or Deficiency of) Revenues ($, in millions)	Percentage of Total Expenditures
1971	16	− 23.1	− .5
1972	12	16.1	.3
1973	8	175.1	3.5
1974	9	156.1	2.9
1975	16	− 28.4	− .4
1976	13	− 154.2	− 2.2
1977	6	230.6	3.1
1978	12	73.6	1.0
1979	9	98.8	1.2
1980	19	− 188.7	− 2.2
1981	10	212.6	1.5
1982	12	168.9	1.2
1983	16	− 164.4	− 1.3
1984	6	309.9	2.4
1989	16	22.4	.2
1990	15	− 51.2	− .3
1991	14 of 19	− 355.6	− 3.0

Source: Published annual financial reports of 28 cities, as compiled by Dearborn et al. (1992).
Note: Data for New York and Los Angeles not included.

reported for two comparable three-year periods (1977–79 and 1984–86), as well as for 1989 and 1991. The three-year periods were chosen to focus attention on secular, rather than cyclical, trends. Both periods begin two years after a recession (the 1974–75 recession in the former case and the 1981–82 recession in the latter case) and encompass years of economic expansion. The year 1989 represents the end of the long expansion and the year just prior to the 1990–91 recession. The year 1991 is a recession year.

MORE CONSERVATIVE FINANCIAL MANAGEMENT

The first two rows in table 9.10 (late 1970s and mid-1980s) present average surpluses (or deficits) over time for the 33 big cities and indicate that during the mid-1980s cities experienced slightly higher average surpluses than those observed in the earlier period. For each city, surpluses (or deficits) are measured as the difference between annual expenditures (excluding capital outlays) and revenues expressed as a percentage of expenditures using data from the annual

Table 9.10 AVERAGE SURPLUS AND PENSION CONTRIBUTIONS IN 33 BIG CITIES

	Late 1970s			Mid-1980s				
	1977	1978	1979	1984	1985	1986	1989	1991
General purpose surplus (higher is better)	0.139	0.134	0.128	0.145	0.147	0.148	0.080	.063
Total	0.069	0.067	0.083	0.075	0.075	0.071	0.020	.024
Contribution to pensions as percentage of wages and salaries	0.112	0.121	0.128	0.150	0.148	0.141	0.122	.110

Source: U.S. Bureau of the Census, *City Government Finances*, various years. Ratios calculated by author from data in table 7, "Finances of Individual City Governments Having 300,000 Population or More" [various years]. (Prior to 1982, table 8, "Finances of Individual City Governments Having 300,000 Population or More, in Detail: 1979–1980".) Information on pension contributions is reported in table 5, "Finances of Individual and Selected Urban Town and Township Governments Having 50,000 Population or More" [various years].

Notes: Entries are unweighted averages across 33 big cities (for list of cities, see note 10 in text). The general purpose surplus is defined as total general purpose revenues minus general purpose current account expenditures divided by expenditures. Total revenue includes both own-source and intergovernmental revenue. Total expenditures are general expenditures minus capital outlays plus long-term debt retired, adjusted for refunding plus contributions to city retirement systems. The total surplus is similar to the general purpose surplus, except that revenues include utility revenues and expenditures include utility expenditures.

Table 9.11 AVERAGE FINANCIAL MEASURES IN 33 BIG CITIES

	Late 1970s				Mid-1980s			
	1977	1978	1979	1984	1985	1986	1989	1991
Capital outlay as percentage of direct general expenditures	19.5	17.7	18.1	18.0	17.1	17.2	19.5	18.3
Short-term debt as percentage of general revenue	6.9	5.0	5.3	6.6	5.7	5.0	2.1	4.3
Debt service as percentage of general revenue	9.7	9.4	9.3	12.4	13.6	14.0	14.3	17.9
Debt service minus interest earned as percentage of general revenue net of interest earnings	6.4	6.0	5.2	5.8	6.0	6.4	5.9	9.8

Source: U.S. Bureau of the Census, *City Government Finances*, various years.
Notes: Entries are unweighted averages across 33 big cities (for list of cities, see note 10 in text).

Table 9.12 CHANGES IN BOND RATINGS IN 15 CITIES

	Bond Ratings	
	1977	1987
Cities with Downgrades:		
Houston	Aaa	Aa
Milwaukee	Aaa	Aa
San Francisco	Aaa	Aa1
Chicago	A1	Baa1
New Orleans	A	Baa
Boston	A	Baa1
Cleveland	A	Baa
Philadelphia	A	Baa
Pittsburgh	A	Baa1
Saint Louis	A	Baa
Buffalo	Baa1	Baa
Cities with Upgrades:		
Phoenix	Aa	Aa1
San Diego	Aa	Aaa
Baltimore	A	A1
New York	Ba	Baa1

Source: Moody's Investors Services, as reported in International City Management Association, *Municipal Year Book*, 1978 and 1988 (Chicago: International City Management Association).
Key to ratings: Aaa, best quality; Aa, high quality; A, upper medium grade; Baa, medium grade; Ba, speculative; B, lacks characteristics of desirable investment; A1 and Baa1, strongest investment characteristics within the category.

Census publication, *City Government Finances*.[24] Because the Census does not distinguish between the various city funds, these measures should be viewed as proxies for comprehensive measures of current account surpluses (or deficits) that are independent of the fund structure in particular cities. The two rows differ only in the treatment of utility enterprises. By excluding all the expenditures and revenues of utilities, the first row focuses exclusively on the general-purpose activities of cities. The second row provides a broader picture based on the combination of general-purpose and utility revenues.[25]

Despite some minor conceptual limitations with this measure, the surplus (or deficit) for each city serves as a measure of the budgetary pressure facing the city, and changes in a city's surplus indicate changes in budgetary pressure over time.[26] The lower a city's general-purpose surplus, the less revenue the city has for capital outlays during the year or for building up fund balances that can ease the budgetary situation in subsequent years. In general, the total surplus measure will be lower than that for general purposes because, unlike general-purpose expenditures, utility expenditures include capital outlays. Because of the inclusion of the capital spending of utilities in the measure of total surplus, the general-purpose measure is probably to be preferred.[27]

By either measure, the mid-1980s witnessed slightly higher surpluses than those observed in the earlier period. The average general-purpose surplus, for example, rose from about 13.5 percent in the 1970s to over 14.5 percent in the mid-1980s. Although the increase in the average city surplus is not large, the fact that it occurred during a period of reductions in federal aid, including aid for capital spending, is significant. The figures suggest that despite such cutbacks, or perhaps because of them, cities apparently managed their finances slightly more conservatively in the mid-1980s than in the 1970s. Strikingly, however, this momentum was not long-lived. Consistent with the Dearborn data, the last two columns of table 9.10 show that the average surplus dropped significantly in 1989 and even further during the recession in 1991.

Closer examination of the period between the late 1970s and mid-1980s shows that even while the average big city was improving its financial position, many cities experienced continuing financial pressure. For example, despite the growth in the national economy, more than a third of the 33 big cities had low or negative budget surpluses in both periods. Contrary to the rosy picture presented in the mid-1980s by Peterson and Dearborn, we find a stubborn persistence of budgetary pressure in many cities, and emerging budgetary problems in a few western cities that had historically been relatively free of such difficulties.

Further evidence of the slightly more conservative financial management during the mid-1980s appears in the bottom row of table 9.10 in the form of a growing fraction of wages and salaries contributed by cities to city-operated pension plans. Because future pension liabilities are accrued annually on behalf of current workers, fiscally responsible behavior requires that money be set aside annually in a fund to meet these future liabilities. Historically, however, many city pension plans have operated on a pay-as-you go basis. For cities with declining work forces, such systems can impose significant financial burdens on future taxpayers. Partly in response to the increased scrutiny of pension funding arrangements by the agencies that rate municipal bonds, many cities increased the amount of funds set aside for future pensions during the mid-1980s. Boston exhibited the greatest change during this period, increasing its contributions from 6 percent of wages and salaries in 1977 to 22 percent in 1984. Other cities such as Cincinnati, Memphis, Miami, Milwaukee, Jacksonville, and Chicago had smaller, but still significant, increases. However, the data for 1989 suggest that the upward trend was not insulated from cyclical pressures; in 1989, average contributions had fallen to the levels of the late 1970s, and they fell even further in 1991. However, the strong performance of the stock market in the 1980s allowed most cities to increase the funded ratio of their pension plans (Dearborn et al. 1992).

CAPITAL SPENDING AS MEASURE OF BUDGETARY PRESSURE

A city facing severe budgetary pressure is likely to cut back spending wherever it can. One possibility is to reduce capital spending. In many cases, cutting back on capital spending may be less politically painful than cutting back on current services such as public safety. Cutbacks in police services, for example, expose the city official to the anger of both voters, in their capacity of service recipients concerned about high and rising crime rates, and powerful public-sector unions concerned about preserving their members' jobs. In contrast, the effects of not spending on capital projects are often less visible. Citizens frequently are not in a good position to understand the consequences of underinvestment in capital, except, of course, in cases where the collapse of a bridge or a broken water main forcefully dramatizes the problem of underinvestment in city capital.

This logic suggests that changes over time in capital spending as a percentage of total spending might serve as an additional measure of changes in the overall financial condition of cities. A reduction in capital spending relative to other spending could indicate more severe budgetary pressure than a situation in which capital spending is maintained. The first row of table 9.11 shows that capital spending declined from 19.5 percent of direct general spending in 1977 to 17.2 percent in 1986. This pattern implies that, contrary to the rosier view indicated previously by the slight rise in budgetary surpluses, the average financial condition of cities may have been tighter in the mid-1980s than in the late 1970s.

Alternatively, the reduced capital spending may be interpreted as another manifestation of the fiscal conservatism of the mid-1980s. According to this interpretation, city officials may have moved slowly on new capital projects for fear of overcommitting city resources, and both the observed reduction in capital spending in the mid-1980s and the higher budgetary surpluses would indicate a more conservative fiscal posture.

This latter interpretation may shed light on the rise in capital spending in 1989. The return of capital spending to its 1977 level, along with the fall in the average budgetary surplus, may indicate more aggressive financial management in the late 1980s than in the mid-1980s. In hindsight and with the knowledge of the slowdown in the economy and the looming recession, this more aggressive fiscal management provides a harbinger of emerging financial problems.[28]

DEBT BURDENS AND BORROWING COSTS

As discussed earlier, the New York City fiscal crisis of 1975 focused attention on that city's heavy reliance on short-term debt to finance current account deficits. Most cities use short-term debt to even out disparities between spending and revenue flows during the fiscal year. Short-term debt has, by definition, a maturity less than one year and, when used appropriately, is paid off by the end of the fiscal year. Problems can arise when cities rely on short-term debt to finance current account deficits, as was true in New York, or when they try to finance long-term capital projects with short-term borrowing.

As shown in the second row of table 9.11, the average amount of short-term debt outstanding as a share of general revenue at the end of the fiscal year in the mid-1980s was about the same as in the late 1970s. However, the number of cities with short-term debt outstanding declined over the period. From a high of 24 cities in 1977, the number of cities fell to 17 by 1986. Several cities such as Detroit, New York, Pittsburgh, and Seattle that made significant use of short-term debt in 1977 (defined as greater than 8 percent of general revenues) apparently changed their ways and reduced their reliance on such debt to more manageable levels in many (but not all) of the other five years (to 1986). A few cities, including Buffalo, Columbus, and Jacksonville, relied extensively on short-term borrowing in both periods. And some cities such as Memphis and Milwaukee relied heavily on short-term debt in the mid-1980s but not in the late 1970s. Thus, the overall picture is a bit mixed; extensive use of short-term debt continued to be a common practice in many big cities, but cities in the aggregate appeared to be somewhat more conservative about their use of such debt in the mid-1980s. The lower ratios for 1989 and 1991 provide no cause for concern.

Debt service costs represent another measure of budgetary pressure. These costs include both interest payments and retirement of long-term debt and represent a city's annual costs of using capital. In the short run, such costs are essentially uncontrollable. The higher a city's debt service burdens, the less flexibility the city has to finance other services and, consequently, the more budgetary pressure it faces. Table 9.11 shows a marked increase in debt service costs over time. From an average of about 9.5 percent of general revenues in the late 1970s, debt service costs increased to about 13 percent in the mid-1980s, presumably in response to the higher interest rates of the 1980s.

These figures overstate the burden of higher interest rates on city finances, however, because cities also benefit by earning higher returns on their invested assets. The net effect is shown in the next line of table 9.11, which reports general purpose debt service costs minus interest earnings as a fraction of general revenues net of interest earnings. This measure shows little change over the two periods; in other words, the combined effects of higher interest rates and changes in debt service did not fundamentally alter the financial condition of big cities from 1977 to 1986. Approximately 94 percent of revenues other than interest earnings were available for current account spending in both periods.

The 1990–91 recession put significant pressure on big cities. As a share of general revenue, debt service increased to 17.9 percent in the typical big city and, net of interest earnings, increased to 9.8 percent (table 9.11). The fall in interest rates reduced cities' interest earnings, but also allowed many to reduce debt service by refinancing some of their outstanding debt.

BOND RATINGS

A final indicator of changes in the financial condition of big cities is changes over time in their bond ratings. Moody's Investors Service grounds its ratings on a city's economic base, measures of indebtedness, administrative factors, and financial factors. Hence, the ratings reflect more than just current financial conditions. Nonetheless, bond ratings partially reflect financial conditions. Moreover, they have direct implications for the city's budgetary condition. By raising the cost of current borrowing, a downgrading of a city's general obligation bond rating increases the pressure on a city's current budget.

Table 9.12 lists the 11 cities whose ratings were lower in 1987 than in 1977 and the four cities whose ratings improved during the same period. Significantly, more ratings were lowered than were raised during the period. The 17 big cities not shown in the table (excluding Washington, D.C.) experienced no change in their bond ratings. Among the cities with declining ratios are three—Houston,

Milwaukee, and San Francisco—that began the period with the highest rating and many cities that had persistent budgetary problems throughout the period. Notwithstanding the fact that bond ratings measure more than just financial condition, the large number of downgrades is consistent with a deterioration in the average financial condition of big cities even in the mid-1980s.

Between 1987 and 1992, seven big cities received upgrades (Boston, Chicago, Cleveland, Columbus, Phoenix, Pittsburgh, and Seattle) and four (Jacksonville, Philadelphia, San Francisco, and San Jose) received downgrades. Philadelphia's rating was reduced to below-investment grade in 1991, where it stayed until 1993.

Summary

The average financial condition of big cities was apparently no more favorable in the mid-1980s than in a comparable period in the late 1970s. Although the average budget surplus (as measured with data from the *Census of Governments*) was slightly higher in the mid-1980s, evidence of persistently skimpy surpluses suggests little improvement in many big cities. In addition, the reduction in capital spending and the finding that more cities experienced downgrades than upgrades in bond ratings suggest that in some ways budgetary pressure may have been more severe in the mid-1980s than in the late 1970s.

This conclusion, plus the observation that the surplus in the average big city declined significantly in 1989, suggests that the financial condition of many big cities was not particularly strong at the start of the 1990–91 recession. During and immediately after the recession, conditions deteriorated further.

FISCAL HEALTH

This focus on city budgets and city financial conditions diverts attention from a more fundamental or basic issue: What has happened over time to the ability of big cities to provide public services at reasonable tax rates? This question can be approached in two ways. First, one can look at changes in the factors outside the control of city officials that determine the fiscal options facing a city, that is, the trade-off the city faces between service levels and tax rates. Second, one can look at actual city performance with respect to service levels and tax burdens. The first approach is the topic of this section, on fiscal health; the second approach is the topic of the following section, on fiscal performance.

Measuring the underlying fiscal health of a city is a complicated task. Hence, rather than undertaking a new analysis of fiscal health, I rely heavily here on the analytical framework and findings contained in the updated edition of *America's Ailing Cities: Fiscal Health and the Design of Urban Policy* (Ladd and Yinger 1991). That book's comprehensive study of 70 major central cities documents a significant deterioration between 1972 and 1982 in the ability of central cities, and more specifically America's biggest cities, to meet, using state and local resources, the service needs of their residents. The Epilogue to *America's Ailing Cities* demonstrates that the economic expansion of the 1980s may have brought some relief to big cities. Nonetheless, many big cities still ended the decade in poor fiscal health.

Standardized Fiscal Health

A city has poor fiscal health if it has limited revenue-raising capacity relative to its expenditure need. The concept of expenditure need recognizes that some cities face higher costs of providing a given package of public services than others because of city characteristics, such as population density or the incidence of poverty, that are outside the control of city officials (Bradford, Malt, and Oates 1969). A city with poor fiscal health would have to impose above-average tax rates to provide a standard package of services or must accept low service levels if it chooses to impose average tax rates. A city with strong fiscal health, in contrast, has substantial capacity to raise revenues relative to its expenditure need and can achieve standard service levels at below-average tax rates.

The measurement of a city's fiscal health is complicated by the fact that the fiscal institutions within which cities operate vary dramatically from city to city. For example, New York City, Baltimore, and Boston are all responsible for providing county services and local schools as well as standard municipal services such as public safety and sanitation, while many other cities provide only standard municipal services. Similarly, San Francisco, Washington, D.C., and Saint Louis are each empowered to use a sales tax and an earnings or payroll tax along with the property tax, while cities like Boston are limited to the property tax. Given this complexity and in order to distinguish the effects of economic and socioeconomic characteristics from those of fiscal arrangements on a city's fiscal health, Ladd and Yinger (1991) begin by measuring a city's *"standardized fiscal health."* Standardized fiscal health is defined by them as the difference between a city's revenue-raising capacity and its expenditure need expressed as a percentage of capacity, where capacity and need are calculated as though all cities operated within the same set of fiscal institutions. This measure reveals the net effect of a city's economic, social, and demographic characteristics, but not of its specific fiscal arrangements, on the city's ability to deliver a standard level of public services at a standard tax burden on its residents.

REVENUE-RAISING CAPACITY

Cities differ from one another first in terms of their *revenue-raising capacity*, that is, the amount of revenue a city could raise from three standard tax bases—property, general sales, and earnings—while imposing a standard tax burden on its residents. With the standard tax burden set at a fixed percentage of resident per capita income, revenue-raising capacity varies across cities for two reasons: differences in the average per capita income of residents and differences in the ability of cities to export tax burdens to nonresidents. For example, at the standard tax burden a city with richer residents can raise more revenue per resident from its residents than can a city with poorer residents. And a city with a large proportion of its property tax base in the form of business property, with a large proportion of its retail sales to nonresident commuters or tourists, or with a large proportion of earnings generated in the city accruing to nonresident commuters, can substantially increase its revenues by exporting tax burdens to nonresidents (see Bradbury and Ladd 1985; Ladd and Yinger 1991).

EXPENDITURE NEED

Just as cities differ in their revenue-raising capacity, they also differ in the amount of money they must spend to achieve a standardized package of public services, that is, in their *expenditure need*. The cost to a city of providing a standard package of services that people value such as protection from crime, a clean city, or adequate education varies with the social and demographic characteristics of the city. For example, a city with the social and economic conditions that breed crime will have to pay more per capita to obtain a given level of crime protection than will a city facing more favorable conditions; a city with densely packed, wooden housing will have to pay more per resident to obtain a given level of fire protection than one with newer housing; or a city with a large proportion of its public school pupils from disadvantaged households will have to pay more per pupil to obtain a given quality of education. Hence, the harshness of a city's environment is a major determinant of public service cost and thereby of a city's expenditure need (see Bradford et al. 1969). To calculate each city's expenditure need, Ladd and Yinger (1991) use regression analysis to isolate the effects of these environmental cost factors that are outside the control of city officials.[29] They then adjust the average cost of providing a standard package of public services upward or downward for each city by the city's index of costs relative to those of the average city.

Several environmental characteristics turn out to be powerful determinants of the cost per city resident of providing various types of city services. Poverty, for example, has a big impact on the costs of providing public safety. A city with a poverty rate 1 percentage point higher than that of another city will have police costs that are 5.5 percent higher on average. Furthermore, a city with a poverty rate one standard deviation above the 1982 mean must pay 36.4 percent more for police services than a city with average poverty. The size of a city, as measured by its population, and the amount of its economic activity, as measured by private employment per capita, also increase the costs of public services. In addition, the larger the population in the city's surrounding metropolitan area relative to the city's population, the higher are the city's costs of providing general and police services. And finally, the composition of city property affects police and fire costs; rental property, for example, is more expensive to protect from crime and fire than is owner-occupied property. Property used for wholesale and retail trade is relatively costly, while property used for services or manufacturing is relatively cheap to protect from fire.

Declining Standardized Fiscal Health, 1972–82

Table 9.13 reports indexes of standardized fiscal health in 1982 and its components for 6 illustrative big cities and averages for 70 central cities grouped by size of city. The indexes are constructed using a 1972 baseline service level, that is, the quality of services that the average city could provide at the standard tax burden in 1972. As a result, the index measures not only the position of one city relative to another but also relative to a 1972 average. A positive fiscal health

Table 9.13 INDEXES OF STANDARDIZED FISCAL HEALTH OF 70 CENTRAL CITIES, 1982

	(1) Number of Cities	(2) Revenue-Raising Capacity	(3) Standardized Expenditure Need	(4) Capacity Minus Need	(5) Fiscal Health Index
Illustrative Cities:					
Atlanta	1	$505	$640	($136)	−26.9%
Baltimore	1	331	483	(152)	−45.7
Boston	1	501	561	(59)	−11.9
Detroit	1	341	654	(313)	−91.9
Denver	1	532	505	27	5.0
Washington, D.C.	1	624	535	89	14.3
All Cities in Sample:[a]					
Average	70	$425	$458	($33)	−10.9%
Standard Deviation	70	80	109	128	32.2
Maximum	70	649	737	290	47.2
Minimum	70	286	243	(386)	−109.7
Cities Grouped by Population (in thousands):[a]					
Less than 100	6	$457	$384	74	16.4%
100–250	19	473	421	52	9.1
250–500	26	420	473	(53)	−13.5
500–1000	14	385	466	(80)	−22.9
Greater than 100	5	341	586	(245)	−72.8

Source: Ladd and Yinger (1991: tables 5.1 and 5.2).
a. Sample excludes Washington, D.C.

index, such as that for Denver or Washington, D.C., implies that the city's revenue-raising capacity was greater than its expenditure need and indicates an improvement in fiscal health relative to the average major central city in 1972. The specific value (5 percent for Denver and 14 percent for Washington, D.C.), indicates the percentage of its revenue the city would have had left over for increases in service quality or for tax cuts in 1982 after it had provided the 1972 average service quality at the standard tax burden.

A negative fiscal health index, such as those for Atlanta, Baltimore, Boston, and Detroit, implies that a city's 1982 capacity was less than its expenditure need and indicates that the city's fiscal health was weaker in 1982 than that of the average major central city in 1972. For example, Detroit's fiscal health index of almost − 92 (table 9.13) indicates that it had a standardized expenditure need that was almost twice as high as its standardized revenue-raising capacity. Detroit would have had to receive a 92 percent boost in its revenue-raising capacity from outside sources to be able to provide services of the quality that the average city could provide out of its own broad-based revenue sources in 1972.

The average standardized fiscal health of the 70 central cities in the Ladd-Yinger study was − 11 percent in 1982 (see table 9.13). This figure implies that the typical central city would have needed a boost in revenues of 11 percent from outside sources in 1982 to provide the 1972 baseline service level at the standard tax burden. In other words, economic and social forces weakened the fiscal health of the typical city during the period.

Of greatest interest for this study are the three largest-size categories of cities.[30] The negative average index in all three categories indicates that the standardized fiscal health of America's big cities in 1982 was significantly poorer than that of smaller central cities (see table 9.13). In contrast to the − 11 percent index for all 70 cities, cities in the largest three size categories had average indexes of − 14 percent, − 23 percent, and − 73 percent, respectively.

As shown in table 9.13, the weaker fiscal health in the larger cities relative to the smaller cities reflects both larger cities' lower revenue-raising capacity and their higher expenditure need. Particularly high police costs, but also above-average costs for fire and general services, account for the high needs. These costs are high both because population itself, holding all other factors constant, emerges as a cost factor and because city population is positively correlated with other characteristics, such as the city's poverty rate or private-sector wage rates, that also increase the costs of providing services to city residents.

Table 9.14 CHANGES IN STANDARDIZED FISCAL HEALTH OF 70 CITIES,
1972–82
(AVERAGE CHANGE BY CATEGORY OF CITY)

	(1) Number of Cities	(2) Potential Revenue-Raising Capacity (%)	(3) Standardized Expenditure Need (%)	(4) Standardized Fiscal Health Index (Percentage Point)
City Size (in thousands):[a]				
Less than 100	6	10.3	12.6	−1.6
100–250	19	10.9	23.2	−9.3
250–500	26	9.5	20.4	−11.4
500–1000	14	8.2	17.0	−10.3
Greater than 1,000	5	−5.6	12.3	−27.2

Source: Ladd and Yinger (1991: table 5.3).
a. Sample excludes Washington, D.C.

The larger cities had relatively poor fiscal health in 1982 both because they had poor fiscal health in 1972 and because they experienced above-average declines in fiscal health between 1972 and 1982. The declines are shown in table 9.14. (Because the 1982 index is constructed relative to the 1972 average, the average decline over all 70 cities is the same as the average standardized fiscal health index in 1982.) Revenue-raising capacity declined only in the cities with populations over 1 million. Nonetheless, large increases in expenditure need led to declines in fiscal health in each size category of city. Interestingly, expenditure need grew fastest not in the largest central cities, but, rather, in the cities with populations between 100,000 and 250,000. Nonetheless, the net effects of social and economic forces on the revenue and expenditure sides of the fiscal picture produced the greatest declines in the standardized fiscal health of the cities of most interest for this chapter, namely those with populations over 250,000.

In sum, America's big cities experienced a significant deterioration in their standardized fiscal health over the 1972–82 period. This finding implies that economic and social trends, such as the decline in real income of residents in many cities and the rising rate of poverty among city residents, worsened the balance between revenue-raising capacity and expenditure need in the typical big city during this period.

STANDARDIZED FISCAL HEALTH OF BIG CITIES, *1982* AND *1990*

During the 1980s cities presumably benefited from the long economic expansion. However, they also suffered from increasing rates of poverty. Recent census data document distressingly large increases between 1979 and 1989 in the poverty rate among persons in many big cities. In 15 of the 33 big cities, poverty rates increased by more than 2 percentage points. The largest percentage point increases were in Detroit (from 21.9 percent to 32.4 percent), Milwaukee (from 13.8 percent to 22.2 percent), Houston (from 12.7 percent to 20.7 percent), Miami (from 24.5 percent to 31.2 percent) and Cleveland (from 22.1 percent to 28.7 percent). As of 1989, more than 20 percent of the population was poor in almost half the big cities.[31]

Unfortunately, some of the data needed to replicate the standardized fiscal health measure for 1990 are still unavailable. The best that can be done is to generate rough estimates for 1990 using the methodology described in Ladd and Yinger (1991, pp. 116–119 and 315–321).[32] Although the 1990 estimates incorporate recent information on city poverty rates, the estimates could still understate the effects of that poverty on expenditure need. That result would occur to the extent that the poverty-related problems of homelessness, crack cocaine, and AIDS placed greater burdens on city services in 1990 than they did in 1982.

The first two columns of table 9.15 report standardized fiscal health in 1982 and updated estimates for 1990 for the 29 big cities for which complete data are available. The figures in both columns indicate the city's fiscal health relative to that of the average major central city in 1972. For purposes of subsequent analysis, the cities are grouped into quartiles of 1982 standardized fiscal health. Cities falling into the lowest quartile in 1982 are New York, Detroit, New Orleans, Philadelphia, Cleveland, Chicago, and Buffalo.

A comparison of columns 1 and 2 shows that according to these estimates the standardized fiscal health of most big cities improved during the 1980s. The only exceptions are New York, Detroit, Milwaukee, and Miami. Nonetheless, despite this improvement, the typical big city still was worse off in 1988 than the average major central city in 1972; the typical big city would have needed an 18 percent boost in its revenues to enable it to provide the same quality of services at the standard tax burden as the average major central city could provide in 1972. In addition, many cities, namely all the ones in the top half of the list, still had very poor standardized fiscal health in 1990. According to these estimates, national economic growth was beneficial, but not sufficiently powerful to offset the other social and economic forces that adversely affected the ability of cities to provide adequate services.

These measures of standardized fiscal health were specifically

Table 9.15 FISCAL HEALTH OF 33 CITIES, 1982 AND 1988
(SORTED BY STANDARDIZED FISCAL HEALTH)

Cities by SFH[a] Quartile (I, Low to IV, High)	Standardized Fiscal Health		Actual Fiscal Health, 1982	Implied State Assistance, 1982 (col. 3 − col. 1)
	1982 (1)	1990 (2)	(3)	(4)
Quartile I				
New York	−104.6	−136.9	−63.2	41.4
Detroit	−91.9	−97.8	−30.8	61.1
New Orleans	−72.7	−34.6	−72.8	−0.1
Philadelphia	−59.9	−42.7	−23.1	36.8
Cleveland	−58.7	−57.1	−29.3	29.4
Chicago	−58.5	−44.1	−43.8	14.7
Buffalo	−52.6	−35.5	−26.2	26.4
Quartile II				
Los Angeles	−48.9	−39.2	−79.7	−30.8
Baltimore	−45.7	−27.8	6.8	52.5
Saint Louis	−37.7	−28.5	−31.3	6.4
Columbus	−36.9	−23.0	−10.4	26.5
Kansas City	−33.6	−14.2	8.6	42.2
Cincinnati	−33.1	−16.4	5.9	39.0
Milwaukee	−33.1	−34.3	12.3	45.4
Quartile III				
Memphis	−30.1	−16.8	−56.1	−26.0
Atlanta	−29.9	−5.3	−65.9	−36.0
Indianapolis	−25.0	−8.4	26.5	51.0
Minneapolis	−14.8	−14.3	−1.5	13.3
San Diego	−13.0	3.2	−16.0	−3.0
Jacksonville	−12.8	5.2	28.8	16.0
Boston	−11.9	13.9	2.3	
Quartile IV				
Phoenix	−11.2	−7.3	11.4	22.6
Portland	−9.8	7.8	−10.2	−0.4
Pittsburgh	−7.8	−5.1	−34.7	−26.9
Denver	5.0	6.5	−4.9	−9.9
San Francisco	7.7	43.6	8.0	0.3
Miami	17.5	15.9	5.6	−11.9
San Jose	18.4	26.4	16.7	−1.7
Washington, D.C.	14.3	42.8	10.0	−4.3
Dallas	N/A	N/A	N/A	N/A
Houston	N/A	N/A	N/A	N/A
San Antonio	N/A	N/A	N/A	N/A
Seattle	N/A	N/A	N/A	N/A
Average (29 cities)	−29.9	−18.1	−15.8	−14.2

Source: Ladd and Yinger (1991: tables A5.1, A9.1, and unpublished entries by Ladd and Yinger).
a. SFH, standardized fiscal health.

designed to eliminate any differences across cities or in a particular city over time in the fiscal institutions within which specific cities operate. Consequently, the negative values of standardized fiscal health reported in table 9.15 indicate the adverse effects on city fiscal conditions of economic and social forces alone. The obvious next question is: To what extent did state government actions offset the deterioration in city fiscal health caused by the deleterious economic and social forces? Ladd and Yinger shed light on this question by calculating a new measure of city fiscal health that accounts for fiscal institutions and state aid.

Fiscal Health Accounting for Fiscal Institutions and State Aid

State fiscal institutions, including aid from state governments, clearly affect the ability of cities to provide public services to their residents. These fiscal institutions include first the set of taxes that the state empowers the city to use. A state law that allows a city to levy an earnings tax on commuters, for example, typically increases the revenue-raising capacity of the city by expanding its opportunities to export tax burdens to nonresidents. A second component of the package of fiscal institutions is the set of services for which the city has responsibility. In addition to providing standard municipal services such as public safety, sanitation, and roads, for example, a city may also be responsible for providing certain social services or local schools. Within the sample of 33 big cities, 6 cities (Baltimore, Boston, Buffalo, Memphis, New York, and Washington, D.C.) have responsibility for local schools, and those that are city-counties such as San Francisco also have responsibility for many of the social services typically provided by counties.

Over time, a state can assist a central city overburdened by large responsibilities by taking over provision of services such as welfare, courts, or social services; this shift in responsibilities reduces the city's effective expenditure need, that is, the cost to the city of providing a given quality of public services. At the same time, however, such a shift may increase state tax burdens on city residents and thereby reduce their capacity to raise revenue for locally provided public services. Stated more generally, a third component of fiscal institutions is the role of overlying jurisdictions; the greater the taxes levied by noncity governments on city residents, the less revenue-raising capacity is left for city services. A final component of the package of fiscal institutions is state aid to cities; with more state aid, everything else held constant, a city is better able to provide a given level of public services.

By modifying their measures of standardized fiscal health to take account of these fiscal institutions, Ladd and Yinger (1991) constructed what they referred to as a city's "actual fiscal health." The term *actual* does not signify anything about the current budgetary situation in the city. Instead, like its standardized counterpart, actual fiscal health measures the constraints facing a city given various characteristics of the city that are outside the immediate control of city officials. In contrast to standardized fiscal health, actual fiscal health treats as a constraint the fiscal rules under which the city operates. More specifically, it measures the balance between a city's effective expenditure need (its need adjusted for its service responsibilities) and its restricted revenue-raising capacity (its capacity restricted by the taxes it is empowered to use and adjusted for capacity used up by overlying jurisdictions and by state aid). Standardized to a 1972 average service level, actual fiscal health measures a city's ability to provide the 1972 baseline service level at a standard tax burden on city residents, given the economic and social characteristics of the city as well as the fiscal institutions within which the city operates.

ACTUAL FISCAL HEALTH AND STATE ASSISTANCE

The actual fiscal health as of 1982 of each big city is reported in column 3 of table 9.15.[33] These measures are interpreted analogously to those of standardized fiscal health. In particular, the −63.2 percent figure at the top of the column means that New York City would have needed additional resources equal to more than 63 percent of its revenue-raising capacity to provide the 1972 baseline service level at the standard burden on city residents. In other words, even accounting for state assistance, New York City was still much worse off in 1982 than in 1972.

The difference between a city's actual and standardized fiscal health can be interpreted as the relative amount of state assistance to the city, where assistance is broadly defined to include indirect assistance through the structure of fiscal institutions as well as monetary assistance in the form of grants. Comparing the bottom line of columns 1 and 3 of table 9.15 shows that between 1972 and 1982 the typical big city experienced a 15.8 percent decline in its actual fiscal health in contrast to a 29.9 percent decline in its standardized fiscal health. In other words, state assistance offset on average about

Table 9.16 ACTUAL FISCAL HEALTH IN 70 CITIES

(AVERAGE BY CATEGORY OF CITY)

	(1)	(2)	(3)
	Number of Cities	Actual Fiscal Health	Change in Actual Fiscal Health (percentage point)
Average	70	−4.9	−4.9
Cities Grouped by Population (in thousands):			
Less than 100	6	14.6	7.0
100–250	19	6.4	−9.2
250–500	26	−9.0	−4.4
500–1000	14	−5.5	−4.6[a]
Greater than 1,000	5	−48.1	−20.8

Source: Ladd and Yinger (1991).
Note: Sample excludes Washington, D.C.
a. Figure excludes Cincinnati because of a possible data problem with the 1972 figure for that city.

half of the deleterious effects of the social and economic pressures affecting big cities. In general, state assistance was largest in the cities with the poorest fiscal health. Interestingly, some cities, such as Memphis, Atlanta, and Pittsburgh had higher standardized than actual fiscal health; in these cities, the fiscal institutions within which the city operates exacerbated rather than mitigated the adverse effects of economic and social trends.

Despite this relatively well-targeted state assistance during the 1970s, the fiscal health of the typical big city declined between 1972 and 1982. Moreover, the actual fiscal health of the big cities was significantly worse in 1982 than that of smaller cities. As shown in table 9.16, which is based on Ladd and Yinger's larger sample of 70 major central cities, the actual fiscal health of the typical large city with population over 1 million was − 48 percent, which contrasts with much smaller negative averages for cities and populations between 250,000 and 1 million and with positive averages for smaller cities.

STATE SUPPORT SINCE 1982

How much the states have actually done to help their cities since 1982 is difficult to determine because, as discussed earlier, state assistance encompasses more than just the provision of state aid; it also includes state assumption of city expenditure responsibilities and authorization to use additional broad-based taxes. Focusing just on state aid, the one component of the assistance package for which recent data are available, no evidence emerges of increased state support for big central cities. Indeed, between 1982 and 1989, state aid to the 32 big cities (excluding Washington, D.C.) declined slightly, from 17.1 percent of city general revenue to 16.9 percent. Aid as a percentage of revenues decreased in 18 cities and increased in only 14 cities. Moreover, no clear pattern emerges across cities grouped by their 1982 fiscal health. States have seen their own budgets squeezed, making city assistance more difficult.

Summary and Role of Federal Aid

The Ladd-Yinger measures of the underlying or structural fiscal health of U.S. cities indicate a significant deterioration over time. They imply that economic and social trends made it more difficult for many big cities to provide a standard package of public services at reasonable tax burdens on their residents in 1982 than in 1972. Although the long national economic expansion of the 1980s apparently reversed this downward trend, the resulting relief was not sufficient to restore the average fiscal health of big cities to that of the average city in 1972. Thus, even at the end of the decade, near the end of the longest peacetime economic expansion in recent history, the economic and social characteristics of many big cities made it extremely hard for them to deliver adequate public services to their residents at reasonable tax burdens.

Fortunately for the residents of big cities, some of the effects of these adverse social and economic characteristics were offset by assistance from state governments. Moreover, this additional state assistance, broadly defined to include assistance in the form of greater local taxing authority or reallocation of service responsibilities as well as grants, was well targeted to the cities in the most dire straits. The magnitude of state assistance during the 1980s cannot easily be determined, but the evidence suggests that assistance fell far short of the amount needed to offset the poor standardized fiscal health of many large cities in 1988, as reported in table 9.15. Hence, it appears that the underlying or structural fiscal health of many, but not all, big cities was quite poor at the end of the 1990s as the economy teetered on the brink of recession.

Federal Aid

What about the role of federal aid? As constructed by Ladd and Yinger, the concept of actual fiscal health accounts for state, but not federal, assistance. This observation raises the possibility that additional federal aid may have made up the gap in revenue-raising capacity in big cities. In fact, in the average major central city (based on Ladd and Yinger's sample of 70 cities), federal aid apparently fully offset the decline in actual fiscal health between 1972 and 1982 (Ladd and Yinger 1991: chap. 11). However, the offset was far smaller for the largest cities (those with population greater than 1 million); federal aid offset only about a third of the decline in the actual fiscal health of these cities.

Although not a panacea for their fiscal problems, federal aid to big cities clearly helped alleviate some of their fiscal pressures during the 1970s. Given this fact plus the poor fiscal health of many big cities in 1988, as reported in table 9.15, one cannot avoid the conclusion that the razing of federal aid programs for cities during the 1980s may create future serious problems for cities. That these problems did not emerge clearly in the 1980s is mainly attributable to the beneficial effects of the long economic expansion. With the current slowdown in the economy, the poor underlying fiscal health of many big cities is becoming more apparent and the effects of the cutbacks will be increasingly felt.

PERSPECTIVE ON FINANCIAL CRISES

The documentation of the poor underlying fiscal health of many big cities adds perspective to the financial crises experienced by several major central cities, particularly Philadelphia and New York, during 1990 and 1991. Although the financial difficulties in these cities may be exacerbated by politics or management practices, the fact that both cities were among the 10 least healthy cities in 1988 suggests that their financial problems primarily reflect underlying structural problems that are largely outside the control of city officials. Stated differently, one explanation for the political difficulty that these cities face in balancing their budgets may simply be that their options are all unpleasant; poor fiscal health implies that a city must choose between severe cuts in public services and tax hikes.

FISCAL PERFORMANCE

By definition, a city in poor fiscal health faces a less favorable trade-off between taxes and public services than a city in strong fiscal health. In other words, the tax effort of the less healthy city must be higher, or the services it provides to its residents must be lower, than those of a healthier city. Over time, a city with declining fiscal health can choose to increase tax burdens and maintain service levels or to hold tax burdens constant and decrease the quality of services it provides to its residents. This section describes the choices cities have made about taxes and service levels and how these choices vary with the fiscal health of the city.

Tax Effort

The concepts of tax burden and tax effort are essentially the same; a city that imposes a higher tax burden on its residents is also making more of a tax effort. For comparisons across states, tax effort is best measured not on a per capita basis but relative to the revenue-raising capacity of the state. Typically that capacity is measured either by state personal income or by some broader indicator such as the representative tax system measure developed by the Advisory Commission on Intergovernmental Relations. For comparisons of tax effort across cities, one must pay even closer attention to the measurement issue.

This conclusion follows for two reasons. First, a portion of the burden of city taxes is not borne by city residents. For a city that exports a large portion of its tax burden to nonresident taxpayers in the form of higher prices paid by tourists or commuters or lower prices of factor inputs owned by nonresidents, total taxes collected significantly overstate the tax burden that falls on city residents. Hence, in such a city total taxes expressed per city resident or per dollar of resident income would yield misleadingly high measures of tax burdens on residents and consequently of tax effort. An accurate measure of tax burdens required some adjustment for tax exporting.

Second, cities differ in the range of public services for which they are responsible, and hence in the taxes required to meet their responsibilities. Unless city tax burdens are adjusted for differing responsibilities, one could easily draw the wrong conclusion from high or low city taxes expressed either on a per capita basis or in relation to resident income. For example, the residents of a city with an overlying county that provides a variety of social services might face a low *city* tax burden, but at the same time an average or high city-plus-county tax burden.[34]

Hence, in measuring city tax burdens, one should adjust both for tax exporting and for differing roles of overlying governments. One way to achieve this end is to express city taxes as a fraction of a city's

Table 9.17 TAX BURDENS IN 33 CITIES: 1977, 1982, 1986
(AVERAGES FOR ALL CITIES AND BY STANDARDIZED FISCAL HEALTH CATEGORY)

	1977	1982	1986
Three taxes	.926	.887	1.058
All taxes	1.153	1.142	1.376
Three Taxes by SFH[a] *Quartiles*			
I (Low)	1.29	1.22	1.38
II	.79	.78	.95
III	.82	.87	.87
IV (High)	.92	.79	1.13

Notes: All entries are city taxes divided by a city's restricted revenue-raising capacity as described in the text. "Three taxes" includes property, sales, and earnings taxes. See table 9.15 for cities in each quartile.
a. SFH, standardized fiscal health.

restricted revenue-raising capacity. This restricted (as distinguished from full) capacity can be measured as the amount of revenue a city could raise from the broad-based taxes it is empowered to use at a standard total state-and-local tax burden on city residents, after adjusting for the capacity "used up" by overlying governments.[35] Because the choice of the initial tax burden is somewhat arbitrary, one should pay more attention to how the measures change over time or how they vary across groups of city than to the absolute levels.[36]

By this definition, tax burdens in the 33 big cities declined between 1977 and 1982, but then increased sufficiently after 1982 to produce a higher tax burden on city residents in 1986 than in 1977. This conclusion holds both for the three broad-based taxes and also for all city taxes shown in table 9.17. The decline in tax burdens in the early period largely reflects the effects of the nationwide tax revolt; between 1977 and 1982, taxpayers nationally became much less willing to bear the burden of state and local taxes. Even though few big cities experienced the property tax rollbacks faced by California and Massachusetts cities, fear of taxpayer revolts apparently made city councils less willing to raise taxes than they might have been in a different tax environment.

After 1982, city officials became more willing to increase taxes. This increased willingness was partially a response to large cutbacks in federal aid under the Reagan administration, but may also reflect rising costs of providing public services and a desire to maintain the quality of public services. Between 1982 and 1986, tax burdens on city residents rose by 19 percent for three broad-based taxes and by 21 percent for all city taxes.[38] Unless these tax increases were offset by comparable increases in local public services, these changes imply

Table 9.18 PER CAPITA EXPENDITURES IN 32 CITIES, 1977–89
(AVERAGES)

	1989 ($)	Percentage Change (constant dollars)		
		1977–82	1982–89	1977–89
All functions (current account)	888	−1.8	12.3	9.8
Common functions	541	−2.9	17.4	12.6
Public safety	269	−5.0	20.7	13.3

Source: U.S. Bureau of the Census, *City Government Finances*, various years.
Notes: Washington, D.C., is excluded. Expenditures were deflated by the national deflator for state and local government purchases. Common functions include police, fire, corrections, inspections, highways, sanitation, parks and recreation, and administration.

that city residents were worse off on average in 1986 than in 1982 or 1977.

The bottom section of table 9.17 summarizes average tax burdens by cities, grouped by their standardized fiscal health. One would expect that cities with poor fiscal health would tax their residents more heavily than would their healthier counterparts. Only if such cities chose to respond to their poor fiscal health by providing much lower services than other cities would this outcome not occur. The table shows that the cities with the lowest fiscal health did in fact impose the highest tax burdens on their residents in all three years. In each year, tax burdens in these fiscally unhealthy cities exceeded the average by about a third. Within this category, the highest 1986 tax burdens were in Philadelphia, Detroit, New York City, and Chicago.

Expenditures and Services

A standard approach for determining what has happened to the quantity and quality of public services over time is to examine per capita spending adjusted for inflation. Moreover, because different cities have differing expenditure responsibilities, one typically looks at several categories of spending: current spending on all functions, which ignores the variation across cities in responsibilities; spending on a set of functions that are common to most cities; and public safety, which is the primary municipal service provided by all cities (see, for example, Peterson 1976). As shown in table 9.18, per capita spending (deflated by the national deflator for state and local government purchases) declined during the 1977–82 period and then rebounded sharply after 1982. Over the entire 1977–89 period, real

Table 9.19 GROWTH IN PUBLIC SERVICE COSTS IN 33 CITIES, 1972–82

	1982 ($ per capita)	Percentage Change		
		1972–77	1977–82	1972–82
Police	206	7.0	44.8	54.9
Fire	141	−3.8	34.8	29.5
General	122	4.3	5.7	10.3

Notes: See text for definition of public service costs. Cost estimates for 1972 and 1982 are from Ladd and Yinger (1991: table A4.1); those for 1977 are from unpublished data from Ladd and Yinger.

per capita spending on common functions increased by about 13 percent.

It would be a mistake, however, to conclude that the quality or quantity of services increased by 13 percent during this period. The main reason is that the state and local deflator does not include the effects on the cost of providing public services of changes in the environmental characteristics of the city. As discussed earlier, a city that has a harsher environment for providing public services, perhaps because a greater number of its residents are poor or because it has more commuters to serve, has a higher cost of services than a city with a less harsh environment. Similarly, deterioration in the conditions under which cities provide services, caused, for example, by an increase in the incidence of poverty, boosts the costs of providing a given quality of public services.

Although measures of service costs for big cities were not available for 1989, the cost increases estimated by Ladd and Yinger (1991) for the periods 1972–77 and 1977–82 are suggestive. As previously noted, these measures are designed to capture the effects on costs of trends that are outside the control of local officials; they reflect changes in variables such as the poverty rate, per resident private employment in the city, and the composition of economic activity in the city. As shown in table 9.19, the costs of general services and of police services rose on average by 4 percent and 7 percent, respectively, in the 1972–77 period, while the costs of providing fire services apparently declined somewhat. In contrast, the following period, 1977–82, witnessed dramatic increases in costs, especially those for police and fire services. The 45 percent increase in police costs presumably largely reflects the rapid growth in many cities' poverty rates during this period. These 1977–82 cost estimates imply that per capita spending on general services would have had to grow by 5.7 percent, that on police by 45 percent, and that on fire by 35 percent, on average simply to maintain service levels during this period. Because deflated spending did not increase at all during that period, the clear implication is that city service levels were substantially lower in 1982 than in 1977.

The absence of information on cost increases for the more recent 1982–89 period makes it difficult to determine how the 12–20 percent growth in spending during that period translates into service changes. The rise in poverty rates between 1980 and 1990 in many big cities implies that costs have probably continued to increase. But even assuming, unrealistically, no cost increases in the recent period, the spending rebound in the recent period falls far short of what would be needed to offset the service declines of the previous five years. Hence, the data suggest that service levels in big cities were lower in 1989 than in the mid-1970s.[39]

CONCLUSION

In sum, the evidence on city tax burdens and service levels is consistent with the conclusions about city fiscal health, namely that the fiscal condition of cities is deteriorating. The data suggest that big cities apparently have responded to their declining fiscal health both by raising tax rates and reducing service levels.

POLICY ISSUES

From a constitutional perspective, cities are creatures of their states. Hence, state governments clearly have a role to play in establishing budgetary procedures (such as requiring budgetary balance, periodic audits, and use of standard accounting principles) and in intervening, as in the case of New York City's 1975 fiscal crisis or more recently in various cities in the Northeast, when a city's budget gets so far out of balance as to jeopardize the city's ability to provide public services to its residents. But, in general, the short-run budgetary conditions of cities are most relevant to city officials who manage the ongoing fiscal operations of the city and to potential or actual investors in the city's bonds who need assurance of the city's ability to meet its debt service commitments. Whereas it may be true that budgetary distress sometimes indicates a more fundamental problem of poor fiscal health, it would be a mistake for state and federal officials to interpret the absence of budgetary distress as a sign of acceptable fiscal health. Instead, policymakers should focus more directly on the basic issue: How difficult is it for cities to provide adequate services at reasonable tax rates?

Case for Additional State or Federal Assistance

As documented earlier, social and economic trends outside the control of city officials have led to a significant deterioration in the fiscal health of many big cities; residents in many big cities now face significantly less favorable trade-offs between tax and service levels than they did in the 1970s.[40] This decline in fiscal health implies that many cities would need substantial additional revenues from higher levels of government to provide the same quality of public services in the 1980s as provided in 1972 by the average major central city at the standard tax burden on city residents.

But the large federal government deficit and relatively tight fiscal conditions in many states should make one cautious about simply calling for more state and federal assistance for cities. One must begin by looking elsewhere for relief. However, neither of the two main possibilities—encouraging the cities to help themselves and relying on the mechanism of resident mobility—is promising.

In principle, cities can help themselves by annexing wealthier surrounding areas, providing public services more efficiently through better management, or promoting economic development. In contrast to cities in the South and Southwest, many cities in the Northeast and Northcentral regions historically were not allowed to respond to the outmigration of middle- and upper-income households by annexing their surrounding areas. This inability to annex certainly contributes to the poor fiscal health of some of these cities. But although it might be logical to propose more annexation, the likelihood of that occurring "must be judged to be somewhere between negligible and nil—and probably closer to the latter" (G. Peterson 1976: 118).

Better management could also improve a city's fiscal options, and cities should certainly be encouraged to introduce management and service delivery reforms to achieve this end. Tougher bargaining with the unions, improvements in productivity, and contracting out for certain services are all worth pursuing and could yield cost savings in some cities. But, realistically, the scope for cost reduction through this route is limited.[41] Similarly, one should not be overly optimistic about the potential for significant impacts of local policies to promote economic development. National trends affecting city economies, such as suburbanization, interregional migration, and the shift from manufacturing to services, are considerably more powerful than the economic development policies within the fiscal reach of cities (Ladd and Yinger 1991: 293).

One might try to dismiss the problem of poor fiscal health by arguing that residents in fiscally disadvantaged cities are no worse off than those in more advantaged cities. This argument relies on the assumption that residents are mobile; if residents can choose where to live, they would not remain in the disadvantaged city, according to this argument, unless they were compensated in the form of nonfiscal benefits such as higher wages or lower rents. But many of the city's residents—especially the poor, the elderly, the handicapped, as well as blacks and Hispanics—face formidable barriers to mobility that limit their ability to improve their fiscal options. Moreover, moving is expensive for individuals and, from the point of view of the larger society, may not be the least costly way of dealing with fiscal disparities across cities.

The bottom line is that cities face significant fiscal challenges and that without additional outside assistance many will continue to experience deterioration in their fiscal health. Additional outside assistance for cities can be justified on the basis of these empirical findings supplemented by the judgment that higher levels of government are responsible for assisting poor people who are disproportionately represented in cities, to help people make transitions imposed by national trends that are outside their control, and to promote the fair treatment of all residents in a metropolitan area. The question then becomes one of whether the additional assistance should come from the states or from the federal government and what form it should take.

Role for State Governments

State governments already provide substantial assistance to their cities. As noted earlier, this assistance includes that provided through fiscal institutions as well through grants programs. For example, some states such as Ohio help their cities by allowing them to levy taxes with high export potential, and other states take responsibility for welfare or other social services. In 1982 state assistance cut the 1972–82 decline in the standardized fiscal health of the average city in half; this statement holds both for the Ladd-Yinger sample of 70 major central cities and also for the smaller set of big cities. More specifically, while social and economic trends led to a 29 percent decline in the standardized fiscal health of these big cities between 1972 and 1982, state assistance reduced the decline to 15 percent (see difference between standardized and actual fiscal health in table 9.15). Between 1972 and 1982, states provided most of the *new* assistance to the biggest cities in the form of monetary grants rather than by modifying fiscal institutions. For cities with populations between half a million and 1 million people, for example, additional assistance through institutions amounted to only .5 percent of cities' revenue-raising capacity while additional grants accounted for over 10 percent of capacity (Ladd and Yinger 1991: table 11.4).

Even after all this state assistance, however, actual fiscal health declined in the average big city between 1972 and 1982, and some cities have significantly poorer actual fiscal health than others. Can and should the states be asked to do more? States have one major advantage over the federal government in providing assistance to cities: they control the fiscal rules under which cities operate. Hence, compared to the federal government, states have a broader array of policy instruments for helping fiscally troubled cities. With detailed knowledge about the fiscal constraints that confront each of their cities, states can design assistance packages that respond to the specific circumstances of individual cities and their metropolitan areas. Moreover, reliance on state governments to provide assistance to cities has the additional advantage of promoting diversity and policy innovation. Therefore, states should be expected to do more.

The most direct way for states to assist cities in poor fiscal health is through an equalizing grant program. Many states now direct more school aid to school districts with smaller equalized tax bases and higher costs of educating students. Building on this model for other public services, states could develop revenue-sharing programs for their cities that direct aid to cities with low revenue-raising capacity and high public-service costs. Including a measure of costs in the distribution formula is essential; cities with above-average revenue-raising capacity are still disadvantaged relative to others if, as is true for many of them, they have disproportionately high costs of providing public services. At least one state, Massachusetts, has experimented with a revenue-sharing program of this type for incremental aid (see Bradbury et al. 1984).

Two particular forms of state assistance through fiscal institutions might improve the fiscal health of some cities. First, states can allow cities to levy an earnings tax that applies to the earnings of commuters. This tax typically increases the revenue-raising capacity of cities by giving them more opportunity to export tax burdens to nonresident commuters. Although some cities already have such taxing power, others with low fiscal health such as New Orleans, Chicago, Buffalo, and Los Angeles could benefit from state authorization to use such a tax, and Baltimore could benefit from having its power to tax earnings extended to commuters. Second, some states also may be able to help their cities by assuming responsibility for redistributive services such as welfare and services such as courts or corrections that provide benefits to people in an area extending beyond city boundaries. Substantial gains from state takeover of welfare services, however, are limited to those big cities that have significant welfare responsibilities. As of 1982, those cities were New York, Washington, Indianapolis, Denver, Philadelphia, and San Francisco.

Role for Federal Government

Ladd and Yinger (1991) have documented that federal assistance to 70 major central cities contributed significantly to the ability of central cities to provide public services during the 1970s. Increases in federal aid during the 1972–82 decade provided approximately the amount of assistance needed to prevent the 5 percent decline in the actual fiscal health of the average central city, where actual health, which was specifically designed to highlight the effects of state assistance, includes the effects of state, but not federal, assistance.[42] Federal assistance to the big cities exceeded that for smaller cities, but still was insufficient to offset the stronger adverse economic and social trends they confronted, leaving many of the big cities worse off in 1982 than the smaller cities, even after accounting for federal aid.

The years since 1982 have witnessed large cuts in federal aid to cities, including the elimination, in 1986, of general revenue sharing (see figure 9.1). These reductions in federal aid have interacted with the continuing decline in the fiscal health of America's big cities to produce the tax increases and declining service levels already documented. Given these outcomes, restoring some of the cuts in federal aid may be defended simply on the grounds of maintaining the average fiscal health of U.S. cities.

An even stronger case for reversing the current decline in federal aid rests on three additional considerations. First, variation in states' own fiscal health leads to variation in their ability to help their cities. Evidence reported in Ladd and Yinger (1991: 302) shows that, compared to richer states, states with low per capita income provide less assistance to their cities through both grants and institutions, after controlling for city fiscal health and other factors. Thus, through no fault of their own or of their state, the residents of unhealthy cities in these states receive lower-quality services or pay higher taxes than residents of equally troubled cities in other states. Equal treatment of city residents in all states requires federal intervention.

Second, the federal government has a unique role to play in assuring minimum standards of living for poor and disadvantaged households (see Brown and Oates 1985; Gramlich 1985b; and Ladd and Doolittle 1982). Because minimum standards must include publicly provided goods such as the quality of municipal water as well as privately provided goods such as food, it follows that direct federal government assistance to poor and disadvantaged individuals is insufficient; assistance is also needed for the cities that are in poorest fiscal health, especially when that poor health reflects a concentration of poor and disadvantaged citizens.

Third, the federal government is in a much better position than state governments to respond to national trends in employment and population, such as suburbanization and interregional migration, and to the impact of these trends on the fiscal health of cities. To the extent that policymakers' objectives in assisting cities include compensating people who are hurt by national trends or minimizing wasteful moving caused by these trends, the federal government has a key role to play.

In sum, federal assistance to cities is needed to ensure fair treatment of city residents in states with different levels of fiscal health, to help poor and disadvantaged city residents, and to offset the fiscal consequences for cities of national economic and social trends. Achieving these objectives does not require more federal aid to all cities, but it does require an increase in federal aid to cities with poor or deteriorating fiscal health. In this era of high federal deficits and widespread consensus about the need to hold down federal spending, it is worth emphasizing that these objectives can be achieved without restoring recent aid cuts in all cities. Ideally what is needed is an aid program that is highly targeted to cities with low standardized fiscal health.[43]

Strategic Considerations

Robert Reischauer (1990) has convincingly argued that the growth in federal urban aid programs during the 1960–78 period was an aberration not likely to be repeated. The main conditions that motivated the expansion—the fact that the federal government had the intellectual and financial resources to take on long-neglected domestic programs, the view that in contrast to state governments that were held in low esteem, cities were a deserving and worthy level of government, and the conviction that direct federal action could solve complex social problems—no longer hold. Instead, large budget deficits and the constraints of the Budget Enforcement Act of 1990 leave the federal government with few resources to undertake new initiatives; states have now replaced cities as the deserving level of government, as is evident from the Reagan administration's consolidation of grants into block grant to states; and there now appears to be a general pessimism about the efficacy of federal government relative to local governments to bring about change. Moreover, during the Reagan and Bush administration, *people* replaced *places* as the primary locus of domestic policy concern; prevailing wisdom during that period held that the federal government's limited resources are better directed toward maintaining the social safety net for individuals than providing assistance to places through programs such as the new defunct general revenue-sharing program.

Although a targeted aid program could be much less expensive than the less-well targeted federal initiatives of the 1960s and 1970s, the U.S. Congress has historically been unwilling to engage in much geographic targeting of resources. Peterson, Rabe, and Wong (1986) attribute this unwillingness to the organization of the U.S. system of representation. Because members of Congress represent specific states or districts, each is concerned about how much money will accrue to his or her district. These constituency interests make it difficult for broad partisan and ideological coalitions to focus federal grants on the few places with the greatest need. In particular, for any urban program to receive support it must spread the funds widely across as many congressional districts as possible. In addition to increasing the costs of the program, this spreading of funds to less needy jurisdictions ultimately weakens support for urban programs by generating perceptions of inefficiency and waste (see Reischauer 1990: 231.)

How, then, should advocates of urban interests proceed? Two approaches are possible. The first is to push for nonurban federal programs that indirectly help cities. This approach explicitly acknowledges the weak political position of cities, that major new urban initiatives are not likely to rank high on the federal agenda, and that geographic targeting of assistance is politically difficult (see Cucitti 1990; and Kaplan and James 1990). Many federal policy initiatives could potentially relieve some of the fiscal pressures in cities.

These include welfare reforms that encourage innovation at the state and local levels, education programs aimed at disadvantaged children and that encourage students to stay in school, federal initiatives relating to infrastructure, and a toughening of the nation's fair housing laws (see Kaplan and James 1990). The potential for these and other federal initiatives to improve the fiscal health of U.S. cities remains to be determined. Nonetheless, given the current political and fiscal situation, advocates of cities might attract more federal resources to urban areas by supporting a variety of nonurban federal initiatives than by pushing for explicit urban programs. The objective would be to promote those programs and policies for which the benefits are likely to flow disproportionately to urban areas and to push the designers of such programs to incorporate the interests of cities.

An alternative approach is to seize the opportunity created by the federal budget deficit to encourage Congress to accept the idea of geographic targeting. This approach accepts the proposition that the federal government is unlikely to commit major new sums of money to urban areas, but rejects the view that Congress is inherently unable to make the difficult choices involved in targeting aid to particular geographic areas. The key is to emphasize the asymmetry between a rapidly growing federal pie and a declining, or slowly growing one.

Congressional reluctance in the past to target aid may partially reflect the understandable desire of all representatives and senators to garner for their districts a fair share of a growing federal pie. When federal aid is increasing, elected officials might legitimately fear that constituents will withdraw political support from a representative who is unable to obtain for the district recognizable benefits from the growing federal largess. However, when federal funds are scarce, inability to garner funds for a particular district need not be judged as a failure, especially if the public understands the principles that motivate the aid program. Indeed, if constituents were fully educated to the fact that funds were being targeted just to the neediest areas, conceivably they might be induced to take pride in the fact that their jurisdiction was not so designated. Thus, the viability of this direct approach depends on (1) developing a consensus that some cities are needy as a result of national trends that are outside the control of city and state officials and (2) developing a distribution formula that would target aid only to the neediest cities.

This research, and even more directly that of Ladd and Yinger (1991), contributes to both parts of the effort needed to mobilize support for a targeted aid program. First, by careful documentation of the trends in the fiscal health of cities, it promotes the development of a consensus that some cities have poor fiscal health through no fault of their own. Second, by emphasizing the expenditure need as well as the revenue-raising side of the fiscal conditions, it focuses attention on the central ingredients of an appropriate formula for targeting aid to troubled cities.

Notes

The paper from which this chapter was adapted was initially written with support from the Ford Foundation through a grant to the Taubman Center for State and Local Government of Harvard University. I am grateful to Jack Strauss, Amy Farmer, Jonathan Shalowitz, and Carl F. Rist, of Duke University, for research assistance.

1. The growth rate of city spending is comparable to the rate of growth of total sales of IBM. IBM's revenue growth over the period 1965–73 was 159 percent (G. Peterson 1976: p 41).

2. The following discussion relies heavily on G. Peterson (1976), Schultze et al. (1972), and Bahl, Jump, and Schroeder (1978, 1979).

3. Total labor costs increase through two mechanisms, a rise in the rate of compensation of labor and an increase in the number of public-sector jobs. The discussion in this subsection focuses only on the rate of compensation. However, the period also witnessed rapid job growth. In the state and local sector as a whole, for example, employment grew at an average annual rate of 4.5 percent between 1962 and 1976, while employment in private industry grew at an average annual rate of only 2 percent (Bahl et al., 1978: table 7, p. 18). Much of the growth in public-sector employment in cities during this period can be attributed to factors discussed in subsequent subsections on the changing mix of city population and the proliferation of public services.

4. The significance of the reduction in working hours should not be underestimated. For example, although the number of policemen in New York City increased from 16,000 to 24,000 between 1940 and 1965, the total number of hours they worked was less in 1965 than in 1940 (cited in Schultze et al. 1972: p 196).

5. But this strategy could backfire. In their capacity as voters, public-sector workers and their relatives tend to support public spending more strongly than other taxpayer voters. Thus, the presence in the city of many public employees can increase the pressure for higher spending. See Gramlich and Rubinfeld (1982) and Ladd and Wilson (1983) for estimates of the magnitude of the effect on preferences of having a public-sector employee in the household.

6. Some of these pressures might be summarized under the rubric of increased work-load pressures. The workload terminology is appropriate but only if it accounts not just for the numbers of people to be served but also for the characteristics of city residents that make it necessary for the city to use additional resources to provide a given level of public services.

7. During the mid-1960s new federal initiatives were begun in the areas of community action programs, mass transportation, manpower development and training, neighborhood youth programs, elementary and secondary education assistance, equal educational opportunity programs, basic water and sewer facilities, community health ser-

vices, and law enforcement. Funding for these efforts remained relatively limited during the 1960s, but expanded greatly during the 1970s.

8. In particular, no county could receive on a per capita basis more than 145 percent of the statewide average, and no jurisdiction within a county could receive more than 145 percent of the county average. These limitations were most binding on those cities such as St. Louis, Baltimore, and Philadelphia that also serve as counties (G. Peterson 1976: p 88).

9. See further discussion and elaboration of the concept of fiscal health later in the chapter.

10. The 33 big cities are: Atlanta, Baltimore, Boston, Buffalo, Chicago, Cincinnati, Cleveland, Columbus, Dallas, Denver, Detroit, Houston, Indianapolis, Jacksonville, Kansas City (MO), Los Angeles, Memphis, Miami, Milwaukee, Minneapolis, New Orleans, New York, Philadelphia, Phoenix, Pittsburgh, Portland, Saint Louis, San Antonio, San Diego, San Francisco, San Jose, Seattle, Washington, D.C.

11. The landmark 1971 *Serrano v. Priest* case in California forced states throughout the country to reconsider their systems of financing elementary and secondary education, and, during the next decade, inspired many state legislatures to increase aid for local schools. Arguing that education was a fundamental interest protected by the U.S. Constitution and that differences across school districts related to property tax wealth were inherently suspect, the California court ruled that California's heavy reliance on local financing of education was unconstitutional. Although the U.S. Supreme Court subsequently invalidated the constitutional logic of the Serrano case in its *San Antonio v. Rodriguez* decision, plaintiffs in various states have since won a number of cases similar to the *Serrano* case based on the stricter requirements of particular state constitutions.

12. The figures for city spending on local schools in table 9.5 are based on the spending of only 5 cities—Boston, Baltimore, Washington, D.C., Memphis, and Buffalo, since they are the only large cities (other than New York City, excluded from the table) that have responsibility for schools. In the other 27 big cities, schools are provided by separate school districts. Hence, school spending in these other cities does not directly affect city budgets. Nonetheless, the general pressures on school spending are likely to be relatively similar in all urban districts with similar growth and demographic characteristics, regardless of the governmental structure of the local area.

13. See Ellwood (1982: table 11.1). For more information on federal grant policy under Reagan, see Ladd (1984).

14. Reischauer (1990) provided an insightful discussion of the forces that led to the rise and fall of federal aid to urban areas.

15. See Bradbury and Ladd (1982a and 1982b) for a discussion of the effects of Proposition 2 1/2 on all Massachusetts communities and the tough choices the state had to make to provide additional state aid in the absence of a state budget surplus. Also see Bradbury and Yinger (1984) for a detailed analysis of the effects of Proposition 2 1/2 and other fiscal changes on the gap between Boston's available revenues and its current services expenditures.

16. One must be careful not to assume that state aid is the only mechanism through which states can assist their cities. See subsequent discussion in text of other mechanisms such as state assumption of responsibility for some of the city's services and authorization for the city to use alternative broad-based taxes.

17. Between 1978 and 1985 property taxes in the average California city declined by about $47 per capita in real terms. Although state aid cushioned these reductions in the early years, once the state surplus was exhausted, state aid to cities fell as well; between 1978 and 1985 state aid to the average California city declined by $20. These revenue reductions were exacerbated by even greater declines in federal aid, about $87 per capita in the average city. Overall, per capita revenues from these three sources

fell by $162 in real terms. This reduction translated into a 39 percent decline in revenues from these sources and a 27 percent decline in total revenues. California cities responded to these reductions by increasing service charges, increasing revenue from their money and property, and increasing revenue from utility users' taxes, transient lodging taxes, franchise fees and other nonproperty taxes (Reid 1987: table 1 and p. 9).

18. The figures in table 9.7 refer to revenues for general purposes. They exclude revenues from enterprises (such as municipal water or power companies).

19. Among the 33 cities in 1986, Atlanta had the highest proportion of its own revenues from charges. Its 41 percent share is largely attributable to charges related to the Atlanta airport.

20. In her 1983 study of 153 U.S. cities, Bradbury found little or no correlation between her measure of weak fiscal health, which she called structural distress, and several measures of budgetary distress.

21. To avoid the adverse budgetary impacts of cyclical swings in the economy, city officials can act conservatively by underestimating revenues and overestimating expenditures as they make their annual budgets or by putting money into rainy-day funds to be drawn down when the economic climate worsens.

22. Examining the financial condition of U.S. cities over time is not easy. The difficulty reflects the fund structure of local government accounting, the failure before 1980 of many cities to report on the basis of generally acceptable accounting principles, differences across cities in the form of financial statements, and inadequacies in the financial data reported in the Census publication, *City Government Finances*. Dearborn has provided us with a consistent dataset over time based on cities' annual reports. For the early years, Dearborn focused exclusively on the general fund. Although this represents the major fund of local governments, its importance varies greatly among city governments. Only 20 percent of total expenditures are channeled through the general fund in Phoenix, in contrast to more than 80 percent in New York (Dearborn 1988: 204). Moreover, any such analysis excludes all special revenue funds at a time when intergovernmental aid, especially from the federal government, was growing rapidly. For recent years, Dearborn has broadened his analysis to include special revenue funds and debt service funds.

23. In a 1988 study, Dearborn himself made a similar error. Focusing on 1984, a strong year, he concluded that "as of 1984 [the major cities] were in perhaps the best financial condition they had been in since 1971, as judged by their success in balancing budgets and maintaining balance-surpluses and liquidity" (p. 281). As shown in table 9.10, however, this assessment was overly optimistic. Although the financial condition of cities was relatively strong in 1984, it was not as strong as in 1977, the year most comparable in terms of its relationship to the economic cycle.

24. Bradbury (1982) used similar measures to examine budgetary distress in 153 major cities.

25. Conceptually, neither surplus measure is unambiguously preferred to the other. One might exclude the revenues and expenditures of utilities on the grounds that utilities function more like private firms than like governmental entities in that they charge prices for services such as water, gas, electricity, or transit and strive to be self-supporting. Because some cities choose to provide these services through public-sector enterprises but others do not, excluding them may enhance comparability across cities. On the other hand, surplus revenues from utilities can provide revenues for general purpose functions, whereas their deficits must be financed from the general purpose budget. In this sense, the financial condition of utilities has a direct bearing on a city's financial condition, and hence should be included in an overall measure of the budgetary condition of a city.

26. Strictly speaking, neither measure is a current account budget surplus or deficit as those terms are usually defined (and as defined by Dearborn et al. (1992) for the general fund just described). Consider the surplus (or deficit) for general purpose functions. Expenditures for this measure are current account expenditures in that they include debt service and contributions to city retirement systems, but exclude capital outlays. The primary source of financing for capital, namely bond proceeds, is also excluded from the revenue side. However, because the revenue measure includes some intergovernmental aid for capital projects and possibly some own-source revenues used for capital outlays, it represents more than revenue for current expenditure. This fact should lead to larger measured surpluses (or smaller deficits) than would occur if current account revenues were correctly measured.

27. In principle, one could delete the capital spending of utilities using the supplemental detail on utilities provided in table 9 of *City Government Finances*, but this adjustment was not made for this study.

28. New York City provides a good example of the potential problem. Mayor Edward Koch's decision to begin a massive capital spending program in the mid-1980s, much of it financed by borrowing, led to huge debt service costs in the early 1990s at a time of economic recession. During the 1991–92 fiscal year, debt service payments were due to rise by $962 million, or to about half of the city's forecasted budget deficit of more than $2 billion (*New York Times,* March 5, 1991).

29. Ladd and Yinger (1991) first use regression analysis to explain the variation in per capita spending across cities and over time. Explanatory variables include demand and resource variables (such as the income of city residents, the tax price of public services, and intergovernmental aid); political and institutional variables (such as an indicator variable for the presence of a city manager); service responsibility variables (such as whether the city has responsibility for providing elementary and secondary education); and cost variables (such as private-sector wage rates, the poverty rate, the fraction of old housing, and jobs in the city per resident). They then simulate what spending would be in each city in each year if the city had average values of the demand and institutional variables but its own city characteristics. The ratio of the simulated expenditure for each city to average expenditure yields a cost index for each city. For example, a ratio of expenditures of 1.4 means that because of city characteristics outside the control of city officials, the city would have to spend 40 percent more than the average city to provide a standard package of public services. Ladd and Yinger were careful not to include cost differences over which city officials have some control. For example, because city officials have some control over the wage rates paid to city workers, Ladd and Yinger measured differences in input prices across cities by private-, rather than public-sector, wage rates; cities in high-wage regions have higher expenditure need, all else constant, because they must pay more than other cities to entice private workers into city jobs.

30. All the cities in the top two size categories in table 9.13 and about half of the cities in the 250,000 to 500,000 size category are in the sample of 33 large cities.

31. The 1979 poverty rates are from U.S. Bureau of the Census (1983: table C, cities). The 1989 poverty rates are from U.S. Bureau of the Census (1990).

32. The figures in column 2 in table 9.15 were estimated by Ladd and Yinger using the following procedure. First, they used regression analysis to determine how a city's 1982 fiscal health is related to the following variables: population, per capita income, poverty rate, share of housing that is old, city share of metropolitan population, unemployment, and 10-year rate of change in population. The estimated relationship was then applied to data on these variables for 1990 (1989 in the case of income) to estimate standardized fiscal health in 1990. Ladd and Yinger (1991: 315–321) used a modified procedure to estimate figures for 1988. The 1990 estimates are preferred to the published 1988 estimates in that they are based on more complete and more recent data from the 1990 Census of Population and Income.

33. Breakdowns by revenue-raising capacity and expenditure need for actual fiscal health are not presented because the components of fiscal institutions are too intertwined to permit a meaningful interpretation of the capacity and need sides of actual fiscal health. For example, a city that has low service responsibilities is likely to have more of its local revenue-raising capacity used up by overlying jurisdictions and consequently to have a smaller revenue-raising capacity than a city with a larger range of responsibilities. In addition, the city may well receive less state aid. Hence, the observation that a city has low actual expenditure needs is not meaningful without reference to its revenue-raising capacity; what matters is the balance between the two as measured by actual fiscal health.

34. Bradbury (1982) dealt with this complexity by looking at aggregate state and local taxes in each city rather than city taxes alone.

35. The expression for restricted revenue-raising capacity is $KC \times Y \times (1 + e')$, where KC is the city-specific standardized tax burden; Y is the per capita income of city residents; and e' is a weighted average of the export ratios (defined as dollars from nonresidents per dollar from residents) from each of the three broad-based taxes that the city is authorized to use. The weights are the proportions of revenue from each source. For further explanation, see Ladd and Yinger (1991: chaps. 6, 7).

36. Technically, a ratio less than one implies that the city is not using its full available capacity, that is, it is imposing a lower tax burden on its residents than the standard burden used to construct the measure of revenue-raising capacity.

37. Conceptually, the measure for the three taxes (property, sales, and earnings) is preferred to the measure for all taxes (which includes selected sales and other miscellaneous taxes), but both are presented to give a more complete picture of the burden of all city taxes. The measure for three taxes is preferred since the denominator of the ratio for both measures is based on export ratios for the three taxes alone; to the extent that the potential for exporting the burdens of other taxes is higher than the average for the three broad-based taxes (as it might well be for selected sales taxes), revenue-raising capacity would be understated and tax burdens for all taxes slightly overstated.

38. The 1986 tax burdens are based on estimates of revenue-raising capacity that reflect actual changes between 1982 and 1986 in the income of city residents and the composition of tax revenues (used for weighting the individual export ratios), but assume no change in the individual export ratios or in the city-specific standard tax burden.

39. For completeness, it should be noted that changes in total current account spending over time may also reflect changes in the services for which cities are responsible. On average, these responsibilities did not change significantly during the 1977–82 period, and the change in the 1982–86 period is not known.

40. This section relies heavily on Ladd and Yinger (1991: chap. 12). Many of the arguments outlined here are developed in more detail in that chapter.

41. Ladd and Yinger (1991: 292) used their statistical analysis of spending to argue that managerial improvements would save only about 4 percent of a typical city's budget.

42. If the tax revolt is interpreted as an additional constraint on city finances, then increases in federal aid suffice only to cut in half the decline in the fiscal health of the average central city from 1972 to 1982.

43. Federal aid should be directed to cities with poor standardized, rather than poor actual, fiscal health to avoid penalizing states that are generous to their troubled cities. However, one might want to adjust the aid to a city by the fiscal health of the city's state, so as to avoid unfair treatment of residents in cities that are located in poor states.

References

Bahl, Roy. 1987. "Urban Government Finance and Federal Income Tax Reform." *National Tax Journal* 40 (March): 1–18.

Bahl, Roy, Bernard Jump, Jr., and Larry Schroeder. 1978. "The Outlook for City Fiscal Performance in Declining Regions." In *The Fiscal Outlook for Cities: Implications of a National Urban Policy*, edited by Roy Bahl. Syracuse, N.Y.: Syracuse University Press.

————. 1979. "Federal Policy and the Fiscal Outlook for Cities." In *Fiscal Crisis in American Cities: The Federal Response*, edited by L. Kenneth Hubbell (1–48). Cambridge, Mass.: Ballinger.

Bradbury, Katharine L. 1982. "Fiscal Distress in Large U.S. Cities." *New England Economic Review* (January/February): 33–43.

————. 1983. "Structural Fiscal Distress in Cities—Causes and Consequences." *New England Economic Review* (January/February): 32–43.

Bradbury, Katharine L., and Helen F. Ladd. 1982a. "Proposition 2 1/2: Initial Impacts, Part I," *New England Economic Review* (January/February): 13–23.

————. 1982b. "Proposition 2 1/2: Initial Impacts, Part II." *New England Economic Review* (March/April): 48–61.

————. 1985. "Changes in the Revenue-Raising Capacity of U.S. Cities, 1970–1982." *New England Economic Review* (March/April): 20–37.

Bradbury, Katharine L., and John Yinger. 1984. "Making Ends Meet: Boston's Budget in the 1980s." *New England and Economic Review* (March/April): 18–28.

Bradbury, K. L., H. F. Ladd, M. Perrault, A. Reschovsky, and J. Yinger. 1984. "State Aid to Offset Fiscal Disparities across Communities." *National Tax Journal* 37 (June): 151–70.

Bradford, D. F., R. A. Malt, and W. E. Oates. 1969. "The Rising Cost of Local Public Services: Some Evidence and Reflections." *National Tax Journal* 22 (June): 185–202.

Brown, Charles C., and Wallace E. Oates. 1985. "Assistance to the Poor in a Federal System." Sloan Working Paper 11-85. College Park, Md.: Department of Economics, University of Maryland.

Browne, Lynne E., and Richard F. Syron. 1977. "Big City Bonds after New York." *New England Economic Review* (July–August): 3–15.

Chernick, Howard, and Andrew Reschovsky. 1988. "The Effect of Federal Tax Reform on State Fiscal Systems: Some Preliminary Evidence." Paper prepared for the session on "Federal, State, and Local Fiscal Relations" of the meeting of the American Economic Association, New York: December.

Courant, Paul, and Daniel L. Rubinfeld. 1987. "Tax Reform: Implications for the State-Local Public Sector." *Journal of Economic Perspectives* (Summer): 87–100.

Cuciti, Peggy L. 1990. "A Non-Urban Policy: Recent Policy Shifts Affecting Cities." In *The Future of National Urban Policy*, edited by Marshall Kaplan and Franklin James (235–50). Durham, N.C.: Duke University Press.

Dearborn, Philip M. 1988. "Fiscal Conditions in Large American Cities, 1971–1984." In *Urban Change and Poverty*, edited by Michael M. G. McGeary and Lawrence Lynn, eds. Washington, D.C.: National Academy Press.

Dearborn, Philip M., George E. Peterson, and Richard H. Kirk. 1992. "City Finances in the 1990s." Project Report No. 6151. Washington, D.C.: Urban Institute.

Ellwood, John William. 1982. *Reductions in U.S. Domestic Spending*. New Brunswick, N.J.: Transaction Books.

Gold, Steven. 1988. "State Fiscal Conditions." *Urban Change and Poverty*, edited by Michael M. G. McGeary and Lawrence Lynn. Washington, D.C.: National Academy Press.

Gramlich, Edward M. 1976. "The New York City Fiscal Crisis: What Happened and What Is to Be Done?" *American Economic Review* 66 (May): 415–29.

————. 1985a. "Reforming U.S. Federal Arrangements." In *American Domestic Priorities: An Economic Appraisal*, edited by J. M. Quigley and D. L. Rubinfeld (34–69).

————. 1985b. "The Deductibility of State and Local Taxes." *National Tax Journal* (December).

Gramlich, Edward M., and Daniel L. Rubinfeld. 1982. "Voting On Public Spending: Differences between Public Employees, Transfer Recipients, and Private Workers." *Journal of Policy Analysis and Management* (Summer): 516–34.

Kaplan, Marshall, and Franklin James. 1990. "Urban Policy in the Nineties and Beyond: The Need for New Approaches." In *The Future of National Urban Policy*, edited by Marshall Kaplan and Franklin James (351–67). Durham, N.C.: Duke University Press.

Ladd, Helen F. 1984. "Federal Aid to State and Local Governments." In *Federal Budget Policy in the 1980*, edited by J. Palmer and G. Mills. Washington, D.C.: Urban Institute Press.

Ladd, Helen F., and Fred Doolittle. 1982. "Which Level of Government Should Assist Poor People?" *National Tax Journal* 35 (September): 323–36.

Ladd, Helen F., and Julie Boatright Wilson. 1983. "Who Supports Tax Limitations: Evidence from Massachusetts' Proposition 2 1/2." *Journal of Policy Analysis and Management*, Winter.

Ladd, Helen F., and John Yinger. 1991 [1989]. *America's Ailing Cities: Fiscal Health and the Design of Urban Policy*, updated edition. Baltimore, Md.: Johns Hopkins University Press.

Newman, Frank, Robert Palaich, and Rona Wilensky. 1990. "Reengaging State and Federal Policymakers in the Problems of Urban Education." In *The Future of National Urban Policy*, edited by Marshall Kaplan and Franklin James (61–88). Durham, N.C.: Duke University Press.

Pagano, Michael A. 1987. "The Effects of the 1986 Tax Reform Act on City Finances: An Appraisal of Year One." Research report of the National League of Cities. Washington, D.C.: National League of Cities.

Peterson, George E. 1976. "Finance." In *The Urban Predicament*, edited by W. Gorham and N. Glazer (35–118). Washington, D.C.: Urban Institute Press.

―――. 1986. "Urban Policy and the Cyclical Behavior of Cities." In *Reagan and the Cities*, edited by George E. Peterson and Carol W. Lewis (11–36). Washington, D.C.: Urban Institute Press.

Peterson, John. 1987. "Examining the Impacts of the 1986 Tax Reform Act on the Municipal Securities Market." *National Tax Journal* 40 (3, September): 393–402.

Peterson, Paul E., Barry G. Rabe, and Kenneth K. Wong. 1986. *When Federalism Works*. Washington, D.C.: Brookings Institution.

Poterba, James M. 1986. "Explaining the Yield Spread between Taxable and Tax-Exempt Bonds: The Role of Expected Tax Policy." In *Studies in State and Local Public Finance*, edited by Harvey S. Rosen. Chicago: University of Chicago Press.

Reid, Gary. 1987. "How Cities in California Have Responded to Fiscal Pressures since Proposition 13." Photocopy.

Reischauer, Robert. 1990. "The Rise and Fall of National Urban Policy: The Fiscal Dimension." In *The Future of National Urban Policy*, edited by Marshall Kaplan and Franklin James (225–34). Durham, N.C.: Duke University Press.

Reiss, Albert J., Jr. 1970. "Assessing the Current Crime Wave." *Crime in Urban Society*, edited by Barbara McLennan (23–44).

Schultze, Charles, Edward R. Fried, Alice M. Rivlin, Nancy H. Teeters, and Robert Reischauer. 1972. "Fiscal Problems of Cities." In *Setting National Priorities: The 1973 Budget*, edited by C. Schultze, E. R. Fried, A. M. Rivlin, and N. H. Teeters (chap. 9). Washington, D.C.: Brookings Institution.

Skogan, Wallace G. 1975. "Measurement Problems in Official and Survey Crime Rates." *Journal of Criminal Justice* 3: 17–32.

U.S. Bureau of the Census. 1983. *County and City Data Book*. Washington, D.C.: U.S. Government Printing Office.

―――. 1992. *1990 Census of Population and Housing*. Summary Social, Economic, and Housing Characteristics, ser. CPH5. Washington, D.C.: U.S. Government Printing Office.

U.S. Congressional Budget Office. 1977. "New York City's Fiscal Problem." Excerpt in *The Fiscal Crisis of American Cities*, edited by Roger E. Alcahy and David Mermelsein. New York: Vintage Books.

ABOUT THE EDITOR

George E. Peterson is a senior fellow at the Urban Institute and a codirector of the Urban Opportunity Program. His research has dealt with the financing of state and local governments and the development of urban policy. He was a member of the National Urban Policy Committee of the National Academy of Sciences. Among his recent publications is *Reagan and the Cities*, and he is the editor of two other volumes in the Urban Opportunity Series—*Drugs, Crime, and Social Isolation: Barriers to Urban Opportunity* with Adele V. Harrell, and *Urban Labor Markets and Job Opportunity* with Wayne Vroman.

ABOUT THE CONTRIBUTORS

Carolyn T. Adams is dean of the College of Arts and Sciences at Temple University, where she has been a member of the faculty since 1976, teaching courses in urban development, urban politics, and public policy. She has authored or co-authored numerous articles and books, including an award-winning cross-national study of *Comparative Public Policy: The Politics of Social Choice in Europe and America*. Her publications focusing on Philadelphia include a co-authored study of the transformation of that city's economy and politics since World War II, titled *Philadelphia: Neighborhoods, Division and Conflict in a Post-Industrial City*.

Peter K. Eisinger is professor of political science and public policy and director of the La Follette Institute of Public Affairs at the University of Wisconsin. He has taught at Columbia University, the University of Essex, and Brown University. He is the author of various articles and books on American urban politics and state and local economic development, including *The Rise of the Entrepreneurial State*.

Christopher Howard is assistant professor of government at the College of William and Mary, and also teaches in the college's Thomas Jefferson Program in Public Policy. He is currently investigating the connections between tax policy and social policy in the United States. Articles that he has authored or co-authored have appeared in the *American Political Science Review, Political Science Quarterly, The American Prospect*, and *Journal of Policy History*.

Byran O. Jackson is now deceased. He was formerly an associate professor of political science at California State University, Los Angeles. He worked as a social science research analyst for the Department of Housing and Urban Development and as assistant professor of political science and adjunct professor of urban studies at Washington University, St. Louis. Jackson has major publications in the area of U.S. housing policy and ethnic politics in U.S. cities. His work on ethnic policies had research support from the Rockefeller, Ford, and National Science Foundations.

Helen F. Ladd is a professor of public policy studies and economics at Duke University. An expert on state and local public finance, she has written extensively on the property tax, education finance, tax and expenditure limitations, intergovernmental aid, state economic development, and the fiscal problems of U.S. cities. Her most recent book, co-authored with John Yinger, is *America's Ailing Cities: Fiscal Health and the Design of Urban Policy* (Johns Hopkins University Press, 1991). She is spending 1994–95 as a visiting fellow at the Brookings Institution.

Michael Lipsky is a program officer in the governance and public policy program of the Ford Foundation. A political scientist, he is the author of *Street-Level Bureaucracy: Dilemmas of the Individual in Public Services*, and *Protest in City Politics*. His most recent book, with Steven Rathgeb Smith, is *Nonprofits for Hire: The Welfare State in the Age of Contracting* (1993). He served on the faculty of the Massachusetts Institute of Technology from 1969 to 1993.

Dale Rogers Marshall is president of Wheaton College in Norton, Massachusetts and professor of political science. She has written widely on urban politics and policy, including *Racial Politics in American Cities* and *Protest is Not Enough: The Struggle of Blacks and Hispanics for Equality in Urban Politics*, with Rufus Browning and David Tabb. She has also served as vice president of the American Political Science Association, president of the Western Political Science Association, and trustee of Cornell University.

Carlos Muñoz, Jr. is professor of Chicano and ethnic studies at the University of California, Berkeley. He is the author of *Youth, Identity, Power: The Chicano Movement*, which received the 1990 Gustavus Myers Book Award. His research interests include urban, ethnic, and racial politics and coalitions. He is currently working on a book on the struggle for a multicultural democracy in America.

Dianne M. Pinderhughes is professor of political science and Afro-American studies, and director of the Afro-American Studies and

Research Program at the University of Illinois, Urbana-Champaign. She is the author of *Race and Ethnicity in Chicago Politics*, and numerous articles on race and public policy, and electoral politics. She also focuses on racial and ethnic interest representation and voting rights politics.

Michael B. Preston is professor of political science and department chair at the University of Southern California. His research interests focus on urban politics, urban problems, and black political participation in the American political system. Recent publications include *The New Black Politics, The Politics of Bureaucratic Reform*, and "The Politics of Economic Redistribution in Chicago: Is Balanced Growth Possible?," in *Regenerating the Cities*, edited by Michael Parkinson and Bernard Foley, and *Racial and Ethnic Politics in California* (with Byran O. Jackson).

Genie N. L. Stowers is a political scientist and associate professor of public administration at San Francisco State University. Her research interests include politically marginalized groups in urban society, their politics, and their ability to influence public policy. Her publications include those focused upon Cuban-American political development, the politics in Miami, and domestic violence policy.

Ronald K. Vogel is associate professor of political science at the University of Louisville. He is author of *Urban Political Economy: Broward County, Florida* (1992). He is currently editing a "Handbook of Research on Urban Politics and Policy" and co-editing "Regional Politics: America in a Post-City Era." His research focuses on urban economic development, metropolitan governance, and national urban policy.